THE
CIVIL RIGHTS
COMMISSION:
1957-1965

MICHIGAN STATE UNIVERSITY PRESS | 1968

THE
CIVIL RIGHTS
COMMISSION:
1957-1965

FOSTER RHEA DULLES

To
Dorothy and Jim

CONTENTS

PREFACE

The initial phase in the history of the United States Commission on Civil Rights developed against the background of the burgeoning Negro Revolution. The establishment of this bipartisan, independent Federal agency; its original investigations and reports, the continuing battles over its recommendations, were framed by Montgomery and Little Rock, the sit-ins and freedom rides, the March on Washington, and by Selma and Watts. Its activities between 1957 and 1965 were coterminous with a civil rights movement that was gathering a steadily increasing momentum. In itself the Commission was but one manifestation of the belated response of a conscience-stricken people to the imperative need somehow to make good the promises of democracy in support of equal protection of the laws regardless of race, color, religion or national origins.

Many closely interrelated factors account for the movement to ensure civil rights that began in the 1950's. The Negro American had been stimulated to a new search for identity and status by events both at home and abroad. He was awakened by what was taking place in Africa, the surge of nationalistic ambitions among people of his own race. He was aroused by the impact of new concepts of equality as American democracy sought to demonstrate its validity in the face of the challenge of international communism. The steps first taken in 1954 when the Supreme Court denied the validity of the historic equal but separate doctrine then triggered a chain of events that could not be halted.

The Commission on Civil Rights has not of course played what could be characterized as the decisive role in the battle against discrimination. No single organization or agency, public or private, may be said to have done so. In gathering the irrefutable facts on which civil rights legislation could be soundly based, in stimulating action on the part of both Congress and the Executive, and in serving as the conscience of the nation in its revelation of the iniquities of discrimination, the Commission nevertheless had a very important influence in furthering the civil rights movement as a whole. Sometimes its reports disappointed northern liberals by not going far enough in recommending new legislation; the same reports invariably angered Southerners by going in their opinion much too far. The Commission sought to represent the voice of moderation between two harsh and seemingly irreconcilable extremes. At the same time, these reports reveal a steadily mounting insistence that equality must be effectively woven into the fabric of American life —equality in voting, equality in education, equality in housing, equality in economic opportunity, equality in the administration of justice. The history of the Commission graphically illustrates the changing temper of the times in its members' growing realization that the challenge of discrimination had to be met if American democracy were to endure.

The Commission has always operated under the most severe handicaps. During the first years it never knew at the end of each temporary lease on life whether its congressional mandate would be renewed or be quietly allowed to lapse. Under such circumstances it was repeatedly forced to begin to phase out current operations with the reduction of staff and personnel, and in each instance

rescue came only at the eleventh hour. Yet in spite of all such uncertainties the Commission persisted in making the most extensive
investigations, gathering facts from every possible source, and submitting the most forthright recommendations without fear or favor.

The importance of the Commission's role is manifest in the
extent to which both Congress and the President ultimately acted
on its recommendations and proposals. Other and often more important forces helped to drive the country along the road toward
equality. The pressure from the civil rights movement in a broader
context was unrelenting; in taking their battle into the streets, the
Negroes themselves exerted a compelling influence. Still and all,
the epochal Civil Rights Act of 1964 and the Voting Rights Act
of 1965 were built on the factual foundations of racial discrimination portrayed in the Commission's reports and in part they embodied these reports' specific recommendations for remedial action.

In the light of subsequent events—the mounting aggressiveness of the Negro protest, the reiterated cry of Black Power, the
rioting in the segregated slum areas of cities throughout the land—
there may also be emphasized the inherent tragedy in the failure
of Congress to act more promptly and more energetically on certain of the Commission recommendations. From the very start the
Commission publicly and authoritatively disclosed not only the
extent of legal discrimination against Negroes in the South, but the
dangerous potential in *de facto* segregation in the black ghettos of
the North. The testimony of many witnesses at the initial hearings
clearly foreshadowed the violent outbreaks which have since taken
place because of the failure to adopt adequate measures to cope
with the crisis of the northern cities.

This book is an account of the activities of the Commission—
not of the Negro Revolution nor of the civil rights movement. My
purpose has been, against this broader background, to outline the
Commission's role between the years 1957 and 1965: its establishment and its internal difficulties, the constant battle against southern opposition; the dilemmas created at times as a consequence of
sharp disapproval on the part of Administration officials in Washington; the record of investigations, conferences and hearings both
in the North and in the South; the many reports and official recommendations. I have tried to tell the story of what the Commission
by and of itself sought to accomplish, and yet relate these activities

to the broad spectrum of the political and social history of the late
1950's and early 1960's. These developments are too recent to be
able to see them or judge them with the perspective of time; they
are charged with an emotional content making impossible an aloof
objectivity. There are inescapable limitations in any present-day
writing in the vital, urgent field of civil rights.

The Civil Rights Commission has been exceptionally generous in making all its records and files freely available. It has not
only provided me with all published reports and the transcripts of
hearings and conferences, it has also given me access to the minutes
of Commission meetings, Staff Activities Reports, memoranda submitted by division heads, and a mass of other material in official
files. Dr. John A. Hannah, who has served since its establishment
as the Commission's chairman, has also let me see the papers and
correspondence relating to Commission affairs which are in his
personal files at Michigan State University. Without such assistance,
forced to rely wholly on the public record, I could not possibly have
written this book. Needless to say neither the Commission nor Dr.
Hannah, nor any member of the staff, in making these records
available, has offered any suggestion as to how they might be used
or interpreted.

The Commission material has been supplemented from other
sources. The more important were Senate and House committee
hearings, relating both to the Commission itself and civil rights
legislation in general; congressional debates; the published papers
of Presidents Eisenhower, Kennedy, and Johnson; newspaper records (many of which were found in the Commission's own files);
contemporary magazine articles; and selected books dealing with
the civil rights movement and the Negro Revolution.

My project has been sponsored by the Michigan State University and the Michigan State University Press. I am especially
indebted to Provost Howard R. Neville, who was instrumental in
promoting such sponsorship; Paul A. Varg, Dean of the College of
Arts and Letters, for his constant encouragement; and Lyle Blair,
Director of the Press. I would also like to thank those members of
the Commission, especially Chairman Hannah, who afforded me
interviews; and also acknowledge the help of Howard W. Rogerson, former Acting Staff Director; and William L. Taylor, Staff
Director. Miss Ruth Jameyson, Administrative Assistant to Dr.

Hannah in his role as President of Michigan State University, was very generous of her time in introducing me to the material available in East Lansing, and the research librarians at the Commission's offices in Washington were equally helpful in enabling me to go through the records which I examined there. Finally I would like to thank Miss Virginia Vorus who somehow managed to type the many revisions through which the manuscript has made its halting way to the press.

F. R. D.

August, 1967
Jamaica, Vermont

I. THE COMMISSION
IS CREATED

On September 9, 1957, President Eisenhower signed the first civil rights act to be adopted in eighty-two years. This measure took an unconscionable time making its way through Congress and was greatly weakened in the course of its laborious progress. Final passage awoke frustrated laments on the part of those who felt it had been so emasculated as to be almost meaningless, and anguished outcries by those who wanted no bill at all. What remained most significant—and surprising—was the fact that any measure "with as much marrow and gristle as this," in the phrase used by Richard Rovere in the *New Yorker,* had actually been adopted by a politically fearful Congress.[1] Few there were with the prescience to realize what it really might mean as a first step, however halting

1. Richard Rovere, "Letter from Washington," *New Yorker,* 33, Aug. 31, 1957, 68–72.

1

and tentative, in breaking through the barrier of legislative apathy in maintenance of equal rights before the law.

One such astute observer was Dean Acheson who stated, "I don't think it an exaggeration to say that the bill is among the greatest achievements since the war, and in the field of civil rights, the greatest since the Thirteenth Amendment."[2]

Title 1 of the new law established a Commission on Civil Rights as an independent, bipartisan, federal agency. The Commission was empowered to investigate allegations that United States citizens were being deprived of the right to vote by reason of color, race, religion or national origin; to collect information on legal developments constituting a denial of the equal protection of the laws; to appraise the laws and policies of the Federal Government in the whole field of civil rights; and, within two years, to report its findings and recommendations to the President and Congress. During the impassioned congressional debate over the new law, the advocates of such a Commission insisted that it was an absolutely indispensable step in meeting the basic problem of civil rights; opponents furiously attacked its establishment as an unwarranted and dangerous intrusion by the Federal Government into matters constitutionally allocated to the states.

The further provisions of the Civil Rights Act of 1957 authorized the appointment of an additional Assistant Attorney General to head a Civil Rights Division in the Department of Justice and extended the jurisdiction of district courts to include civil actions designed to secure relief from violation of any civil right. It also empowered the Federal Government, through the Attorney General, to seek court injunctions against interference with the right to vote, but in a bitterly disputed compromise, allowed the presiding judge in criminal contempt proceedings to determine whether or not such cases should be decided by a jury.[3]

In comparison with these relatively weak and legalistic provisions, the importance of the Commission lay in its future potentialities. Empowered to assemble authentic and documented information, to be incorporated in the public record, this new Fed-

2. Dean Acheson, "A Word of Praise," *Reporter*, 17, Sept. 5, 1957, 3.
3. *Public Law 85–315*. For digest of law and its legislative history, see most conveniently, *Revolution in Civil Rights*, published by *Congressional Quarterly Service*, Washington, 1965.

eral agency would be able to build up an unassailable factual record of the status of civil rights throughout the country. From this base it could then point the way toward more effective policies, on the part of both the Executive and Congress, than anything contemplated in the existing halfway measure. The creation of the Commission would indeed prove in time to have been the most enduring and useful feature of this first legislative step toward meeting what had by 1957 become universally recognized as the gravest domestic problem facing the American nation.[4]

The mounting pressures in the civil rights field that led the Eisenhower Administration to take this important step were an immediate outgrowth of the overall resistance throughout the South to compliance with the Supreme Court's historic decisions in 1954 overruling the traditional doctrine that "separate" could be legally reconciled with "equal" in the protection of the laws. These decisions were the projection of a trend already very clear—both legally and politically—which was to have a revolutionary effect on race relations within the United States and on the whole structure of American society.

The doctrine of equality among all men has a philosophic and religious background that may be traced far back in history. The Stoics of ancient Greece and such Romans as Cicero and Seneca accepted its validity, and equality has always been a tenet of Christian faith as proclaimed by St. Paul. Yet equality clashed irreconcilably with the accepted existence of slavery, forcing upon both philosophers and religious leaders an unhappy realization of the seemingly unbridgeable gap between the ideal and the real. When slaves became for the most part Negroes, which was not necessarily the case in ancient times, their status in society was then complacently rationalized on the ground that Negroes were of an inferior race to which the principles of equality, theoretically applicable to all men, did not extend.

When slaves were introduced into America with the trans-

4. For general background of creation of Commission, see *Report of the United States Commission on Civil Rights—1959*, Washington, 1959, ix–xv; also abridgment of this Report, *With Liberty and Justice for All*, Washington, 1959, 1–7.

portation of Negroes from their African homelands, the peoples of the colonies, and subsequently those of the United States, confronted this age-old historic dilemma in seeking to harmonize freedom and bondage. The Declaration of Independence stated that "all men are created equal"; the Constitution impressively spoke of a government established by "We the People." Nevertheless, the existence of slavery in American society was an irrefutable fact. To attain agreement on any constitution at all, its framers were compelled to acknowledge that Negroes could be lawfully held in bondage and deprived of their civil rights. The Constitution adopted in 1789 contained no guarantee of equal protection of the laws.

Not until the Civil War, the emancipation of the slaves, and the adoption of the Fourteenth Amendment did the doctrine of equality become a part of the American credo. Only then was equal protection of the laws accepted as a guiding principle in the growth of an emergent democracy. Yet quite obviously the principle long remained more honored in the breech than the observance in application to Negroes. The South continued to maintain in theory and in practice the basic position that their segregation was wholly justified because of the inherent superiority of the whites. And losing all interest in seeking to uphold the safeguards written into the Fourteenth Amendment, the North went its own way for almost a century with little concern for what might be happening to the Negroes given a nominal freedom by force of arms.

True, Congress passed the Civil Rights Act of 1875 which was very much like that to be finally enacted in 1964. However, when the Supreme Court declared it unconstitutional on the ground that such a law constituted an unwarranted invasion of states' rights, there was little outcry or criticism. Fifteen years later the House adopted a voting rights bill, once again foreshadowing the legislation of the 1960's with a provision for Federal supervision of congressional elections, but in the Senate, many northern Republicans combined with southern Democrats to defeat it.

Charles A. Dana of the New York *Sun* fearfully envisaged the possibility that the southern states might "be subjected to the political domination of the Negroes" rather than continuing "to be governed by white men as now." "No one liked to contemplate," wrote a contemporary historian, Harry Thurston Peck, "even a partial return to the hideous scenes of the Reconstruction Period, when ape-like blacks had leagued themselves with the vilest whites in a repulsive and disgraceful political orgy."[5]

The social discrimination practiced by southern whites nevertheless remained relatively limited in the 1870's and 1880's. Only during the Populist era, ironically enough, did the vagaries of politics really solidify the southern determination to keep the Negroes in their place. The 1890's then witnessed the rapid proliferation of the so-called Jim Crow laws extending the segregation practiced in the schools to transportation, restaurants, places of amusement, and other public facilities. These same years also saw enactment of new and more rigid state laws (Mississippi taking the lead) designed wholly to deprive the Negroes of their right to vote through "grandfather clauses," poll taxes, and literacy tests. In spite of the promise of the Civil War amendments, Negroes in the South— some ninety percent of the total at this time—were relegated to second-class citizenship quite as though the principle of equal protection of the laws had never been enunciated.[6]

They had no recourse in law. The Supreme Court repeatedly sustained the legislation imposing segregation. So long as Negroes were afforded facilities on a par with those enjoyed by whites, such facilities were construed as equal even though they were separate. The key decision, *Plessy v. Ferguson,* decided in 1896, applied to accommodations on railroads, but its implications reached out to all public facilities. Justice Harlan, grandfather of the Justice Harlan of the 1950's and 1960's, in a sharp dissent denied that the states could in any way regulate their citizens' enjoyment of civil rights on the basis of race. "Our Constitution," he said, "is colorblind." But reflecting the temper of the times, the Court denied that segregation was "unreasonable or obnoxious to the Fourteenth Amendment." "If one race be inferior to another," Justice Brown stated in writing the majority opinion, "the Constitution of the United States cannot put them on the same plane."[7]

In their campaign to suppress Negro rights, fire-eating dema-

---

5. Harry Thurston Peck, *Twenty Years of the Republic,* New York, 1926, 201, 297.

6. See C. Vann Woodward, *The Strange Career of Jim Crow,* rev. ed., New York, 1965.

7. Quoted in Alan P. Grimes, *Equality in America,* New York, 1964, 57–58.

gogic southern politicians left no doubt of their passionate support of white supremacy. Said Senator Vardaman of Mississippi:

> . . . It matters not what his advertised mental or moral qualifications may be, I am just as much opposed to Booker Washington as a voter, with all his Anglo-Saxon reenforcements, as I am to the cocoanut-headed, chocolate colored, typical little coon, Andy Dotson, who blacks my shoes every morning. Neither is fit to perform the supreme function of citizenship.

And again on another occasion:

> God Almighty created the negro for a menial—he is essentially a servant.[8]

Nor were such ideas restricted in this period to Southerners. The American people generally accepted the premise of white racial superiority. They were ready to subject not only Negroes but members of all the colored races to discrimination as inferior human beings. This was the era when both at home and abroad the master race felt it had to take up "the white man's burden." Prejudice and bigotry were never more widely prevalent.

Conditions did not improve during the Progressive era. A reformist spirit did not embrace race relations. The South strengthened its segregationist laws; lynchings (one thousand in the years 1900–1914) continued as the ultimate expression of lawless brutality in seeking to hold down the Negroes, and the North looked the other way.

In 1908 Charles Francis Adams stated that "We are confronted by the obvious fact, as undeniable as it is hard, that the African will only partially assimilate and that he cannot be absorbed. He remains an alien element in the body politic."

Moreover most of the Negroes themselves resignedly accepted their lowly status in American society. Their leading spokesman in those days, Booker T. Washington, argued that their position was that of hewers of wood and drawers of water. They were entitled to just and humane treatment, but in a white world could not expect enjoyment of their rights as equal citizens.

8. Quoted in B. Franklin Frazier, *The Negro in the United States*, rev. ed., New York, 1957, 157, 158.

"At the beginning of the twentieth century," Rayford W. Logan has written, "what is now called second-class citizenship for Negroes was accepted by Presidents, the Supreme Court, Congress, organized labor, the General Federation of Women's Clubs—indeed by the vast majority of Americans, north and south, and by the 'leader' of the Negro race."[9]

About this same time, however, a movement to redress this glaring inequity in American society was launched under the militant leadership of a group of Negro intellectuals, of whom the most notable was William E. B. DuBois, and it soon led to the formation of the National Association for the Advancement of Colored People and the Urban League. This movement won the sympathy of some few liberal-minded whites but could make little headway. The discriminatory laws throughout the South, and in some northern states, remained undisturbed; segregation continued to have the blessing of the supreme arbiters of the law. Foreign observers increasingly noted the startling gap between democratic professions and overt discrimination in race relations, but the American nation as a whole placidly accepted the injustice done the Negroes.

Little change took place in the 1920's. During and after the First World War, a vast northern migration of Negroes seeking jobs got under way. There were race riots, lynchings, and growing unrest in what were already becoming the black ghettos of many cities. The North was finally beginning to feel the impact of the "Negro problem" and fumbled uncertainly over what could be done about it. "No matter which way we turn in the North or the South," wrote that astute French observer, André Siegfried, "there seems to be no solution. The colour problem is an abyss into which we can look only with terror."[10]

Nor did the New Deal come to grips with racial discrimination for all its other social advances. Mounting concern was everywhere evident but little action was taken except for Roosevelt's belated establishment of a Fair Employment Practices Commission. The challenge was nevertheless inescapable.

In concluding his epochal study *An American Dilemma*, published in 1941, Gunnar Myrdal wrote not without hope of the

9. Rayford W. Logan, *The Negro in American Life and Thought; The Nadir, 1877–1901*, New York, 1954.
10. André Siegfried, *America Comes of Age*, New York, 1927, 108.

future that "the Negroes in America have on their side the law of the land and the religion of the nation. . . . America can demonstrate that justice, equality and cooperation are possible between white and colored people. . . . America is free to choose whether the Negro shall remain her liability or become her opportunity."[11]

The Second World War and its aftermath provided the impetus for the civil rights movement. Negroes were fighting in the armed forces to defend democracy against the menace of Fascism. Their segregation was a shocking denial of the democratic faith so loudly proclaimed. As postwar America then felt itself threatened by communism, discrimination appeared to be an even more blatant contradiction of principles professed in opposition to the new totalitarianism. And finally with the rise of the independent nations in Africa, which the free world hoped would follow a democratic course rather than be swept into the communist camp, discriminatory treatment of Negroes in the United States became wholly irreconcilable with the efforts to win the friendship of these African nations. How could America stand before the world as the champion of liberty and justice while it denied real freedom to a tenth of its own people because of their race and color?

At the same time the Negroes were themselves insistently demanding recognition of their rights. The experience of the war and the sense of racial pride awakened by what was happening in Africa gave a revolutionary turn to this new movement. The Negro American would no longer passively accept the denial of his equality.

If it may be said that the conscience of the American people was finally awakened in the 1950's to the wrongs done to the Negro, after generations of apathy, evasion, and indifference, the impact of events played a major part in that awakening. The practical exigencies of both domestic and foreign politics focused attention on conditions which the nation had for long successfully ignored. Only in these circumstances was the country prepared to accept both a legal and a moral obligation to uphold the principle of equality.

In 1946 President Truman established a Committee on Civil

11. Gunnar Myrdal, *An American Dilemma*, 2 vols., New York, 1944, I, 510; II, 1021.

Rights and a year later it issued a report, *To Secure These Rights,* declaring that the equal protection of the laws was a national problem. "We need to guarantee the same rights," it stated, "to every person regardless of who he is, where he lives, or what his racial, religious or national origins are."[12] The report was cast in a broader mold, but at its core was the status of the Negro. When eight years later the Supreme Court, which had been slowly moving to declare invalid certain other aspects of racial discrimination, crossed the Rubicon in outlawing segregation in the nation's schools, it made an immense forward stride. In *Brown v. Board of Education* it unanimously rejected the old doctrine of "separate but equal," declared that "separate educational facilities are inherently unequal," and without equivocation stated that Negroes so discriminated against were clearly deprived of the equal protection of the laws. Subsequently the Supreme Court called upon the schools to take such steps as were necessary to break down the barriers of educational segregation "with all deliberate speed."[13]

The South was prepared to strike back at this assault on the bases of its entire policy toward the Negro. Whatever the implications for the North, which were soon to become very important, ending segregation in the schools would undermine the whole southern way of life. The South adopted a program of massive resistance, revived the old doctrine of state interposition against Federal law, and launched a new campaign through its White Citizens Councils to bolster white supremacy. At the same time the Negroes, acting through such old or new organizations as the NAACP, the Congress of Racial Equality (CORE), and the Student Nonviolent Coordinating Committee (SNCC), were to insist upon implementation of the new interpretation of equality which the Supreme Court had made the law of the land. The lines of racial conflict were dangerously drawn.

The White Citizens Councils voiced the most extreme doctrines of racial superiority. While theoretically they eschewed the tactics of the old Ku Klux Klan, their campaign was one of un-

12. *To Secure These Rights: The Report of the President's Committee on Civil Rights,* New York, 1947, xi.
13. *Brown v. Board of Education,* 347 U.S. 483 (1954), and *Brown v. Board of Education,* 349 U.S. 294 (1955), quoted in Grimes, *Equality in America,* 76–77.

relenting economic pressure ("We won't gin their cotton, we won't allow them credit, we won't sell them homes") and of intimidation and threats against those Negroes seeking to assert their rights. At least indirectly, the White Citizens Councils inspired a mounting wave of violence: the burning or bombing of Negro churches and homes; and attacks, sometimes fatal, upon civil rights workers.

For their part the Negroes were ready to carry the campaign for acknowledgment of their rights into the streets with demonstrations against every form of discrimination. A first significant instance of this was the 1955 nonviolent boycott of the bus system in Montgomery, Alabama because of its segregated seating arrangements. Under the leadership of Dr. Martin Luther King, Jr., who would the next year form the Southern Christian Leadership Conference, the Negroes conducted their campaign peacefully. Although for a year the threat of possible violence constantly hung over Montgomery, the boycott attained its objective when a court order prohibited further segregation on the buses. More important, this disciplined Negro demonstration dramatically focused nation-wide attention on racial discrimination in the South and set a contagious pattern for further Negro boycotts and demonstrations.

Even as President Eisenhower's Cabinet was the next year considering the possible establishment of a civil rights commission, another dramatic development on the campus of the University of Alabama aroused the public. By Federal court orders the university authorities enrolled a Negro, Autherine Lucy, but the student protests against her attendance at classes were so violent that the authorities soon felt compelled to suspend Miss Lucy, as the official notification read, "for your safety and for the safety of the students and faculty members." The Court promptly ordered her reinstatement, but with student hostility unabated, the university trustees seized upon the pretext that Miss Lucy had made derogatory statements about the university to expel her permanently. The entire nation was deeply shocked.[14]

A comment by Miss Lucy's backwoods farmer parents strikingly revealed the contrast between the new militancy of the Negroes in seeking their rights, and their former spirit of passive

14. Sherman Adams, *First-Hand Report,* New York, 1961, 338.

resignation. "We raised ten head of children, nine of them still living," they said, "and every one of them was taught to stay their distance from white folks, but to give them all respect. If Autherine has changed from this, she didn't get her new ideas from home."[15]

This was the background and these were the immediate circumstances that lay behind the decision of the Eisenhower Administration to sponsor new legislation in the delicate and dangerous field of civil rights. The Truman Committee on Civil Rights had recommended the creation of a commission to study the whole problem and make recommendations for its solution,[16] and every year during the ensuing decade individual Congressmen introduced bills to implement this proposal. But Congress veered away from taking any action whatever on such a controversial issue. Eisenhower himself moved very reluctantly, but the course of events finally persuaded him that he had no alternative other than to press directly for legislation that would in some measure at least meet the demands of the Negroes and their northern sympathizers.

Taking what Sherman Adams, his Special Assistant, has described as "a bolder step than many of his close counselors deemed advisable," the President thereupon asked Congress in his 1956 State of the Union message to create a civil rights commission which would be empowered to investigate the charges "that in some localities Negro citizens are being deprived of their right to vote and are likewise being subjected to unwarranted economic pressures." There were protracted cabinet discussions over the exact form such legislation should take and the possible incorporation in the proposed bill of other features than establishment of a civil rights commission. After the most careful weighing of political implications, the Administration policy makers agreed on a measure basically foreshadowing the law finally passed, and on April 9 Attorney General Brownell sent this draft to both the Senate and House.[17]

"Investigations and hearings," Brownell stated in support of a civil rights commission, "will bring into sharper focus the area of

15. *New York Times*, Feb. 26, 1956, quoted in Frazier, *The Negro in the United States*, 690.
16. *To Secure These Rights*, 154–55.
17. Adams, *First-Hand Report*, 335-39.

responsibility of the Federal Government and of the States under our constitutional system. Through greater public understanding, therefore, the Commission may chart a course of progress to guide us in these years ahead."[18]

In spite of the mounting racial tension—or perhaps because of it—Congress moved with agonizing slowness in considering the Administration's bill. The House passed it in July 1956, but faced with a possible southern filibuster, the Senate allowed it to die in committee. Both political parties nevertheless stressed the need for action in their party platforms in this election year, and on starting his second term President Eisenhower reintroduced his former proposals.

He was still acting with careful circumspection. He took no stand on the historic Supreme Court decisions and what has been described as his "profoundly reticent view . . . toward the whole struggle for civil rights" was attributed to political caution.[19] The President later sought to justify a position deeply discouraging to the civil rights advocates who thought they had his full support. "The Administration," he wrote in *Waging Peace,* "had steered a difficult course between extremist firebrands and extremist diehards. This was due to conviction, not politics."[20]

Attorney General Brownell, in any event, once more testified in favor of the Administration bill and tried to speed its way through Congress. Again the House was ready to act; again the Senate balked. The political situation became incredibly confused, with conflicts between Northerners and Southerners, amendments and counter-amendments to the bill, divisions within House and Senate, Administration ambiguities in outlining policy, complex backstage maneuvers in which principle and partisanship became inextricably entwined. Nevertheless a coalition of liberal Republicans and northern Democrats kept up a steady pressure and an acceptable compromise was ultimately worked out largely through the influence of Lyndon Johnson, Majority Leader in the Senate, and William Knowland, the Minority Leader. After further impassioned debate in both branches of Congress, the House ap-

18. Quoted in *With Liberty and Justice,* 1, from House Report 291, 85th Congress, 1st Session, April 1, 1957, 14.
19. Emmet John Hughes, *The Ordeal of Power,* New York, 1963, 200.
20. Dwight D. Eisenhower, *Waging Peace,* New York, 1965, 154.

proved this compromise by a vote of 297 to 97, and the Senate by one of 60 to 15.[21]

At the committee hearings, and then on the floor of Congress, the bill's advocates and opponents agreed on the potential importance of the Civil Rights Commission, but their sharply contrasting arguments over whether such an agency should be created fell into what was to become an increasingly familiar pattern. Spokesmen of northern religious groups and labor unions, of such organizations as the Civil Liberties Union and the NAACP, together with an impressive array of liberal politicians, marshaled compelling evidence on the need for the Commission. Southern lawyers and state attorney generals, members of conservative rightist groups, and congressmen from below the Mason-Dixon Line declared vehemently that it was totally unnecessary and wholly subversive of states rights. Repeated debate took place over the relevance of the Commission to the civil rights bill as a whole. Southerners insisted on the basic contradiction in setting up a commission to make further investigations when other sections of the bill adequately safeguarded civil rights. Northerners countered by saying that minimal action had to be taken immediately, but a commission was essential to discover what further measures might have to be adopted to meet the problem more effectively.[22]

Among members of the House, Rodino of New Jersey argued persuasively that the Commission would be of "great value" in focusing attention on areas where improvement was still essential and in encouraging general discussion on the whole civil rights problem. Varik of Ohio stated with even greater emphasis that the Commission would fill a vital need and could make "a tremendous contribution to national welfare." In the Senate, Hubert Humphrey, who had actually proposed such an agency eight years earlier, was one of the Commission's staunchest adherents, and equally outspoken among Republicans were Javits of New York and Goldwater of Arizona. Lyndon Johnson, so influential in win-

21. *Revolution in Civil Rights,* 27–30; Douglas Cater, "How the Senate Passed the Civil Rights Bill," *Reporter,* 17, Sept. 5, 1957, 9–13.
22. *Hearings before Subcommittee No. 5, House Committee on the Judiciary,* 85th Congress, 1st Session; *Hearings Before the Subcommittee on Constitutional Rights of the Committee on the Judiciary; Senate,* 85th Congress, 1st Session.

ning passage of the bill as a whole, came out in emphatic support
of the proposed agency. "It can gather facts instead of charges,"
he commented in a much-quoted statement, "it can sift out the
truth from the fancies; and it can return with recommendations
which will be of assistance to reasonable men."[23]

The tone of the Southerners' testimony in committee hearings
and their remarks on the floor of Congress were rather different.
They attacked the Commission as "another tentacle of the Federal
octopus" with unlimited powers of "smear and harassment." One
irate South Carolinian asked what could be the possible objective
"in giving some little 2-4 whippersnapper the power to go all over
the United States and summon me, and my wife and my children
and grandchildren. . . ." Another caustic critic from this same state
declared that if investigations were necessary, they were better left
to the FBI than "the adolescent, uninformed, and inexperienced
Civil Rights Commission."[24] Virginia's Attorney General characterized the proposed agency as a Frankenstein monster: "You are
asked to create a Commission of Civil Rights and empower it to
perpetuate civil wrongs."

Northerners sought to assuage such fears of the Commission's
powers by emphasizing that it actually had only a two-year lease on
life. Southerners were not mollified. The minority report of the
House Committee on the Judiciary stated that anyone believing
the Commission would be allowed to expire after two years could
rightfully be accused of believing in fairies. "There will be so many
leftwing pressure groups howling for its permanency as now demand its creation," the report said. "Its hordes of employees and
snoopers will perpetuate themselves on the public payroll."[25]

Even when they had virtually given up the fight as the civil
rights bill reached the final stage of Senate debate, Southerners
continued to snipe at the Commission as a "roving election-year
Gestapo." Thurmond of South Carolina, who on August 29th
staged a one-man filibuster with a recording-breaking marathon
speech of 24 hours and 18 minutes, was still crying out in alarm
over giving any Federal agency "carte blanche authority to probe

23. *Hearings before . . . House Committee,* 1089, 667; *Congressional Record,*
    Senate, Aug. 7, 1957, 13851, 12637.
24. *Hearings before . . . House Committee,* 633, 696, 1097, 1166, 1242, 1245.
25. *House Report 291, Committee on the Judiciary,* April 1, 1957; 41–44.

and meddle in every phase of the relations between individuals."
Talmadge of Georgia continued to inveigh against the probable association with the Commission of "self-serving meddlers, interloping
agitators, and groups of one extreme persuasion or another."[26] And
in a final despairing statement, Johnston of South Carolina declared that he was prepared to introduce a new amendment to the
bill whose purpose would be "to meet the funeral expenses of the
members of the Civil Rights Commission in the unlikely event that
the Commission should ever come into being."[27]

The Commission survived all such attacks; it came through
the debates virtually unscathed. As finally established, it retained
broad though carefully defined functions. It was a fact-finding
and appraising agency, without any powers of enforcement, but
it could issue subpoenas in the course of its investigations and
call upon witnesses to testify under oath at its hearings. It was
authorized to consult with government officials, Federal and state,
and to set up Advisory State Committees to give aid and assistance.
The six members of the Commission, to be appointed by the President and confirmed by the Senate, were to serve without pay other
than *per diem* expenses when actually engaged in Commission
work, but the Staff Director, whose key position was from the first
fully recognized, could receive a salary as high as $22,500 annually.
Its life remained limited: a final report was to be made to the
President and Congress not later than two years following passage
of the enabling act, that is, by September 9, 1959.[28]

These were the responsibilities and powers of the Civil Rights
Commission. Though the primary task was the investigation of
voting complaints, any denial of the equal protection of the laws
fell within its scope.

26. *Congressional Record,* Senate, Aug. 6, 13848, 13374, 13725.
27. Quoted in Rovere, "Letter from Washington," 72.
28. *Public Law 85–315.*

II. GETTING UNDER WAY

It was one thing to have Congress create the Civil Rights Commission and quite another to have the Commission become fully operative. This was to prove a long and often frustrating task for all concerned. Not until ten months after passage of the Civil Rights Act—more than a third of the Commission's allotted span of life—could full-scale activities finally get under way.

There was the problem of finding the best possible appointees, including a Staff Director; their confirmation by the Senate; and the little matter of congressional appropriations for the conduct of Commission affairs. Even when these issues were settled, it was still necessary to formulate policy, set up an effective organization, and develop the actual procedures for carrying out the Commission's prescribed functions. A hesitant Congress wished to withhold funds until the Commission was fully organized; such organization could

not possibly be effected until adequate funds were assured for
staffing and investigations. For his part Eisenhower continued to
move with disconcerting caution and failed to exert any decisive
pressure to speed things up and enable the Commission to get at
its work.

A new and explosive crisis relating to civil rights took place
just as the President was engaged in his search for the men he
wanted for the Commission. This same September, 1957, Governor
Faubus of Arkansas challenged the Eisenhower Administration
over enforcement of a court ruling that called for the integration
of the all-white Central High School in Little Rock. Refusing to
accept the court decree, Faubus ordered out the state's National
Guard to block any attempt at entry to the school by nine Negro
children. The President made every effort to induce the Governor
to retreat from his defiant position, including representations at a
dramatic personal interview, but the Arkansas segregationist stood
his ground. When finally faced with an injunction against any further interference with the school's integration program, he withdrew the state troops but reiterated his unqualified opposition to
the court order. When the high school then opened following a
tense weekend, an unruly and threatening mob of five hundred
surged about the adjacent streets. The school officials felt obliged
to send the Negro children home for their own safety.

Although a few months earlier President Eisenhower emphatically stated that he could not imagine any circumstances that
would lead him to send Federal troops to enforce court orders,
the defiance of national authority in Little Rock left him no choice.
He moved reluctantly—but at the final moment decisively—to
federalize the National Guard and send in paratroopers to sustain
the court's ruling and provide protection for the Negro students.
The shame of Little Rock echoed around the world, but so also did
the dramatic interposition of Federal authority.[1]

In these untoward circumstances, having taken what Sherman
Adams described as "a constitutional duty which was the most
repugnant to him of all his acts in his eight years in the White
House,"[2] Eisenhower was especially anxious to find men to serve

1. Adams, *First-Hand Report*, 343–59; Hughes, *The Ordeal of Power*, 241–45;
   Eisenhower, *Waging Peace*, 162–67.
2. Adams, 355.

on the Civil Rights Commission who, as he described it, might have an "ameliorating effect" on the prejudices and passions aroused by the Little Rock crisis. "I want to get the spectrum of American opinion on the matter," he told a press conference on October 30; he was seeking men of "thoughtful mien" who would command full public confidence. Asked about the availability of such rumored appointees as Adlai Stevenson, Thomas Dewey, and Governor Shivers of Texas, he refused to comment but admitted ruefully that it was "difficult to get exactly what you want."[3]

Finally on November 7, Eisenhower announced the names of the six members of the Commission and said that it would be headed by Justice Stanley Reed, recently retired from active service on the Supreme Court. Within a month, however, Justice Reed withdrew his name. On further thought, he told the President, he had come to the conclusion that service on the Commission would be "incompatible with my obligations as a Judge" and that he feared "the harmful effects of possible lowering of respect for the impartiality of the Federal Judiciary."[4] Eisenhower then designated John A. Hannah, the President of Michigan State University, as Chairman. The other Commission members were Robert G. Storey, Dean of the Southern Methodist University Law School, who was to serve as Vice-Chairman; John S. Battle, a former governor of Virginia; Father Theodore M. Hesburgh, President of Notre Dame; J. Ernest Wilkins, an Assistant Secretary of Labor; and as the new sixth member, Doyle E. Carleton, one-time governor of Florida. They were sworn in at a ceremony at the White House on January 3, 1958.

The Commission could not have been more carefully balanced. It was bipartisan, as legally required, with three Democrats, two Republicans, and an Independent; and equally divided between Northerners and Southerners who might be expected to reflect their regions' conflicting views on integration versus segregation. It was heavily weighted in favor of the law and the academic profession, but two members were political figures, and in the person of Ernest Wilkins, one was a member of the Negro race.

In spite of general approval for these appointments, a number

3. *Public Papers of the Presidents,* 1957 (Eisenhower), National Archives, Washington, 1957, 781–83.
4. *Ibid.,* 829.

of newspapers and magazines expressed their doubt whether with such emphasis on balance and conservatism the country could expect very much from the Commission's ultimate recommendations. An editorial in the *Nation* noted that since the members were "deliberately chosen for their devotion to the cause of moderation, the Commission is not likely to break many lances crusading for civil rights." The *U.S. News and World Report* was also skeptical whether the new agency could be very effective. Expressing the Negro point of view in an article in the *New Leader,* Louis E. Lomax struck a somewhat different note. "It may yet produce some good," he wrote of the Commission, "not because of its intrinsic merit but because public opinion will not let it fail." Perhaps *Time* most accurately reflected public opinion when with its own moderation, it characterized the Commission members as "earnest and juridically minded men" who might have "considerable influence." Few observers anticipated that the Commission would have the highly significant role that it was actually to play in ensuing years.[5]

The choice of the Chairman, by virtue of his position in such a closely divided group, was obviously of utmost importance. A moderate Republican and former Assistant Secretary of Defense in the Eisenhower Administration, Hannah brought to his new task direct experience in government as well as in university administration, and an acknowledged ability for getting things done through quiet, effective pressure without essential compromise. One contemporary article described him as "soft spoken, affable, persuasive, and has the easy style of an able diplomat"; another said that he had the reputation "for standing up to pressure in tough situations." His basic sympathies were clearly in support of civil rights, as demonstrated by his record in promoting integration both in the armed forces and also at Michigan State, but he at the time believed that such social changes could only be brought about by slow, gradual, evolutionary progress. "While President Hannah has firm convictions on human rights," wrote the Lansing *State Journal,* "he is by no means to be considered a zealot."[6]

5. *Nation,* 186, Jan. 18, 1958, 42; *U.S. News and World Report,* 43, Jan. 3, 1958; Louis E. Lomax, "The Prospects for the Commission," *New Leader,* Feb. 3, 1958, 19–20; *Time,* 70, Nov. 18, 1957, 28.
6. Editorial from Flint *Journal,* inserted in *Congressional Record,* 85th Congress, 2nd Session, Vol. 4, Appendix 59; *U.S. News and World Report,* 43, Jan. 3, 1958; *State Journal* (Lansing, Mich.), Nov. 10, 1957.

That civil rights was not one of his major concerns was suggested in later testimony before a Senate committee. "I should say, Senator," Hannah told this committee, "that when I accepted this appointment from President Eisenhower six years ago, I didn't know very much about civil rights, but I have spent a lot of time worrying about it since. . . ."[7]

Hannah accepted his appointment—as indeed was true to a varying degree in the case of all Commission members—very reluctantly. He resisted for a long time, he wrote Governor Mennen Williams of Michigan, but finally agreed to serve "in the conviction that this is the most important single problem facing our country from the standpoint of our domestic tranquility and from the standpoint of long-time relationships with the uncommitted areas of the world that are so vital to the long-time well-being of the country."[8]

As to what the Commission might accomplish, Hannah expressed guarded hopefulness in an interview with the Flint *Journal:*

I have no illusions that this Commission will be able to produce the final solution in a few short months. However, I approach the task with the attitude that men of good will should be able to make some useful contribution in the national interest.[9]

Robert Storey came to the Commission with an impressive record in the field of law. He had been counsel to Justice Jackson in the Nuremburg trials, was a past-President of the American Bar Association, and currently President of the Southwest Legal Foundation as well as Dean of the Law School at Southern Methodist University. A Democrat and a Southerner, Storey was nevertheless a moderate on civil rights issues and notably judicial-minded. In his able conduct of Commission hearings, he was constantly to stress at one and the same time his own southern background and sympathies, and his sworn obligation as a member of the Commission to uphold the Constitution. He was held everywhere in the highest respect.

7. *Hearings Before Subcommittee on Constitutional Rights of the Committee on the Judiciary, Senate,* 88th Congress, 1st Session, May 21, 22, 23, and June 5, 6, 12, 1963, 237.
8. John A. Hannah to Mennen Williams, Jan. 14, 1958, in Hannah files, Michigan State University.
9. Quoted in *Congressional Record,* as above, 59.

Father Hesburgh, politically independent, a widely recognized though still relatively young educational leader, had interests both at home and abroad which went far beyond his responsibilities as President of Notre Dame. He enjoyed close associations with the Vatican and served as its delegate at meetings of the International Atomic Energy Agency. An article in *Look* magazine would somewhat later characterize him as a man of "confident authority . . . cool and outspoken."[10] Deeply committed to the principle of racial equality, Father Hesburgh firmly believed as a matter of religious faith that individual rights stemmed not from laws and constitutions but from the spiritual nature of man as created by God.

Former Governor Battle, at the time an attorney in Charlottesville, Virginia, was the Commission's most uncompromising spokesman of the South. He was an avowed segregationist and sincerely convinced, as he had no hesitation in stating, that a separation of the races was not only too deeply rooted in the southern way of life to be changed, but that it represented the only answer to the Negro problem. However, he was not a violent racist and was deeply concerned with the maintenance of law and order. For all his southern sympathies, *Time* stated, he is "a resonant voice for political moderation."[11] His service on the Commission, undertaken out of a strong sense of duty, placed him in a highly difficult position. This was to be clearly revealed not only in his dissent to some of its later recommendations but in his criticism of the general spirit of its approach to civil rights.

Ernest Wilkins was a lawyer associated for several years with the Department of Labor. His appointment did not awaken great enthusiasm in the Negro press. One commentator stated that while Wilkins was "no Uncle Tom," he was by no means a militant fighter in the civil rights cause.[12] Nevertheless, he appeared to interpret his role on the Commission as that of a spokesman for his race and his firm insistence on full Negro representation on the Commission's staff and advisory committees led to occasional sharp clashes with Governor Battle. However, Wilkins' service with the Commission was short-lived. Becoming seriously ill in the August

10. *Look,* Oct. 24, 1961.
11. *Time,* 70, Nov. 18, 1957, 28.
12. Lomax, "The Prospects for the Commission," 19–20.

after his appointment, he was compelled to resign and died five months later on January 19, 1959.

His successor in this first stage of the Commission's life was George M. Johnson, another Negro and also a Republican. Following extensive legal experience in California, he was the Dean of Howard University's Law School from 1946 to 1958, and, resigning this position, joined the Civil Rights Commission as its Director of Research and Planning before being appointed one of its members. Where his sympathies lay on civil rights matters was no more in question than in the case of Wilkins, but Johnson proved to be rather more tactful in expressing his views and more judicial-minded.

Doyle Carleton, whose term as Governor of Florida ran from 1923 to 1933, was a practicing attorney in Tampa and one of that city's outstanding and most honored citizens. His views on civil rights were much the same as those of Battle, with whom he worked in favor of a compromise plank at the Democratic Convention in 1952, but he never urged them aggressively and played a less positive role in the Commission than his fellow governor. Asked about his position on integration when he joined the Commission, he refused to commit himself other than to state quietly: "I have always been a Southerner."[13]

The popular estimation of these appointees as men ready to follow a reasonable course in trying to meet the problems the Commission faced, augured well for their prompt confirmation by the Senate. Optimists, however, reckoned without the strong position of Southerners in the Senate Judiciary Committee. Its intransigent chairman, Eastland of Mississippi, repeatedly postponed committee hearings and did everything he could to slow up the laborious process of senatorial action.

When hearings were at last held on February 24, 1958, the committee members for the most part treated the President's nominees with respect. Senator Ervin of North Carolina, although an implacable foe of the Commission, went so far as to say he was "pleased with the caliber of the men who have been selected." Eastland, however, was a good deal less gracious. He pressed Father Hesburgh mercilessly on his views on integration and was hardly mollified by the latter's acknowledgment that while he firmly believed in the Constitution, he realized that the "implementation

13. *U.S. News and World Report*, 43, Jan. 3, 1958.

of its provisions in regard to civil rights presented no end of problems." Hannah was attacked more directly. Incensed by reports that he was criticizing the Judiciary Committee for its dilatory tactics and was ready to cooperate with the Department of Justice in enforcing integration, Eastland subjected the Chairman to a sweeping cross-examination. Hannah insisted that the Commission would maintain complete independence in all its operations, had no intention of letting itself become the tool of the Department of Justice, and would not seek to impose on the South any preconceived integrationist pattern. Eastland nevertheless remained convinced that Hannah was wholly committed to the civil rights cause and strongly biased against the South.[14]

He would continue to maintain his opposition on the floor of the Senate. Even after Senator McNamara of Michigan came to Hannah's defense, stating that he had "never heard a word uttered against Dr. Hannah's sense of justice and fair play," Eastland repeated his accusations. "The facts show," he said on May 14, "the bias and prejudice on the part of the Chairman toward the southern people."[15]

In spite of such attacks, the Judiciary Committee eventually reported favorably on all the nominees to the Commission and recommended their confirmation. The Senate thereupon endorsed this report by a voice vote on March 4.

The Commission had a harder time in regard to the appointment and confirmation of a Staff Director. The President finally chose for this important post Gordon M. Tiffany, a former Attorney General of New Hampshire, who was recommended by the Council of State Governments, with which he was associated as a member of the Board of Managers. He was a close friend of Sherman Adams, though it was specifically denied that this had been a factor in his selection, and active in his state's politics.[16] Eisenhower sent his name to the Senate on February 18, but the subcommittee of its Judiciary Committee did not get around to even preliminary hearings until April 2—some six weeks later.

14. *Hearing Before Committee on the Judiciary, Members of the Commission on Civil Rights, Senate,* 85th Congress, 2nd Session, Feb. 24, 1958, 1–20; *New York Times,* Feb. 25, 1958.
15. *Congressional Record,* 85th Congress, 2nd Session, Senate, May 14, 1958, 7751, 8668, 8702.
16. *New York Times,* Feb. 19, 1958.

Tiffany earlier stated in an interview with the Boston *Sunday Globe* that if he became Staff Director he was determined to be "fair and open-minded and pursue a course of moderation." He now told the subcommittee that he did not consider himself an expert on civil rights, felt that policy making was up to the Commission members, and visualized his own task as that of maintaining an efficient organization and developing workmanlike day-by-day operations.[17] His conciliatory attitude nevertheless did not convince the southern members of the committee that he was the right man for the job. They held their fire both at this preliminary hearing, and at a subsequent session before the Judiciary Committee as a whole. However, the narrow majority of the final report recommending confirmation, delayed until early May and adopted by a vote of five to four, promised trouble on the floor of the Senate.

The attack then launched against Tiffany reflected both political and sectional undertones. Senator Russell of Georgia pointed out in an impressive speech that the Staff Director was the key man on the Commission. "His views and activities," he declared, "will have more effect upon the work of the Commission and its final recommendations than will any other individual, including the Chairman of the Commission."[18] Accepting this thesis, the foes of the Commission saw all their worst fears confirmed in the President naming as Staff Director a Republican from New Hampshire who might be expected to reflect both the views of his party and those of his section of the country. Russell restricted his criticism to what he considered Tiffany's lack of stature for such an important post, but Senator Eastland went much farther afield. After renewing his vituperative attacks on the Commission itself, he personally assailed Tiffany and charged him with radicalism and bias. "I do not believe that Mr. Tiffany is a Communist," Eastland generously admitted, but then went on to say that an apparent interest in communist-front organizations clearly disqualified him from serving on the Commission.[19]

The Republican senators came valiantly to Tiffany's defense

17. Boston *Sunday Globe,* March 2, 1958; *New York Times,* April 3, 1958.
18. *Congressional Record,* 85th Congress, 2nd Session, Senate, May 14, 1958, 7751.
19. *Ibid.,* 7748–59.

and stoutly upheld his integrity and professional competence. Senator Dirksen further urged his confirmation as a New Englander, an Episcopalian—and a father. "I think that makes a great deal of difference," he said. "Mr. Tiffany has two children. I think of a father, always, as one who has a little more human sympathy. Children will coax it out of him, if it cannot be coaxed in any other way."[20] This unusual argument would not appear to have proved wholly persuasive. The Senate voted favorably on Tiffany's confirmation on May 14, but the South cast thirteen adverse ballots. The issue was at last settled, however, and on June 9—nine months to the day after the creation of the Commission—the Staff Director was sworn in.[21]

In the meantime, the difficulties the Commission experienced in the delay over Tiffany's confirmation were compounded by the failure of Congress to appropriate operating expenses. The President allocated $200,000 from emergency funds to get things started, but to enable the Commission fully to carry out its duties, he asked for a prompt appropriation of $750,000. Congress dallied; Eisenhower did not press matters. The Commission could not proceed with any assurance until it knew just where it stood and what future funds were available.

Criticism of this delay soon became widespread. As early as February, Representative Yates of Illinois, charging "gross inaction," held the Administration responsible for the snafu which found the Commission unable to move ahead because it had neither a Staff Director nor appropriations, and Congress justifying procrastination in granting the necessary funds because the Commission was not yet organized. "The facts show," Yates stated, "that the White House has been derelict in failing to press for implementation."[22]

A month later an editorial in the *Christian Century* further pressed such charges against a "limping Administration" for failure to come to the rescue of "the so far peculiarly ectoplasmic" agency. "Precious time has been lost," this magazine declared. "Let Congress now appropriate operating funds. Let the grievances pour in.

20. *Ibid.*
21. *New York Times,* June 15, 1958.
22. *Congressional Record,* 85th Congress, 2nd Session, House, Feb. 15, 1958, 1967.

Let the committee get down to work. Let the truth break through."[23]

As other critics also voiced their concern over executive inertia, Eisenhower felt advised to issue a reassuring statement. "Surely it has had a hard time getting off the ground," he said on March 26 in answer to questions about what was happening to the Commission. "We had to give it, you might say, a loaned budget, but I have great hopes for what it will do in both these fields, watching and seeing what are the legal difficulties that may occur, as well as what can be done in what you might call the educational and even, indeed, the spiritual field."[24]

This was neither a very clear statement nor a ringing call to action. It reflected the natural caution of a man who was still asking the Negroes for "patience and forbearance" in the whole field of civil rights.[25] However, the friends of the Commission found their own patience exhausted with the request for funds lying deeply buried in committee, and they brought the matter to the floor of the House through an amendment adding the $750,000 for the Commission to a general appropriation bill for the Executive Office funds.

The Southerners put up another last-ditch fight arguing that the Commission had been an evil thing when it was first created and was no less evil now. But while their ranks held firm, they were very much in the minority and on April 1 the House approved the amendment. The concurrence of the Senate was delayed another two months as the general money bill was subjected to further hearings and floor debate, but this disputed measure was finally approved with the appropriation for the Commission intact and the President signed the bill into law on June 25. The Commission now had the funds it needed, and with the Staff Director's appointment already confirmed, was at long last ready to swing into operation and embark upon its long-delayed program of investigations, hearings and reports.[26]

23. *Christian Century,* 75, March 5, 1958, 268–69.
24. *Public Papers of the Presidents,* 1958 (Eisenhower), 238; *New York Times,* March 27, 1958.
25. *New York Times,* May 13, 1958.
26. *General Government Matters Appropriation for 1959, Additional Hearings Before the Subcommittee on Appropriations, House,* 85th Congress, 2nd

The Commission itself had been slowly, hesitantly seeking to prepare the way for such activity ever since that distant day— January 3, 1958—when its members held their initial meeting and were sworn into office at the White House. Hardly foreseeing the frustrating delays to which they would be subjected, Hannah was on that occasion quite hopeful. "We are not only going to get along well," he said in a first press conference, "but come to conclusions agreeable all the way around."[27] But the Senate's tardiness in confirming the Commission members, the problem of the Staff Director, and the inaction on appropriations soon tempered his optimism. In February, Hannah wrote Sherman Adams that without a Staff Director he was "becoming increasingly restive"; a month later he complained to Secretary of Labor Mitchell that the Commission was "stalemated by the hurdles created by Senator Eastland and some of his colleagues."[28]

A first need was to find a habitation and a home, and when quarters in Washington were finally secured at 726 Jackson Place, to get someone to handle correspondence. Hannah appealed to the White House for help. "It is hoped," he wrote Douglas Price, in the Executive Office, "that you will make arrangements for a person to at least temporarily sit in the offices of the Civil Rights Commission to answer the telephone, receive mail, etc."[29] In response to this poignant appeal, an executive secretary from the State Department, Mrs. Carol Arth, was loaned to the Commission to take charge of office organization, personnel, and public liaison.

The Commission members adopted the practice of meeting about once a month and were soon deeply involved in consideration of the interrelated problems of recruiting the necessary staff and planning a general program. Very little could be done until a Staff Director was officially confirmed, but once the President named Tiffany for this post, the Commission sought to alleviate this difficulty by first calling him in as a consultant and then making

---

Session, 39–40; *Congressional Record,* 85th Congress, 2nd Session, House, March 31, 1958, 5817–20; *New York Times,* April 2, 1958.

27. *New York Times,* Jan. 4, 1958.
28. Hannah to Sherman Adams, Feb. 20, 1958; Hannah to James P. Mitchell, March 21, 1958, in Hannah files.
29. Hannah to Douglas Price, Jan. 6, 1958, in Hannah files.

him Staff Director-designate. The southern opposition to Tiffany's
appointment nevertheless called for caution in giving him too
much responsibility while his name was still before the Senate
Judiciary Committee. The Commission consequently felt it necessary, as Hannah wrote in the letter to Mitchell already quoted, to
behave "in a very circumspect manner so as to avoid irritating
Senator Eastland's colleagues."[30]

In spite of Hannah's original optimism there was not complete harmony within the Commission as it sought to map out its
program and make its plans. Sharp controversy arose between Battle
and Wilkins, especially in regard to Negro representation on the
staff, and on this and other issues the Chairman's major role was
that of moderator and peacemaker in attempting to bring about a
consensus between northern and southern members. "In some of
our earlier meetings," Hannah was later to recall, "we found that
we were far apart in our basic thinking. At times it appeared it was
going to be very difficult, indeed, to make real progress." Yet progress was made. The Commissioners were all men of goodwill; Governor Battle later emphasized what he called the forgiving spirit of
his colleagues, and they became mutually convinced that the country faced no more important problem than civil rights and that
somehow it must be solved.[31]

In building up the staff each Commissioner personally appointed a legal assistant, who was also to serve as a regular staff
member, and joint action was taken upon the persons to head up
the different divisions. Mrs. Arth was prevailed upon to remain
in charge of office personnel and liaison; George Johnson, later appointed a Commissioner, took over planning and research; and
Colonel A. H. Rosenfeld, an attorney and former army officer, became responsible for complaints and field surveys.

A further move, which Dean Storey called "the smartest thing
we ever did" and the *New York Times* hailed as the first really important forward step since the creation of the Commission, was the
decision to set up State Advisory Committees.[32] While the legal staff
at headquarters undertook a thorough inquiry into all Federal and
state laws bearing on civil rights, these committees could assume

30. Hannah to Mitchell, March 21, 1958, in Hannah files.
31. Commission files.
32. *New York Times*, April 27, 1958.

"a grass-roots information-gathering job." Henry M. Shine, Jr., a Texas attorney who had been with the Hoover Commission on Government Reorganization, was given primary responsibility in organizing these committees and later became an Assistant Staff Director in charge of their activities.

The selection of people for these committees, who served without pay, proved to be an onerous job taking up much time. Each Commission member had general supervision over eight states in seeking out suitable men and women. But all appointments were subject to approval by the Commission as a whole. The State Advisory Committee personnel included lawyers, labor leaders, clergymen, former government officials, civic leaders, and whenever possible, one or more Negroes. Among the more prominent individuals induced to serve were Robert G. Sproul, President-emeritus of the University of California; Edwin D. Canham, Editor of the *Christian Science Monitor;* Rabbi Abraham J. Feldman, of Connecticut; and Charles E. Wilson, former Secretary of Defense. The first committees were set up in Texas, Indiana, Virginia, Michigan, and Florida—home states of five of the Commission members—and by August comparable groups were organized throughout the country except for Mississippi and South Carolina. They were authorized to carry on civil rights investigations in their particular localities, make periodic reports on their findings, and generally cooperate with the Commission itself.[33]

While this organizational work was proceeding in regard to the State Advisory Committees, the staff at Commission headquarters was gradually working out plans under the supervision of the Staff Director-designate for the investigation of complaints, for field surveys bearing upon the deprivation of the right to vote, and for possible future hearings. The files of current Staff Activities Reports, copies of a *Newsletter* carrying general information, and the minutes of the official meetings of the Commission, give a picture of busy activity all along the line. The administrative setup still remained on a tentative and somewhat uncertain basis pending Senate confirmation of the Staff Director and congressional appropriation of a long-term budget, but when these issues were

33. Article prepared for *New York Times,* dated Sept. 19, 1958, in Hannah files; *With Liberty and Justice for All,* 3–4.

settled at the end of June, the Civil Rights Commission was in a position to make definite operational commitments.

It then gave Tiffany full authority in all matters of staff organization and officially established a Secretarial and Liaison Office; an Office of Complaints, Information and Survey; and an Office of Laws, Plans and Research. Although authorized to appraise Federal laws and policies in the whole field of civil rights, the Commission decided to concentrate in three major areas: voting, education, and public housing. Staff "depth study teams" would undertake preliminary surveys, field investigations would be made of complaints of the deprivation of the right to vote, and when the proper time came, the Commission would hold public hearings. In reporting at the tenth Commission meeting on August 19-20, 1958, Tiffany stated that half of the contemplated staff positions were filled and a vast amount of basic civil rights information was already assembled. "The ground work is largely completed," he said, "we are reasonably on top of the job."[34]

The Commission from its earliest days received a steady flow of complaints about alleged violations of civil rights. For the most part, they came from inmates of prisons and mental institutions, or obvious cranks. Moreover the Commission was in fact empowered to investigate only "allegations in writing under oath or affirmation" relating to the deprivation of the right to vote. It did not receive any sworn complaints falling in this category until August. The Commission thereupon authorized their official investigation —first in Alabama and Mississippi, then in Florida, Tennessee and Louisiana—and decided to hold a first public voting rights hearing in Montgomery which was tentatively scheduled for December, 1958.

In the field of education, the Commission restricted its program to consideration of the progress that was being made in public schools that had already adopted a program of integration in conformity with Federal court orders. With this in view, it planned to hold a conference, in Nashville, Tennessee, to which would be invited officials from such school systems for an exchange of views on their common problems. While this conference would not include delegates from the Deep South, which was still so adamantly

34. Minutes of tenth Commission meeting, Aug. 19-20, 1958.

opposed to any move toward integration, the Commission felt that it would provide important data on what was happening in the border states, and also be of great benefit to school systems in a transitional stage through a sharing of their experiences.

In the third area of major concern, segregation in public housing, the Commission planned not only general investigations, but hearings in New York, Chicago, and Atlanta. This would significantly extend its activities to the North and the Commission already considered housing "the frontier problem of civil rights."[35]

This was the agenda worked out and agreed upon by early September. The Commission had full authority to make these investigations and hold these conferences and hearings. It also had the further responsibility, as set forth in the Civil Rights Act, to report its activities, findings and recommendations to the President and Congress. The deadline remained September 9, 1959—little more than a year away. This was an almost overwhelming task.

35. Minutes of eleventh Commission meeting, Sept. 9–10, 1958; *With Liberty and Justice for All*, 4.

III. THE INITIAL HEARINGS

The Washington headquarters staff made the most careful preparations for the Commission's first public project—the hearing on voting rights in December, 1958, to be held in Montgomery. It investigated the complaints received from Alabama, ultimately totaling ninety-one; interviewed those complainants who would be subpoenaed as witnesses at the hearing; and arranged for the filing in advance of their sworn statements. In these circumstances there appeared to be some justification for the later criticism of a southern newspaper that the Negro witnesses "frequently seemed to have been meticulously coached."[1] The Commission nevertheless felt that such careful procedures were essential for an orderly and productive hearing.

1. Birmingham *News,* Dec. 9, 1958.

At the same time that the Commission's field agents were lining up the Negro witnesses, they sought to obtain the cooperation of county voting registrars in making their records available and in agreeing to accept subpoenas for their own appearance at the hearings. Here they encountered a defiantly obstructive attitude. The registrars withheld their records and refused to give out any information. In Macon County, where most of the Alabama complaints originated, this policy was followed on the orders of Attorney General John Patterson, a month later to become Governor Patterson. He was prepared to challenge the Commission's power to subpoena or question any judicial officer of the state. In two other counties—Barbour and Bullock—Circuit Judge George C. Wallace, destined to an even more conspicuous career as a segregationist leader when he in turn became Alabama's governor, officially impounded all registration records. "They are not going to get the records," Wallace declared with the belligerence which was to become his hallmark. "And if any agent of the Civil Rights Commission comes down to get them, they will be locked up. . . . I repeat, I will jail any Civil Rights Commission agent who attempts to get the records."[2]

In these somewhat unpropitious circumstances the Commission, having issued its subpoenas to voting complainants and voting officials alike, met on the morning of December 9 in the Federal Building at Montgomery to open the hearing.[3] All six members (they had to stay at Maxwell Air Base because the city's hotels were all segregated) were present, and they agreed that Dean Storey would preside and take the major responsibility in interrogating the witnesses. The courtroom assigned for the hearing was crowded, some two dozen newspaper reporters were on hand, and in the background whirred four television cameras.

Chairman Hannah made an opening statement (setting a pattern that generally marked all subsequent hearings) and strongly emphasized that the Commission was not a protagonist of any one view on civil rights, had no affiliation with the Department of Justice, and was solely and exclusively "a fact-finding body." It had

2. Montgomery *Advertiser*, Dec. 6, 1958; *Report of the United States Commission on Civil Rights, 1959*, 70–71.
3. *Hearings Before the United States Commission on Civil Rights: Voting, Montgomery, Alabama, Dec. 8–9, 1958 and Jan. 9, 1959*, Washington, 1959.

been established, Hannah told a tensely expectant audience, in the hope that through dispassionate evaluation and appraisal "some sort of reason and light" could be brought to bear upon issues which had heretofore been "frequently and passionately debated but seldom soberly assessed." He then turned the session over to Storey, who after swearing in the subpoenaed Negro complainants and state officials, called the first witness.[4]

He was William P. Mitchell, Secretary of the Tuskegee Civic Association, who had forwarded the original voting complaints from Macon County to Washington. He was himself a registered voter, after three years of litigation, but his testimony concentrated on the difficulties that Negroes generally experienced in trying to secure the right to register. This was then brought home with more compelling force in the questioning of some twenty-six witnesses who in spite of every effort had not been able to register. What gave the testimony of these Negroes an especially dramatic impact was their social status. They were well educated, many of them graduates of Tuskegee Institute; for the most part they were professional men and women—teachers, ministers, doctors, civil service employees; they were almost invariably tax-paying property owners; some of them had been registered voters in other states before moving to Alabama; and all of them met the state's residence and other legal requirements for voting. Yet in each and every case their local registration board rejected their applications or else took no action on them whatsoever.

The complainants described their experiences in almost identical terms. They invariably experienced great difficulty in finding out when the local Board of Registrars would hold one of its infrequent sessions. They had to submit their applications in a room much smaller than that available for whites, only two could be processed at a time, and they had to wait endlessly in a standing line. All Negroes were required to copy a specified article of the Constitution and then fill out a long and complicated form. The process usually took close upon two hours. A single mistake in writing the section of the Constitution or filling out the application blank—a misspelling, a wrong date, anything else—could be seized upon at the whim of the registrar to reject an application.

4. *Ibid.,* 4.

As witness after witness described such frustrating experiences, the emotional undercurrents not far below the surface occasionally broke through. Storey pursued his interrogations with judicial impartiality, but other members of the Commission began to break in to ask why the Negroes wanted to register and why they felt their applications were rejected.

Amelia JoAnne Adams was a shy young girl of twenty-two, studying for a master's degree in organic chemistry at Tuskegee Institute. In a hardly audible voice (Storey repeatedly asked her to speak a little louder), she told of making out her registration application, which included copying out Article 2 of the Constitution in $8\frac{1}{2}$ pages of careful longhand, and then expectantly waiting for the news of either acceptance or rejection. It never arrived. Her questioning then continued:

COMMISSIONER WILKINS: *Do you have any opinion as to the reason why you haven't heard from it?*

MISS ADAMS: *Well, I can read; I can write, and I think I possess all my mental faculties. So, the only thing I can think of is the fact that I am a Negro.*

CHAIRMAN HANNAH: *I would like to ask . . . Why do you want to register to vote?*

MISS ADAMS: *Well, the Government of the United States is based on the fact that the governed govern, and only as long as the people are able to express their opinions through voting will the country be able to remain the great power that it is.*[5]

And then there was Charles B. Miller, a young man of thirty with a college degree, who had served a year overseas with the army in Korea. Dean Storey asked him why he wanted to vote:

MR. MILLER: *I have dodged bombs and almost gotten killed, and then come back and being denied to vote—I don't like it. I want to vote, and I want to take part in this type of government. I have taken part in it when I was in the service. I think I should take part in it when I am a civilian.*

VICE-CHAIRMAN STOREY: *Do you know of any reason why you haven't heard from your application?*

MR. MILLER: *The reason, I believe—I would state that wholeheartedly —that I am a Negro.*[6]

5. *Ibid.,* 53–54.
6. *Ibid.,* 104.

The first morning of the hearing was entirely devoted to this testimony of Negroes from Macon County. It remained a relatively quiet and subdued session. In the afternoon, when the Commissioners interrogated the county officials who were subpoenaed to appear, the atmosphere abruptly changed. The smoldering feud between the Commission and the state of Alabama came out into the open.

The first new witness was Probate Judge Varner, seventy years old, of Macon County. In giving his testimony he was described by *Time* magazine as "studiously loquacious," but the purport of his answers to questions about registration procedures was that he only kept the records and otherwise knew nothing whatsoever of what went on. How often did the registrars meet? "I don't pay any attention to it." How many registrars were there? "I don't actually know how many there are. I don't pay any attention to it." When Commissioner Wilkins pushed him a little harder about the registration forms, Judge Varner again answered: "I don't know how they fix the papers. I don't even remember what's on the paper. It's been so long since I looked at one."

Governor Battle then intervened to ask if there was any distinction in the registration requirements as applied to whites and Negroes. Judge Varner answered: "Not so far as I know." Tempers then flared when an insistent Wilkins asked how he could possibly know whether the rules were applied without distinction if he never saw the records, never saw the applications, and was never present in the registration room.[7]

The next two witnesses—Grady Rogers and E. P. Livingston —were members of the Macon County Board of Registrars and were if possible even less cooperative. Before they were called a heated controversy broke out between Storey and Attorney General Patterson over whether or not they had actually taken the general oath required of all witnesses and whether in any event they could be legally questioned at all. The situation was highly confusing. Storey staunchly held his ground but the end result was that the two registrars not only withheld their records, which they said were impounded that very morning by the state Circuit Court, but they also refused to give any testimony on registration proceedings.

7. *Ibid.,* 131–32, 143, 147, 150.

Against a background of rising tension in the crowded little courtroom, with Storey being repeatedly forced to call for order, the two witnesses averted every question either by stating that an answer might tend to incriminate them, or by declaring that as judicial officers of the state of Alabama, their actions could not be inquired into by the Commission. When Battle asked if they did not have anything to say about the testimony of the Negro complainants who alleged they were denied the right to register because of their race, they still refused any comment.[8]

The Commission then called upon several probate judges and registration officials from other counties to testify but they were hardly more helpful than those from Macon County. They did not have their records with them; they generally declined to answer any questions on matters of substance. Wilkins did succeed in drawing from the probate judge of Lowndes County the reluctant admission that among the fourteen thousand Negroes in that county, not a single one was registered. When further pressed, he conceded that this situation "might be unusual, peculiar in some places, yes." One of this county's registrars was more explicit when this damaging line of inquiry was continued. On Storey's asking whether registration procedures were applied equally to white and black applicants, he bluntly answered, "We have no blacks."[9]

The impasse between the Commission and the Alabama officials was complete. The latter would give no explanation as to why the registration boards so generally ignored the applications of Negroes, or why, as in the case of Lowndes County, Negroes did not even try to register. They maintained this was none of the Commission's concern, and standing on what they asserted to be their constitutional rights, had nothing further to say. After a long afternoon of futile questioning even Governor Battle, for all his southern sympathies, became thoroughly exasperated.

He gravely warned the state officers that while he felt quite as strongly as they did that segregation of the races was "the right and proper way of life in the South," their refusal to cooperate with the Commission in its investigation of voting was "an error in doing that which appears to be an attempt to cover up their actions in relation to the exercise of the ballot by some people who may be entitled thereto."

8. *Ibid.,* 152–62.
9. *Ibid.,* 187, 200.

Their attitude, he said, might well encourage punitive legislation in Congress, and this would "react adversely to us in Virginia and to you in Alabama. . . ." "Will you kindly re-evaluate the
situation," Governor Battle pleaded, "and see if there is not some
way you . . . may cooperate a little bit more fully with this Commission and not have it said by our enemies in Congress that the
people of Alabama were not willing to explain their conduct when
requested to do so."[10]

His warning and his plea went unheeded. At the close of the
day's session Attorney General Patterson pugnaciously denied that
Alabama had "anything to hide." All its citizens, white and black,
were treated fairly, he said, and it was his duty to do everything possible to prevent this "unlawful invasion" into the duties of the
state's judicial officers on the part of the Federal Government.
There could be no surrender of principle to expediency: "The time
for retreating has come to an end."[11]

The Alabama registration officials' contumacious defiance of
the Civil Rights Commission and its Attorney General's outspoken
challenge to its authority were headlined and editorialized about
from coast to coast. The *New York Times* spoke of the "intolerable
contempt for law in resistance to this ultra-moderate Presidential
Commission," while the Washington *Star,* after voicing the strongest criticism of Patterson's attitude, commented wryly that "something is going to fall on Alabama, and this time it will not be
stars." Nor was this condemnation of the local officials' attitude
limited to the northern press. Such prominent southern newspapers
as the Louisville *Courier-Journal,* the Richmond *Times-Dispatch,*
and the Atlanta *Constitution,* while reaffirming their opposition to
the investigation, expressed great concern over developments at
Montgomery. "The irresponsible defiance of this Commission in
Alabama," the *Constitution* declared, "has done the South's cause
more harm than anything since the hate bombings." Even Alabama
papers were critical. Governor Battle, the Birmingham *News* said,
"raised a sober point as the dark velvet skies gentled down over
Montgomery."[12]

10. *Ibid.,* 206–7.
11. *Report,* 86.
12. *New York Times,* Dec. 10, 1958; Washington *Star,* Dec. 9, 1958; Birming-
    ham *News,* Dec. 9, 1958; *Report,* 85–86.

Two days later, replying to questions at a press conference, President Eisenhower himself termed the conduct of the Alabama officials "reprehensible" and said he did not know what would come of it all. "I think it is a rather sad sort of thing," he commented, "because all the way around we are running into this refusal of complying with the basic laws of the land."[13]

Amid all this excitement, the second session of the Commission's hearing was anticlimactic. A number of Negroes from other Alabama counties testified along very much the same lines as had those from Macon County. They told of comparable delays and postponements in the meetings of registration boards, interminable standing in line, long drawn-out procedures, complicated forms—and then the wearying wait for answers to their voting applications which never arrived. Many of the Negroes had tried to register again and again without making any progress. The growing sympathy of the members of the Commission as they heard the same story told over and over, was clearly revealed when Father Hesburgh interrupted the testimony given by a Bullock County farmer on his many futile attempts to register:

COMMISSIONER HESBURGH: *Mr. Sellers, are you going to keep trying?*
MR. SELLERS: *Oh, yes, I'm determined to register.*
COMMISSIONER HESBURGH: *God bless you.*[14]

The continued hearing did not produce any new or startling testimony, but before it came to an end, it was enlivened by a statement from Chairman Hannah. He announced that the Commission greatly regretted the failure of certain persons to produce their records or to testify, and that it had consequently decided to turn the complete record of the hearing over to the Attorney General of the United States "for such action as he deems appropriate to the end that will assist this Commission to have made available to it the information that is required to enable it to carry out the mandate of the law."[15]

Although Hannah gave no hint of any disagreement among the Commissioners, this step did not actually have their unanimous

13. *New York Times,* Dec. 11, 1958.
14. *Hearings,* 275.
15. *Ibid.,* 281.

support. A vote on it at a meeting the night before was four to two. Wilkins would have liked to see a stronger motion; more important, Battle opposed on principle the reference of the dispute to the Attorney General. However, Storey and Carleton, as well as Hannah and Hesburgh, approved the stand taken.[16]

Attorney General Brownell acted promptly. He filed a civil suit in the appropriate United States District Court and after hearings, Judge Frank M. Johnson, Jr., ordered the Alabama officials in three counties to make their records available for inspection by the Commission before January 9. Four staff members thereupon sought to examine them, but still hampered by the obstructive attitude of the registrars, they could do little more than make a rather cursory sampling. At a special meeting in executive session to hear their report, the Commission subsequently passed —this time unanimously—another motion stating that compliance with the court order was not satisfactory and requesting the Attorney General to take further action. Battle's position now was that the controversy was no longer one between the Commission and the judicial officers of the state of Alabama, but a question of the latter's obedience to a Federal court order.[17]

However meager the sampling of registration records presented to the Commission, they nonetheless appeared to substantiate the charges of discrimination made by the Negro complainants at the public hearing. Among one batch of rejected applications, seventy-three were those of Negroes (several of whom had tried to register several times) and only eleven were those of whites. Conversely, in another sample of seventeen applications which were accepted in spite of mistakes in filling out the forms, all but one were those of whites. The Commission's field agents nevertheless remained very circumspect in interpreting this evidence. With the utmost caution they went no further than to say that in these particular records there were "indicia justifying an inference of racial discrimination. . . ."[18]

Their restraint was hardly paralleled by subsequent action on the part of the Alabama legislature. A few weeks later it unanimously passed a bill calling for the complete destruction of all

16. Minutes of fifteenth Commission meeting, Dec. 8, 1958.
17. Minutes of sixteenth Commission meeting, Jan. 8, 1959.
18. *Hearings*, 318.

papers relating to rejected voting applications. This was a move which jarred rather sharply with Attorney General Patterson's statement that Alabama had nothing to hide. Indeed it seemed to give further substance to the charges made by the Negro witnesses at the Commission hearings that they were indeed being deprived of the right to vote by reason of their color.

In commenting on these developments in the section of its 1959 report dealing with this inquiry into voting rights, the Commission said in a triumph of understatement:

"The Alabama story is not ended."[19]

While field investigations on the voting issue continued in several other southern states, the Commission decided to hold another public hearing in Louisiana where seventy-nine sworn complaints on denial of the right to register had originated. It was scheduled for Shreveport on July 13, 1959 but the situation was to prove even more difficult than that in Alabama. The Louisiana officials were completely uncooperative in the preliminary investigations, tried to force the Commission to reveal the names of Negro complainants, instituted a civil suit challenging the constitutionality of the Civil Rights Act itself, and finally appealed to a Federal District Court for a temporary order enjoining the Commission from holding the hearing.

Sixteen hours before proceedings were scheduled to begin at Shreveport, Federal District Judge Benjamin Dawkins issued such an order. He ruled that the inability of state officials, charged by voting complainants of having violated the law, to cross-examine their accusers violated their legal rights as set forth in the Federally enacted Administrative Procedure Act. This court order was of dubious constitutionality. Dawkins himself admitted that it might be set aside if appealed to a higher court (adding rather significantly "it is all part of the game"), but the delay and cost involved in making such an appeal led the Commission to the reluctant decision to suspend the hearing. While the legality of its procedures was ultimately to be fully upheld in the Supreme Court, the Commission had temporarily fallen victim to a southern roadblock.[20]

Thanks to the preliminary investigations and preparation of

19. *Report,* 97.
20. *Ibid.,* 98–106.

testimony, the Commission nevertheless had a very good idea of what was taking place in Louisiana. As subsequently brought out in the official report, the evidence revealed not only an organized campaign to prevent the registration of Negro voters, but an effort in some of the Louisiana parishes to purge the rolls of such Negroes as had succeeded in registering in the past. The state legislature had created a joint committee with the declared purpose of reducing Negro registration, and it was busily distributing a new manual instructing local registrars on how the voting laws might be more rigidly interpreted to maintain "the purity" of the ballot.

One statement in the manual suggested the spirit behind this campaign: "We are in a life and death struggle with the Communists and the NAACP to maintain segregation and to preserve the liberties of the people." In two parishes where no Negroes were as yet registered, the door was kept closed by the ruling that applicants had to be vouched for by two enrolled voters. Without a single member of their own race on the list, a Negro in these parishes had little hope of ever being able to register. Where registrations had been allowed in the past, members of the White Citizens Councils challenged them on the ground that mistakes were made in the original application forms. In one case the charge—and one can imagine the delight with which the Commission's staff member discovered its actual wording—was an "error in spilling."[21]

Such information as was obtained in Louisiana, and investigations in other states, strongly substantiated the evidence of discrimination against Negroes brought out so directly in the Alabama hearing. The overall picture of how literacy tests were openly used to keep non-whites from registering clearly revealed a widespread denial of equal protection of the laws throughout the South. There was nothing surprising in such revelations. Ever since the first days of grandfather clauses, discriminatory poll taxes, and other voting restrictions, the country as a whole knew that many southern states were depriving the Negro of his right to vote in direct violation of the safeguards of the Fifteenth Amendment. What the Civil Rights Commission was doing, however, was to substantiate assumed knowledge by sworn affidavits and incontrovertible legal evidence. It was gathering facts instead of charges, as Lyndon Johnson phrased

21. *Ibid.,* 102, 104.

its objectives, and sifting out the truth from fancies. Moreover, the Commission's case was strengthened by the obstructive attitude of the officials in Alabama and Louisiana in seeking to block this fact-finding. Their attitude hardly persuaded the Commission— and subsequently neither Congress nor the country at large—that on the voting issue the South did not indeed have something to hide.

IV. EDUCATION AND HOUSING

The approach of the Civil Rights Commission to the problems of equal protection of the laws in education and housing differed sharply from its investigation into voting. Limiting itself to the border states in the former problem, and concentrating largely on the North in the latter, the new hearings lacked something of the drama and direct conflict marking those on voting in Montgomery. Nevertheless they had their moments of underlying tension and produced startling evidence of the discrimination against Negroes in fields which were in some measure even more important than the deprivation of the right to vote.

The conference on the progress of school integration reflected a conscious decision to avoid getting enmeshed in the problems of the Deep South. Alabama, Florida, Georgia, Louisiana, Mississippi, and South Carolina still maintained complete segregation in all their schools in 1959. Virginia was deeply committed to a special campaign of "massive resistance." None of these states would therefore be involved in a conference directed, in the Commission's phrase, toward "problems of schools in transition from the educator's viewpoint." Ignoring the wholly recalcitrant states, the Commission was taking a long, hard look at the experience of a selected number of those seven hundred school districts, in thirteen states, which had already taken some steps toward integration in formerly all-white schools.[1]

This conference, in Nashville on March 5–6, 1959, was attended by school officials, representatives of educational organizations, and other invited guests. They heard a series of reports—and were then free to ask questions and discuss them—on the course of integration in seventeen cities, towns and rural communities ranging from Washington, D.C. to San Angelo, Texas, and from Anderson County, Tennessee, to Hobbs, New Mexico.

Many of the accounts of school integration in the face of social tension and incipient racial conflict, sometimes spilling over into open violence, vividly illustrated the emotions and prejudices that underlay every phase of the struggle for civil rights.

The general purport of the conference reports was that in response to the Supreme Court decisions of 1954 and 1955, even in those states that accepted an obligation to integrate, the school districts were placing a great deal more emphasis on "deliberate" than on "speed" in applying the Court's famous formula. Overall statistics showed that out of 8,692 school districts in southern and border states, less than one thousand were desegregated as of May, 1959. What the conference most significantly brought out, however, was the extent to which under the most favorable circumstances the results still remained in so many cases no more than token integration. The general approach of most school boards appeared to be the admission of a few Negro children into the lower grades and their advancement into the upper grades at an ever more gradual pace. The racial pattern of existing school districts, reluctance on the part of many Negro parents to have their children transferred, and continuing community opposition to any social

1. *Conference Before the United States Commission on Civil Rights: Education, First Annual Conference on Problems of Schools in Transition, Nashville, Tenn., March 5–6, 1959,* Washington, 1959.

mixing of the races were among the more obvious reasons for this slow progress. The reports to the conferences also emphasized the many other problems associated with even such limited acceptance of integration. Among them were the possible lowering of educational standards, enforcement of discipline in mixed classes, the difficult position of Negro teachers, and strained community relations.

Any progress whatsoever, the school officials made clear, was dependent on careful preparation of a suitable plan; full cooperation on the part of all concerned, including the local PTA's, and sympathetic support by newspapers willing to minimize publicity. Nothing was more important than the leadership of individual superintendents and principals. In one instance, that of integration in the schools of Leavenworth, Kansas, described as "a southern town situated in the North," a forthright witness pointedly testified that in facing the challenge of integration, the school officials were "so far ahead of the organizations who specialize in morality and human relations that there is no comparison." The schools were integrated in Leavenworth, he said, but not the churches.[2]

Washington, which completely reformed its educational program to do away with a previous dual system, and Baltimore, where a general policy was adopted of letting every pupil attend a school of his choice unless there was overcrowding, were leading border cities with relatively successful integration. Another, whose program was extensively discussed at the conference, was Wilmington, Delaware.

Within two years of the original Supreme Court decision, Superintendent Miller reported, Wilmington's schools were desegregated with a very considerable transfer of students and also an interchange of white and Negro teachers. The plan proceeded smoothly, he testified, in large part because great care was taken in having the teachers, both white and colored, make extensive home visits to explain to parents just what was being done. Another significant factor was that the plan was instituted promptly, and was well under way before the heightening of social tensions that in more recent years bedeviled the whole civil rights movement and perceptibly slowed down school integration.[3]

2. *Ibid.*, 27.
3. *Ibid.*, 73.

A less happy situation prevailed in Nashville itself where the school board had initiated only a first step toward integration. Moreover what had been done was at the cost of so much conflict that the Superintendent of Schools, William Henry Oliver, said he was reluctant even to discuss the matter since it had contributed to the breakdown in the health of one board member and the death of another. In a moving statement he declared:

Many among us, including principals, teachers, and other board members have suffered in lesser ways, but the memory of long hours of labor, followed by almost sleepless nights, disturbed and harassed by insults and threats by mail, by telephone and in person, remind us that it has not been easy or pleasant. And, if we could forget or ignore these personal things, the pictures remaining in our minds of frightened, terrified children; of disturbed, perplexed parents; of glaring headlines in the nation's newspapers; of almost empty classrooms; of a beautiful modern school building blasted by dynamite—these and many other things remind us that the initiation of desegregation in Nashville's schools was not a simple matter. Furthermore, we know that the job is not done. We have only a little more than begun it.[4]

Indeed very little was accomplished on a statistical basis. The Nashville plan desegregated one grade a year, beginning with the first grade, and allowed the possible transfer of other pupils at their parents' request. Oliver nevertheless reported that at the time only seven of the thirty-two predominantly white schools admitted any Negro children—twenty in the first grade and fourteen in the second. Moreover, among one hundred fifteen Negro students eligible for transfer to white schools, all but ten wanted to remain in their own schools. Asked about the prospects for future progress in desegregating Nashville's schools, Oliver could only say, somewhat ambiguously, that popular prejudice was still the greatest barrier to resolving the problem but that he also felt that the people of Nashville, standing firmly for law and order, were prepared to set aside their prejudices to cooperate with the school officials in compliance with the law.[5]

The testimony of Dr. Jack F. Parker, principal of a junior high school in Oklahoma City, indicated a better situation than that

4. *Ibid.*, 86.
5. *Ibid.*, 91–92, 95.

at Nashville and yet also suggested how slowly the processes of integration worked even in a state perhaps more western than southern. Among ninety-one schools, only three secondary and five elementary were desegregated, and the contacts in these schools between Negro and white children remained very limited. Questioned on relative standards of student work, Dr. Parker reaffirmed what appeared to be a very general view among the officials of desegregated systems. The Negro children tended to be concentrated in the lower ability groupings and created some special problems, but he felt this was due to an environment lacking many of the advantages of white homes rather than being due to race. The schools themselves, Dr. Parker said, did not in any way suffer from the admission of Negro children.[6]

The testimony of Ben L. Smith, Superintendent Emeritus in Greensboro, North Carolina, emphasized that token integration was still about all that could be expected in the circumstances of the times. He was proud of the prompt action the Greensboro School Board had taken with the support of "an enlightened and liberal-minded community," but the fact remained that in comparison with twenty-seven all-white schools, only two schools were currently integrated, and they had but five Negro students. Father Hesburgh praised the Greensboro officials for acting as courageously as they had, but expressed the view that the results seemed rather meager. Although Smith agreed this was so, he countered that the pace could not be forced. Negro as well as white attitudes were deeply involved; integration was not a numbers game. "I think that people want to obey the law," he said, "but there are a great many people—and people that approve what has been done—that would not like to see . . . Negro pupils forced against their wills, the wills of their parents, into a situation which might prove inhospitable for them, definitely." His final word was that the Negro leaders themselves were very hopeful. "They are not so much concerned about where we are now," he said, "but the direction in which we are going. . . ."[7]

The most dramatic report at the conference was that of R. G. Crossno, a member of the Board of Education in Anderson County, Tennessee, where twelve Negro students had been admitted to the

6. *Ibid.*, 96–103.
7. *Ibid.*, 106, 109–11.

formerly all-white Clinton High School under circumstances commanding nationwide attention. His story was one of mass intimidation largely inspired by a professional agitator, violent mob action, and the ultimate bombing of the high school. "I regret that I do not have words at my command to adequately describe the reactions of our people to this bombing," Crossno told a rapt audience. "The words stunned, shocked, dismayed and hysterical, are some that could be used." The School Board, however, made immediate arrangements to reopen the school in a vacant building in nearby Oak Ridge, and after discussion with state officials, appealed to Washington for help in rebuilding their bombed-out building.

Crossno made the emphatic point that while he did not feel that Anderson County was entitled to a reward for obeying the law ("we not only feel that such is an obligation but a privilege"), the Federal Government nevertheless did have a certain responsibility for conditions which resulted from its own intervention in local affairs. He was highly critical of Washington's failure to lend its efforts toward creating an atmosphere in which integration could work, the lack of consistency in Supreme Court decisions, the breaking-off of existing lines of communication between the races, and an officially "frigid attitude" toward school systems seeking to comply with the law. Unlike most Southerners, Crossno felt that having gone so far, the Federal Government should expand its role in safeguarding those who were directly involved in the processes of integration. He was a pioneer in insisting both that bombing a school should be made a Federal crime, and that the National Government should play an active role in meeting the emergency such a deed created. Asked whether his ideas did not mean "Federal troops running around the country on every kind of proposition," he answered bluntly that he would rather have Federal troops running around than state troops.[8]

Further testimony etched more deeply the general picture of school boards in these predominantly border states—typical of neither the Deep South nor the urban North—trying to obey the law with at least token integration in the face of continued popular prejudice. In some instances a reluctant willingness to place obedience to the law above the traditions of the past was evident, but in

8. *Ibid.*, 126–36.

many others popular opposition still led to the picketing of desegregated schools, if not more drastic action. The conference showed,
however, that the school officials strongly felt that integration did
not affect educational standards. "It has no more effect on them,"
one superintendent said, "than it has on the yardstick by which a
pupil's height is measured." The real problem was how to counter-
act the deficiencies in most of the Negro children's cultural background.

The Civil Rights Commission acquired a great deal of information on the problems of schools in transition. More significant perhaps was the value of the conference in providing an opportunity
for the school officials to exchange views on what was being done.
Superintendent Oliver of Nashville, who was at first reluctant even
to attend the conference, particularly stressed its importance from
this point of view. This was his first opportunity, he said, "to sit
down with a group of fellow school men and listen to what they
have to say and find out what they think and how they are dealing
with this problem."[9] The conference concluded with repeated ex-
pressions of the hope that since this meeting was so successful, there
would be others of the same sort.

The Commission's hearings on housing were the most comprehensive of those held in 1959.[10] In the hearings on voting, the Commission was concerned with enforcement of the Fifteenth Amendment; in the conference on education, its interest was compliance
with the Supreme Court decisions. Housing was a less tangible
problem, affecting the North even more than the South, and the
Federal Government had not as yet attempted to take any practical
action to combat segregation in urban centers. It would not move
on this important front until President Kennedy's limited Executive Order in 1962 barring discrimination in Federally assisted
housing.

"The ghettos of our cities—North and South, from coast to
coast," President Johnson could still say seven years after the Commission's first housing hearings, "represent fully as severe a denial

9. *Ibid.*, 187.
10. *Hearings Before the United States Commission on Civil Rights—Housing.
New York, New York, Feb. 2–3, 1959; Atlanta, Georgia, April 10, 1959;
Chicago, Illinois, May 5–6, 1959,* Washington, 1959.

of freedom and the fruits of American citizenship as more obvious injustices. . . . We must give the Negro the right to live in freedom among his fellow-Americans."[11]

Nevertheless a host of witnesses made abundantly clear, in the hearings in New York, Atlanta and Chicago in 1959, this paramount need to end discrimination in housing. State and city officials, officers of innumerable quasi-public organizations concerned with housing and racial relations, representatives from the Urban League and NAACP, often found themselves at odds with officers of real estate boards, banks, savings and loan associations, but all agreed that here was a problem whose solution was vital to the nation's social and economic health. Their testimony was voluminous; their supporting statements bristled with statistics. The evidence foreshadowing future crises was all there.

As described to the Commission, prevailing conditions in the three cities where the hearings were held differed greatly. In New York, local legislation outlawed discrimination in public housing and, under certain circumstances, in private housing as well. The municipal administration could claim with considerable justification that it was a pioneer in seeking to enforce fair housing practices. Still, Harlem had a deserved reputation as a notoriously segregated area. Chicago had no anti-discrimination legislation whatsoever, and its Negroes were largely concentrated in a few sections of the city as run-down and poverty-stricken as any slums in the country. Little or nothing was being done about it. In Atlanta, regardless of legislation or the lack of legislation, local custom rigidly enforced segregation as the "traditional southern way of life." Yet within this established framework, housing facilities for Negroes in Atlanta were generally better, outside of a number of very poor districts, than in any other large city north or south.

Conditions differed in each of these cities, but one thing they did have in common was segregation—which invariably meant overcrowding, property deterioration, and the creation of slums. Even those who most deplored segregation recognized that whatever the conditions might be, many Negroes preferred living in communities made up of people of their own race. "We have colored people in Harlem," Roy Wilkins of the NAACP testified, "who wouldn't

11. *New York Times,* May 1, 1966.

move out of Harlem if you gave them a goldplated apartment."[12] Nevertheless these same witnesses strongly maintained that segregated housing was an unjustifiable violation of the principle of equality and made Negroes second-class citizens.

Other speakers at the hearings declared that the question of equal opportunity in housing could not be disassociated from the still broader problem of urban renewal in the interests of low income groups whether made up of whites or blacks. The existence of slums; the entrapment of the poor in great metropolitan centers circled by zoned suburbs for the middle and upper income classes; and existing programs for slum clearance, low-cost housing, and highway construction, obviously formed a complex of inextricably interwoven issues. Nevertheless the evidence submitted to the Commission demonstrated beyond question that segregation stood at the very heart of the great overall problem of the modern American city, and that Negroes were the greatest victims of urban congestion. Cut off from any freedom of movement by what was repeatedly called "a white noose," perhaps even more in the North than in the South, they could not escape the ghettos where all the evils of the slum—unemployment, poverty, juvenile delinquency, dope addiction, vice and crime—were so greatly aggravated.

It may again be said that in bringing out this evidence of urban segregation and the widespread blot of Negro ghettos, the Commission was no more breaking new ground than in its exposure of the extent to which Negroes were being deprived of the right to vote in southern states or in its publicizing of continued segregation in public schools. The Negro ghettos were self-evident —from Harlem to Watts. They had also been repeatedly described and their demoralizing influence sensationally depicted in such autobiographies as Claude Brown's *Manchild in the Promised Land*, *The Autobiography of Malcolm X*, and Sammy Davis' *Yes, I Can*. But the Commission's official hearings not only spread upon the public record undeniable facts about the segregated slum, but authoritative evidence of the responsibility for its existence.

The hearing in New York on February 2–3, over which Father Hesburgh presided, opened with official greetings from

12. *Hearings*, 339.

the city fathers. However, the initial statement of the first of its long array of witnesses, Earl W. Schwulst, President of the Bowery Savings Bank and Chairman of the National Commission on Race and Housing, provided the keynote for most of the subsequent debate and discussion. Describing the results of earlier surveys by his own organization, Schwulst stated that its "most important and I would say overriding finding" was "that housing is apparently the only commodity in the American market which is not freely available to minority groups, and particularly not freely available to those minority groups who are non-white." He recognized that the lower incomes and the lower cultural status of large numbers of the families composing the minority groups contributed to such discrimination. But in his opinion, race was the principal factor so far as the Negroes were concerned. Even with ample funds the non-white could not buy a house as he could purchase a dishwashing machine, a television set, or a Lincoln Continental. His color was the significant and insuperable barrier.

This inability freely to buy a home, Schwulst's testimony continued, was due to two basic fears. The first was that any movement of non-whites into a white neighborhood would tend to scale downward the social status of the whites, and the second and corollary fear was that it would depreciate property values. Schwulst did not believe that these fears were necessarily valid. Where the whites in any community were nevertheless convinced that an influx of Negroes would have such consequences, they became—almost invariably—a self-fulfilling prophecy.

The President of the Bowery Savings Bank further stated, his testimony substantiated by many other witnesses, that the segregation imposed on Negroes was reenforced by the policies and practices of real estate brokers, mortgage lenders—and the Federal Government. While the latter sought to meet the problem of low income housing through slum clearance, urban renewal projects, and loans extended by the Federal Housing Administration or the Veterans Administration, it at the same time tacitly accepted the prevailing patterns of racial discrimination even though the housing benefits it offered had been made possible by public taxation.[13]

13. *Ibid.,* 32–36.

Many other witnesses testified along these same lines; others developed quite different approaches. The testimony eventually touched upon every conceivable facet of the housing situation in New York. Cardinal Spellman made a moving plea for an end of bigotry and prejudice; Senator Javits emphasized the effect of discriminatory policies on other nations' image of America. Representatives of Jewish organizations pointed out that Jews continued to suffer from discriminatory housing practices through restrictive covenants and other devices. Spokesmen for Negro groups vividly described actual living conditions in the segregated areas.

One of the most distressing accounts of Harlem was given not by a Negro but by a Puerto Rican, a long-time resident of New York and a representative of an organization of his own people. Pedro Canino testified:

> It is my happy lot to live in East Harlem, the happy hunting ground of the predatory landlord. . . . East Harlem is a rent jungle, where four filthy rooms and a kitchen bring the landlord the unheard of rental of $139 a month. East Harlem is a place where ten and eleven human beings have been crowded into one room. East Harlem is a place where a decontrolled apartment is divided into eight cubbyholes, filthy cubbyholes at that, where tenants are afraid to put their lights out at night for fear of rats, where the bathtub on the side is disconnected, where the stove has only two working burners and there is no door to the oven. The living-room in this filthy den was at one time—and I am referring to a specific case—$20 per week. Multiply $20 by 8, if you will, and then multiply $160 by 4, and then you get and you arrive at a criminal bleeding of a trusting, helpless minority, both Negro and Puerto Rican.[14]

From a quite different perspective, Justice Justine W. Polier of the Domestic Relations Court told of the delinquency and crime that such segregated slums as Harlem so naturally fostered. She described the wide prevalence of broken families, the pitiful lot of children feeling unwanted and discouraged about the future, and the vulnerability of young people to antisocial conduct. On the other hand, she bore witness to what could be done—and in some instances was done—when the problems of a segregated area were faced honestly. "We have learned," she said, "how much talent this community formerly failed to develop and how many children

14. *Ibid.*, 391.

can be salvaged if the bars of prejudice and resulting discrimination are lowered."

In bringing her testimony to a close, Justice Polier sought to appraise the responsibility for continued segregation in New York. "I think this city can properly pride itself," she concluded, "on being a leader in the United States to date to use the democratic process of law to end discriminatory housing authorized or tolerated —and I say this regretfully—by Federal, state and local governments, which have all contributed in the past to the discriminatory pattern in housing."[15] Father Hesburgh warmly thanked Justice Polier for "your wonderful and your compassionate statement." When the questioning came to an end, the audience shattered all precedent by breaking into applause.

Much of the evidence at the hearing dealt with the difficulties that Negroes in New York faced in trying to buy homes outside the segregated areas. Loan companies refused to grant them mortgages or charged them disproportionately high interest rates. Real estate operators engaged in "block busting" when Negroes somehow did succeed in buying houses in white communities.

A number of witnesses described the latter practice. Whenever a Negro family moved in, the real estate operators persuaded the remaining white home owners in the block that they would be engulfed by a Negro invasion, bought up their houses as a result of consequent panic selling, and then resold the property to Negroes at greatly higher prices. These witnesses maintained that the influence of the real estate operators was thrown so strongly against any intermingling of the races that community integration became impossible even though if left to their own devices, Negroes and whites might have been able to live in harmony. One woman described how the white housewives in a fringe area banded together in refusing to let themselves be persuaded by the real estate brokers into selling out, and then welcomed Negro home owners into what became an acceptable biracial community.

Jackie Robinson was a witness in New York. He eloquently told of his own difficulties in buying a home, even though as Vice-President of the Chock Full O'Nuts Corporation his financial status could not be questioned. He also related his frequent trips to Wash-

15. *Ibid.,* 202–12.

ington to promote the idea of open occupancy in public housing. "The officials have been very polite to me," he said, "but, regardless of the reason, nothing has been done."[16]

The feeling that the Federal Government was not living up to its responsibilities in providing open occupancy in housing settlements, or otherwise combating discrimination, was a reiterated theme. Frank S. Horne, Executive Director of the New York Commission on Intergroup Relations, perhaps emphasized it most strongly, "I think the real sin," he stated, "has been that the great weight and power of the Federal Government has been thrown on the side of the segregated mind."[17]

The Atlanta hearing on April 10 took a quite different turn from that in New York by concentrating to a great extent on developments which made it possible—though without breaking the traditional pattern of segregation—for Negroes to move from congested city areas into the suburbs. The members of the Commission attending this hearing were Hannah, Storey and Carleton (together with Johnson as a member-designate), and their interest was clearly aroused by what they considered a highly constructive step in meeting the problem of Negro housing even though it could not be described as ending discrimination.

Non-whites in Atlanta had previously been confined to a single section surrounded by all-white neighborhoods. But largely through the efforts of a West Side Mutual Development Committee, made up of three whites and three Negroes, the bottleneck preventing any expansion of the colored section was broken. The committee developed a plan whereby the whites would open up certain suburban areas to the Negroes in return for their undertaking not to try to move into other exclusively white districts. For those Negroes who could afford it, this made possible the creation of what was described (and duly exhibited to the Commission) as "a magnificent colored section."[18]

Representatives of the Negro community were not so enthusiastic over this plan as the whites. On the premise that segregation was too deeply rooted to be disturbed, they nevertheless agreed that this cooperative approach to the housing problem enabled non-

16. *Ibid.*, 270.
17. *Ibid.*, 122.
18. *Ibid.*, 442ff.

whites in Atlanta to obtain better homes than would be available to them in any other southern city. In return for such practical benefits, they were apparently ready to accept continued discrimination; that is, to settle for an immediate good rather than yearn for a distant and seemingly impossible utopia.

The difficulty, however, was that the "magnificent colored section" did not resolve the problems of those Negroes too poor to escape from congested slums into the suburbs. The even tenor of the hearing was consequently shattered when a spokesman for their interests, I. V. Williamson, President of the Negro Real Estate Board, gave his testimony. He questioned much of what had gone before, stated that most Negroes were still caught in the trap of having to pay far more than the whites for comparable houses, and vigorously attacked residential segregation whatever form it might take. He declared:

> It is bulwarked behind indifference, it is propped by popular prejudice; it is renewed by the separate institutionalisms it breeds and nourishes; it is protected by the fear of change. And, unfortunately, it is hallowed by the long and continuing support it has had from Government. But the case against its perpetuation rests on sound economic, legal and moral principles.[19]

When Hannah, acknowledging that he philosophically agreed with Williamson's principles, asked if what was being done in Atlanta was not a step in the right direction, the witness answered that it might be the best that could be expected under existing circumstances, but it did not by any means encourage non-segregated housing. Storey now took over the questioning to suggest that segregation existed voluntarily in Atlanta and was enforced by local custom rather than any legislative fiat. Williamson insisted that there was nothing voluntary about it: "you have your political heads of government saying directly what custom is." He cited the impossibility of getting police protection when Atlanta mobs attacked Negroes and bombed Negro homes.

Tempers suddenly flared:

VICE-CHAIRMAN STOREY: *You don't charge the bombing of that house to political heads, do you?*
MR. WILLIAMSON: *I charge this, that in the last 8 years more than 12*

19. *Ibid.*, 546–47.

> *houses have been bombed in Atlanta, and there have been no arrests and no convictions.*
>
> VICE-CHAIRMAN STOREY: *You listen to my questions. Do you charge the bombing of these houses to political heads of government? . . . You don't mean to say that, do you, Mr. Williamson?*
>
> MR. WILLIAMSON: *Yes, I do . . .*
>
> VICE-CHAIRMAN STOREY: *Will you listen to me one more time? Do you charge the bombing of these houses to the political heads of government?*
>
> MR. WILLIAMSON: *Well, it is the lack of police protection.*
>
> VICE-CHAIRMAN STOREY: *Just one more time, please, and I want to be just as courteous as I can. Do you charge them—and I am not trying to create any passion or tension; I am just after facts—do you charge that to the political heads of government?*
>
> MR. WILLIAMSON: *The continuation of it, yes; the continuation of it, yes; the continuation of it, I charge that to the political heads of government.*

Hannah intervened to pour a little oil on these troubled waters—the questioning was leading down a road the Commission did not want to travel, discrimination in housing was an important issue and yet what was described as existing in Atlanta represented a better situation than prevailed in many northern cities. It was perhaps essential to move one step at a time. "The only reason for my saying that," Hannah concluded, "is that I am afraid we have split apart here, and if we leave it at that point, we may do more harm than good."[20]

The hearing continued on a calmer note.

The story of Chicago, as told in the hearing in that city on May 5–6, paralleled in many ways that of New York, but conflicting testimony gave a very confusing picture of general conditions. In describing Chicago's extensive urban renewal program, witness after witness agreed that conditions were somewhat improving for both whites and Negroes, but they failed to give any clear-cut indication of how the problem of segregation, in the absence of any specific legislation, was actually being met. On one occasion Father Hesburgh, presiding over this hearing as he had over that in New York, commented that this confusion among the community leaders over their goals appeared to be the crippling factor in the situation.

20. *Ibid.,* 557–58.

He referred with some asperity to "conflicting opinion as to what is being done, whether or not progress is being made, whether we are on the right path or not."[21] With the frank admission that discrimination against non-whites was more prevalent than in New York, conditions in Chicago were anything but happy.

Several witnesses expressed the view that segregation was by the Negroes' own choice, as was also suggested in New York, and that it followed a traditional pattern established when the first immigrants came to Chicago. Philip M. Hauser, Chairman of the Department of Sociology at the University of Chicago, developed the thesis that people of the same ethnic and racial backgrounds desire to live together, but that just as the one-time insulated immigrants gradually moved into other parts of the city, so would the Negroes break out of the segregated areas as their economic status gradually improved.[22]

George Johnson, once again sitting with the Commission as a member-designate, sharply challenged this thesis. He pointed out that the European immigrants, even though they had once been discriminated against (in Dr. Hauser's phrase) as "Polacks, Sheenies, Bohunks, Wops," possessed a mobility which the Negro lacked. No matter how successfully he adjusted himself to urban life, or was able to raise his standard of living, he remained trapped by his color. Never, Johnson bluntly stated, does the Negro "lose his high visibility."[23]

Other testimony, covering now familiar ground, stressed the stubborn obstacles forever confronting Negroes who sought to move out of segregated areas—trouble in obtaining mortgage loans, prices higher than those charged whites, and other more subtle but equally restrictive forms of discrimination. And once again there was much discussion of how, as one speaker described it, open occupancy "leads inevitably to total Negro occupancy." It was evident as the hearing continued that Chicago real estate interests exercised a pervasive influence in blocking any move toward breaking down the patterns of segregation.

At one point a witness revealed that no Negroes were members of the Chicago Real Estate Board. When its President was then

21. *Ibid.,* 810.
22. *Ibid.,* 632–33.
23. *Ibid.,* 639.

asked whether there was any reason for this other than racial prejudice, he flatly refused to elaborate any further. As the argument
over this issue nevertheless continued, Governor Battle broke in
to ask whether the Real Estate Board was a wholly voluntary organization. Told that it was, he commented wryly: "I must say,
coming from the South as I do, I find this discussion very interesting."[24]

Rabbi Richard G. Hirsch, of the Chicago Federation, Union
of Hebrew Congregations, developed further Governor Battle's
implication that the North might be quite as prejudiced as the
South in its attitude toward the Negro. After stressing what he felt
were the inherent evils of discrimination, he declared that it was
time "we in the North learned that the distance between Poplar-
ville, Miss., and Trumbull Park in Chicago is not so vast as some
of us in our complacency would like to believe." His strictures on
the consequences of segregated housing were among the most
forceful of any of those presented at the Chicago hearing:

> *To what avail is the principle of non-segregated education when,*
> *because of segregated housing, 100,000 Negro children attend Chicago*
> *public schools where there are no white children? To what avail do we*
> *assure equal voting rights when, because of segregated housing, the*
> *power of the vote in local government is manipulated, discounted, and*
> *vitiated? . . . To what avail do we establish recreation, welfare and*
> *civic institutions when, because of segregated housing, the group which*
> *needs understanding the most is not even able to participate?*
>
> *The leadership of our country must recognize the housing problem*
> *for what it is—the crucial challenge to American democracy.*[25]

Such an interpretation of the vital importance of housing has
become commonplace. But this hearing was in 1959 and not the
late 1960's. The evidence of conditions in Chicago revealed, even
more than had the hearing in New York, that the time was long
overdue for the North to realize that its Negro problem was just as
serious as that of the South.

One constructive suggestion for handling urban segregation
was put forward by Saul D. Alinsky, Executive Director of the
Industrial Areas Foundation, whose own activities in this field were

24. *Ibid.,* 752.
25. *Ibid.,* 815.

subsequently to become increasingly well known. To meet the problem of the flight of whites from any neighborhood where Negroes obtained homes and to prevent open occupancy from becoming total Negro occupancy, he proposed a quota system for the acceptance of Negroes into all-white communities. This was the only practical alternative, he maintained, to continued racial segregation. Asked how any such quota system could be handled or enforced, he expressed the opinion that with its potential control over the sale and purchase of homes, any organized community that so desired could work things out on a wholly voluntary basis. Success depended on neighborhood goodwill and tolerance. When Alinsky concluded his statement, Father Hesburgh expressed the Commission's gratitude for "your fine imaginative presentation."[26]

A great deal more testimony was forthcoming. Several witnesses described what they called the "gentleman's agreement— with teeth," whereby real estate dealers in Chicago agreed that they would not sell or rent to a non-white in any city block until it had been "cracked" by the presence of a Negro family through some other means. Others told of programs for slum clearance and low-cost housing which actually consolidated the patterns of segregation rather than eliminating them. The spokesmen of civil rights groups, as in New York, maintained that the Federal Government evaded its responsibilities and urged that mandatory fair practices should be the condition for the receipt of Federal funds in any housing project. The hearings came to an end with Father Hesburgh emphasizing in his final statement that the Commission had learned a great deal. It was convinced, he said, that no facet of the civil rights problem—whether housing, voting, education, or the public administration of justice—could be separated from another. This was "a total problem."[27]

During 1959 the Commission on Civil Rights engaged in other activities involving surveys of existing laws, field investigations, and supervision of the work of its State Advisory Committees. A conference in Washington early in June brought together members of the Commission, its staff and representatives of the advisory

26. *Ibid.*, 769–81.
27. *Ibid.*, 886.

groups for an overall survey of the whole civil rights field. But the public hearings so graphically illuminating denial of the right to vote in southern states, the conference at Nashville revealing the slow progress of integration in public schools, and the hearings exposing discrimination in housing were the year's outstanding developments.

The Commission carried out its program with a great sense of urgency. Because of the unavoidable delays in getting started, everything it sought to do was crowded into a few brief months. There was no time, as Chairman Hannah stated, "to cover the waterfront." Nevertheless, the Commission succeeded in accomplishing a great deal and successfully met its deadline. Summarizing the scope and impact of existing Federal legislation, outlining the results of both field investigations and public hearings, pulling together its overall findings, hammering out its final recommendations, it duly rendered its prescribed Report on September 9, 1959.

V. THE FIRST REPORT—
1959

This First Report of the Commission on Civil Rights reflected sharp differences of opinion between the Commission's northern and southern members, but it also revealed an unexpected degree of unity on broad principles. It was a good deal more forthright than had been generally anticipated in describing the lack of equal protection of the laws for the country's Negro minority and in emphasizing the need for further civil rights legislation. The Report was especially outspoken in calling for measures that would combat the denial of the right to vote, which had been so dramatically disclosed in the Alabama hearings.[1]

Newspapers throughout the country gave the Report extensive

1. *Report of the United States Commission on Civil Rights—1959.* Washington, 1959; *With Liberty and Justice for All—An Abridgement . . .* , Washington, 1959.

coverage (even though it was somewhat overshadowed in the news columns by President Eisenhower's return from a European tour and the imminent arrival of Khrushchev for his famous visit to the United States), and Congress welcomed it with "gales of oratory." Southern spokesmen, with Senator Thurmond attacking it as "radical, vicious, unconstitutional and obnoxious," blasted its recommendations; Northerners, following the lead of Senator Humphrey who praised the Commission for "its courage, for its forthrightness, and for its vision," generally hailed these same recommendations as well-balanced and eminently reasonable.[2]

A magisterial editorial in the *New York Times* stated that the Report made "important, though unhappy reading"; expressed a sense of shame about its basic findings relating to civil rights; and, noting the angry attacks of the Southerners, nevertheless declared that "on the whole the proposals and recommendations of the Commission are moderate in nature and worthy of serious consideration."[3]

An unusual feature of the Report was the way in which the dissenting opinions were handled. They were embodied in the text— as *Life* said, the "disagreements show"[4]—but rather than being pulled together in a separate minority report which might have emphasized the division within the Commission, they were set forth in separate statements or in some cases footnotes. Moreover, where agreement on "recommendations" were impossible because of a three-to-three split, the Northerners made their own "proposals," and in spite of the failure of the Southerners to accept them, they became a part of the main Report. Only Governor Battle set forth a specific dissent, not only on the voting recommendation but on the tenor of the Report as a whole.

"In my judgment," he said in a frank statement in which neither of his two southern colleagues concurred, "it is not an impartial factual statement, such as I believe to have been the intent

2. *Congressional Record,* 86th Congress, 1st Session, Senate, Sept. 14, 1959, 16878–18026, 18897, 19427–95. The release date was broken and Senator Eastland had the Report printed in part in the *Congressional Record* before it was officially submitted to the President.

3. *New York Times,* Sept. 9, 1959.

4. *Life,* 42, Sept. 21, 1959.

of Congress, but rather, in large part, an argument in advocacy of preconceived ideas in the field of race relations."[5]

That the Report was indeed such an argument could hardly be denied. A good deal more questionable, however, was whether Battle was correct in ascribing to Congress any intent to limit the role of the Commission to that of rendering an impartial, factual statement. Congress had called upon the Commissioners to make such recommendations as they saw fit in the light of their findings. The liberal majority responsible for the passage of the Civil Rights Act obviously expected such recommendations to suggest ways for more effective enforcement of equal protection of the laws, especially in the field of voting rights. The legislative history of the Act from its very inception made this abundantly clear. Nevertheless, the way in which the dissents were muted had the effect of making it seem as if the northern position on civil rights, which the Report so generally reflected, constituted a majority view even when the voting marked an even division.

Senator Russell quickly noted this. In his outspoken criticism of the "alleged" Report, he said that it had been "cunningly drafted" to suggest that the three Northerners "who were in favor of the most vindictive and punitive measures" actually constituted the Commission and that the three Southerners defending more moderate views were somehow outsiders.[6]

If this were a conspiracy, however, the Southerners were part of it. When the Report was about to be submitted to President Eisenhower, the Commissioners agreed that at the expected press conference, Chairman Hannah should seek to clarify the distinction between the recommendations which had at least majority support and the proposals that expressed the views of the Northerners alone. However, he was also to emphasize (Battle concurring) "the unanimity of thought" which characterized the Commission's general position.[7]

The process whereby the Report was drawn up involved a great deal of work on the part of the members of the Commission's staff. They made innumerable drafts of individual sections, especially the findings and recommendations; and then carefully incorporated the

5. *Report*, 551; *Liberty and Justice*, 195.
6. *Congressional Record*, Senate, Sept. 14, 1959, 17933, 19432.
7. Minutes of 24th Commission meeting, Sept. 8, 1959.

revisions and suggestions of individual Commissioners. Finally the Commission itself held a long session at which remaining differences were hammered out and a definitive agreement reached on both the substance and form of the official text. It was quite true, as Senator Russell divined, that the staff members were prepared to go much further on some recommendations than the Commissioners themselves. The latter keenly felt their responsibility for moderating any extreme views and coming as close as possible to a general consensus. Hannah adroitly exercised his most persuasive influence as Chairman in support of a Report which would at once reflect a basic unity and also give both Northerners and Southerners the opportunity to express differing attitudes when they could not be reconciled.

As early as the close of 1958 the staff made a first "mock-up" of the projected Report, and throughout the opening months of the next year drew up successive revisions. Their job had to be completed by July 15 if the final draft was to be ready for submission in printed form on the prescribed date. With a primary responsibility for getting everything in shape as soon as possible, Staff Director Tiffany kept his various task forces under constant pressure. "Perfectionists," read one of his memos, "must simply resolve to do the best they can in the time available."[8] To help expedite matters two special advisors were recruited: Robert S. Rankin, Chairman of the Department of Political Science at Duke University (a subsequent Commission member), and Herbert Kay, from the *Life-Time-Fortune* group of magazines.

The Commission met to put the seal of approval on the final draft in a two-day session, July 14–15, at Land O' Lakes, Wisconsin. The minutes reveal the differences as well as agreements among the Commissioners. Battle strongly expressed the opinion, later included in his formal dissent, "that we have gone very far afield; that the Report is an eloquent preachment for integration all the way through." He reserved the right to express his generally critical views but nevertheless accepted the format which provided for dissents on specific issues through separate statements or in footnotes.

The most critical problem was that of voting recommendations. On this point Battle acknowledged the need for further protection of the Negroes' rights but he would have left to Congress the question of how this might be done. The other members of the

8. Minutes of 18th Commission meeting, March 4, 1959.

Commission felt this approach to be an evasion of responsibility and the debate over what stand should be taken was the most prolonged and intense of the entire meeting. The minutes also show, among other disagreements, an irreconcilable conflict in the field of higher education, resolved only by an understanding that on this issue both Northerners and Southerners should state their opposing views.

If these debates found the two camps within the Commission strongly upholding their respective positions, the discussion apparently never became acrimonious. The meeting ended with both Hannah and Storey expressing the opinion that it was remarkable how great a measure of agreement was attained. Battle voiced his appreciation for the tolerance and forbearance with which his colleagues had treated his support of the southern position to which he remained so deeply committed.[9]

The first part of this long Report (668 pages in all) dealt with the constitutional background of civil rights. Succeeding sections in turn took up voting, public education and housing, with, in each instance, a further examination of historic developments in these special areas, an analysis of current circumstances, and then formal findings and recommendations. The latter were accompanied by the separate and supplementary statements—or footnotes—in which individual members expressed their dissenting or amplifying views.

The Report's introductory material postulated the right of all persons within the United States to equal protection of the laws as being implicit in the Constitution itself. It was argued that this was not only sound historically but had a very significant pragmatic importance. The Report succinctly stated:

By returning to these fundamental principles of the Founding Fathers, we can perhaps disentangle ourselves from much of the current disputation about recent decisions of the Supreme Court. Over the years the Court has given differing interpretations of the Constitution, and men may honestly differ about the wisdom of these interpretations. But the principles remain steadfast.[10]

The three southern members of the Commission allowed this statement to stand but they expressed their dissent to its implica-

9. Minutes of 23rd Commission meeting, July 14–15, 1959.
10. *Report,* 8; *Liberty and Justice,* 15.

tions in a closely argued footnote. With greater validity and logic than the Northerners displayed, they disputed its historical basis. The discussions during the Constitutional Convention, especially those relating to the compromises on the slavery issue, clearly indicated in their opinion that the principle of equality was not a part of our fundamental law. It became so, they maintained, only with the adoption of the Fourteenth Amendment in 1868.[11]

This chapter of the Report then concluded—without dissent —on a ringing note:

In a world where colored people constitute a majority of the human race, where many new free governments are being formed, where self-government is everywhere being tested, where the basic human dignity of the individual person is being denied by totalitarian systems, it is more than ever essential that American principles and historic purposes be understood. These standards—these ideas and ideals—are what America is all about.[12]

The further development of constitutional requirements in a second chapter was less controversial. Its carefully documented record of civil rights since the adoption of the Civil War amendments included an account of immediate postwar legislation affecting the Negro; Supreme Court decisions such as *Plessy v. Ferguson* with its endorsement of the "separate but equal" doctrine, and the further adoption of "Jim Crow" laws leading to increasing racial discrimination in so many phases of southern life. The Report then strongly emphasized—and this again without dissent— the magnitude of the injury done the Negroes by the consequences that flowed from the whole course of American history since their first arrival in the United States:

It is reflected in the poor education, low income, inferior housing and social demoralization of a considerable part of the Negro population. What compounds the problem is that these unfortunate results of slavery, discrimination, and second-class citizenship are in turn used by some more fortunate Americans to justify the perpetuation of the conditions that caused the injury.[13]

This part of the Report was not an entirely negative accounting of the position of the Negro. It related what had been recently

11. *Report* (footnote), 1–2; *Liberty and Justice* (footnote), 9–10.
12. *Report*, 9; *Liberty and Justice*, 15.
13. *Report*, 16; *Liberty and Justice*, 21.

achieved in meeting the problems of segregation and discrimination, and expressed confidence that this progress would be
continued. The Commission was hopeful. It affirmed a strong belief
in constitutional rights, and declared that in looking to the future,
it shared Lincoln's faith that the whole American people will be
"again touched . . . by the better angels of our nature."[14]

From these generalities the Report moved on to the most important section—that on voting. Here again there was first a historical analysis. After discussing the adoption of the Fifteenth Amendment and its express prohibition of any denial or abridgement of
the right to vote because of race, color, or previous condition of
servitude, the Report demonstrated the breakdown of this guarantee
throughout the southern states. This involved a careful analysis of
such restrictive legislation as grandfather clauses, literacy tests and
poll taxes whose admitted purpose was to keep the Negro from the
polls. Statistical evidence and the testimony of the complainants at
the Alabama hearings were then presented to show that in spite of
Supreme Court decisions outlawing discriminatory practices, the
southern states were still using literacy tests and other devices to
block Negro voting.

Some improvement was recorded for recent years with an increase
in the number of registered Negro voters in the southern states
rising from 595,000 in 1947 to 1,200,000 in 1956. However, this total
still represented no more than twenty-five percent of the non-whites
of voting age. Far more shocking, as the Commission graphically
revealed, was the incontrovertible evidence that in a number of the
states in the Deep South, the percentage of Negro votes fell almost
to the vanishing point. Nearly thirty percent of Alabama's population of voting age were Negroes, but they constituted no more than
8.1 percent of those registered. Non-whites made up 41 percent of
the population of Mississippi and only 3.9 percent of the voters.
Moreover, in forty-nine scattered counties in the South where a
majority of the citizens of voting age were Negroes, less than five
percent of them were registered. In sixteen such counties there were
no colored voters.[15]

The complete accuracy of these statistics could sometimes be

14. *Report,* 17; *Liberty and Justice,* 22.
15. *Report,* 40–54; *Liberty and Justice,* 34–46.

challenged. Senator Johnston of South Carolina gleefully discovered
that the report gave his state an extra county! Nevertheless they
gave authoritative confirmation of conditions that were heretofore
generally known but not officially authenticated. And these cold,
impersonal figures were given even greater weight by the testimony
drawn from the Alabama hearing as to just why these disenfranchised Negroes were unable to exercise their rights as American
citizens.

As a consequence of these findings on voting, the Commission
then stated what it felt should be done. In the first instance, it made
four specific recommendations generally growing out of its own
experience. They called for a nationwide compilation by the Bureau
of the Census of all voting statistics, including a count by race, color
and national origin; congressional action to require registration
boards to preserve all their records for a period of five years; an
amendment to the Civil Rights Act prohibiting any action which
would deprive or threaten to deprive any individual or group of
individuals from the right to register and vote; and authorization
for the Civil Rights Commission to apply directly to Federal District
Courts for enforcement of its subpoena power at all future hearings.[16]

No dissents and no objections were recorded to these somewhat
technical recommendations. The Commission then added a fifth
and much stronger one. In light of the fact that substantial numbers
of Negroes were unable to register, and that the remedies written
into the existing Civil Rights Act were wholly ineffective (indeed,
not a single Negro was registered under its provisions), it recommended that the President be empowered to appoint temporary
Federal registrars who would administer registration proceedings
wherever there was a pattern of discrimination, and have the further
authority to issue certificates to all would-be voters they found
qualified.

The Civil Rights Commission, the Report proposed, should be
given the function of determining if such a pattern of discrimination
existed. Whenever nine individuals in any district, county or parish
attested through sworn affidavits that they were deprived of the
right to register because of their race, it would make a complete

16. *Report,* 136–39; *Liberty and Justice,* 91–94.

investigation of the complaints. If they were found to be justified, the Commission would so certify to the President.

Battle emphatically dissented from this recommendation on the ground that while he believed every citizen should have the right to vote, existing laws were sufficient to protect such a right. In his opinion, the appointment of Federal registrars would mark the intrusion of the Federal Government into a vital part of the election process carefully reserved to the states. Far more significant than his dissent, however, was the conspicuous fact that neither of the other Southerners went along with it. Storey and Carleton joined Hannah, Hesburgh and Johnson to give this most important recommendation of the entire Report a five-to-one majority.[17]

The three northern members of the Commission would have gone a good deal further. They felt that the appointment of Federal registrars was no more than a stopgap measure and that the only real solution to the voting problem was the removal of all restrictions whatsoever on the exercise of the ballot. To this end they proposed a constitutional amendment declaring that the right of citizens to vote should not be denied or abridged for any cause except inability to meet state requirements as to age and length-of-residence, or legal confinement at the time of registration or election. Hannah repeatedly tried to win the support of the three Southerners to this proposal. But Storey and Carleton, while reserving the right to change their minds, strongly felt that such an amendment would be in order only if it were demonstrated that the Federal Government otherwise lacked the power to meet the issue. In a separate statement Battle simply said that he heartily agreed with his southern colleagues' objections. The vote on this proposal was consequently three-to-three.[18]

Once again it may be emphasized that while the Commission was unable to agree on a possible constitutional amendment, the near unanimity on the paramount need for Federal action to assure the Negroes their right to vote was of utmost importance. Moreover a plan to protect such rights without cumbersome court procedures struck directly at the heart of the voting problem. The recommendation for the appointment of Federal registrars provoked more con-

17. *Report*, 141–42; *Liberty and Justice*, 96.
18. *Report*, 143–45; *Liberty and Justice*, 97–99.

troversy and debate than any other feature of the Report—controversy and debate that were to continue for six years.

No such decisive majority could be reached on any significant phase of the problem of education.[19] The Supreme Court decisions, calling for school integration with "all deliberate speed," were far more debatable than the clear-cut constitutional guarantee of the right to vote. Since their enforcement would deeply affect the whole pattern of life in the South, its representatives on the Civil Rights Commission found themselves in sharp disagreement with any proposals by the Northerners for further action. Battle, Storey, and Carleton even objected to the Report's introductory material on the school integration crisis. They said it was argumentative, colored by prejudiced sociological and philosophical views, based upon very limited information, and drawn up without due consideration of conditions in large areas of the country where the problem was most acute.[20]

In this background material the Report first drew upon the testimony of the school officials at the Nashville conference. Statistical evidence was then presented dealing with current conditions in the seventeen states (and the District of Columbia) which in 1954 had dual systems of education. There were over ten million students in these states, and a quarter of them were Negroes. Eleven of the states and the District of Columbia, the report stated, were making some effort to comply with the Supreme Court decisions on integration, but six remained "adamantly non-compliant."

The testimony of school officials and available figures further showed that the pace of integration was actually slowing down. In all too many cases nothing had happened beyond a first token step. The proportion of Negro students in desegregated schools in those parts of the country where something was being done, remained little more than fifteen percent. And this figure was as high as it was only because of the very good record in Missouri and the District of Columbia. Less than one percent of the colored students in North Carolina, Arkansas, Tennessee, and Virginia were enrolled in integrated schools.[21]

19. *Report,* 147–335; *Liberty and Justice,* 101–37.
20. *Report,* 328; *Liberty and Justice,* 135. Paraphrase from latter source which makes stronger statement.
21. *Report,* 299, 309; *Liberty and Justice,* 106, 119, 128.

Turning to the Deep South, the Report went no further than to emphasize strongly the consequences of that area's program of massive resistance. Louisiana, Florida, Alabama, Mississippi, Georgia, and South Carolina still maintained officially segregated school systems. Among all those states which had traditionally maintained dual systems, that is, only one-quarter of their biracial school districts had even begun to integrate five years after the Supreme Court called upon them to do so with "all deliberate speed."[22]

Further discussion of the educational issue centered on the measures which the South was taking to avoid compliance with the law. Some states were seeking to strengthen their anti-integration bulwarks by revival of the historic doctrine of state interposition to circumvent the enforcement of Federal legislation; others were continuing segregation through more subtle legal subterfuges. The Report described how a number of schools closed completely to avoid the admission of colored students; how under pupil placement programs race became the controlling factor; and how the provision of tuition grants drawn from state funds supported new private schools limited to white children. These were some of the means whereby integration could be wholly avoided or at best introduced on a purely token basis.

The Commission found the educational record—with a somewhat ambiguous choice of words—to be "dismaying, but not necessarily discouraging." It sought to find reassurance in the view that even though little more than token integration had been achieved, no reasonable citizen could expect great changes overnight—even when "overnight" appeared to have been five years. Obviously treading on uncertain ground, the Commission then emphasized the importance of bringing into play the democratic processes of discussion and persuasion, concluding that in this general area of educational reform, "the goal is clear, but for those disposed to move cautiously, if at all, the way is murky."[23]

A good deal of this "murkiness" seemed to characterize the Report. The discussion of this admittedly complex and frustrating problem of how public school integration could be effectively achieved was confused and inconclusive.

The Commission did make two recommendations. The first was that it should itself serve as a clearing house to collect more

22. *Report,* 298; *Liberty and Justice,* 119.
23. *Liberty and Justice,* 122 (not in *Report*).

accurate information on programs and procedures for compliance with court orders, and provide an advisory and conciliation service to assist school districts in carrying out desegregation plans. The second was that an annual census should be made showing the number and race of all students enrolled in public educational institutions throughout the country.

This was as far as the Commission as a whole could go in the general field of education. The three northern members were not, however, content with such innocuous recommendations and felt that something more decisive could be said at least in the case of institutions of higher education. They proposed that in order to encourage integration on this level, the Federal Government should withhold all supporting funds from any university or college, public or private, which continued to practice any form of racial discrimination.

The Southerners dissented emphatically to this proposal. They were opposed to any program of economic coercion which sought to bring about compliance with the Supreme Court decrees on school integration. Furthermore, they declared that this problem had not been sufficiently explored in staff studies and was beyond the scope of the Commission's duties.[24]

Even though the idea of withholding Federal support from educational institutions discriminating against Negroes was not to die, and would in time win increasing support, the fact of the matter was that in 1959 the Commission did not go very thoroughly into any of the issues centering on school integration. It did not have the time to do so, and apart from the conference at Nashville, held no public hearings on the issue. The basic assumptions that public education should be preserved without impairment and that compulsory segregation could not be reconciled with equal protection of the laws were implicit in the Commission's findings. Except for the supplemental statement of the Northerners in respect to higher institutions of learning, however, the Report did little more than rather vaguely outline the problem.

On the housing issue the Commission relied principally on the hearings held in New York, Atlanta, and Chicago.[25] They

24. *Report,* 326–30; *Liberty and Justice,* 133–37.
25. *Report,* 331–543; *Liberty and Justice,* 139–89.

produced, as has already been shown, thoroughly convincing evidence of the urgency and complexity of the overall problem. Cities throughout the country were experiencing unparalleled growth and overcrowding, greatly accentuated by the influx of Negroes. The members of the Commission, both Northerners and Southerners, were obviously deeply affected by the testimony of so many witnesses in New York and Chicago describing the squalor of the slums. They agreed there was no greater need in the country as a whole than more effective programs for slum clearance and urban renewal. Having set forth this view, the Report continued:

> But at this point, the problem of discrimination in housing rises to block a rational solution. Racial discrimination enters into and magnifies every one of the above factors producing the general housing crisis. While it is important to see these problems in their general shape in order to keep their racial aspects in perspective, it is also necessary to understand the special housing needs and problems of minorities, particularly of the racial minorities, in order to see the nation's housing crisis in its full dimensions.[26]

This rather general and carefully phrased statement was supported by a wealth of statistics showing what was happening in the cities, particularly to the Negro population. A most telling figure was the estimate that between 1935 and 1950 some nine million new private dwelling units were built in the United States, but only one hundred thousand—or slightly more than one percent of the total—were for non-whites even though they constituted ten percent of the overall population. What this meant in overcrowding for the Negroes, generally restricted to old, run-down, unsanitary houses, could hardly have been more pointedly suggested.[27]

The Report also incorporated the evidence produced at the public hearings upon the extent to which discrimination in housing affected not only poor Negroes but also those whose economic and social status would otherwise have enabled them to buy homes or rent apartments wherever they chose. Although other minority groups, especially Jews, suffered discrimination, both official statistics and individual testimony clearly brought out the almost universal segregation of Negroes. The Report further drove home

26. *Report,* 340; *Liberty and Justice,* 143.
27. *Report,* 347–48; *Liberty and Justice,* 144.

the lesson that this was, if anything, more true of the North than
of the South, and that the black ghettos of the metropolis were as
shocking a travesty upon the ideal of equality as any other phase
of the whole Negro problem.

The policies—state and municipal—of the three cities where
the hearings were held came in for lengthy examination. In accordance with the congressional mandate to appraise the laws and policies of the Federal Government, the Commission also looked very
closely into the records of the various Federal agencies in the
housing field.

President Eisenhower had set forth in 1954 the goal of a national housing program which would "assure equal opportunity for
all our citizens to acquire, within their means, good and well-
located homes." The Commission found, however, that little progress had been made in implementing the anti-discriminatory
features of this long-range goal. While the Federal housing agencies
were willing to cooperate with states and municipalities which
adopted anti-discrimination laws, they also worked with those that
did not do so and thereby condoned and sometimes even encouraged
segregation. This was not necessarily for want of sympathy with
the ideal of equal opportunity. The Federal agencies' policies, it
was said, were due to a lack of any clear directive, the general practice of following local custom whatever it might be, and a basically
conservative attitude.

The Report cited the testimony of Norman P. Mason, Administrator of the Housing and Home Finance Agency. He accepted
the need in all government programs of equal treatment for all
persons without regard to race, color or creed, and he felt that his
own agency should take the lead in such matters. But in assaying
the difficulties of conforming to this ideal, he doubted the value
of trying to act "precipitously."[28]

The findings included very detailed information on the practices of the various Federal agencies. The Federal Housing Administration still extended Federal mortgage loan insurance to
segregated housing, and both the Urban Renewal Administration
and the Federal Highway Aid Program followed policies that often
accentuated existing patterns of segregation. The Public Housing

28. *Report,* 459–61; *Liberty and Justice,* 170–71.

Administration generally left the whole question to local authorities. It did insist that where housing settlements were separately designed for whites and non-whites their facilities should be equal, but this was as far as it was prepared to go.

The Commission was able to report that between 1952 and 1959 there had been an increase from 76 to 428 racially integrated projects sponsored by the PHA and praised this seemingly good record. However, its Report added rather despondently: "Whether 'open occupancy' will prove to be merely another name for all-Negro projects remains to be seen."[29]

On the basis of voluminous evidence, the Commission reached two hardly surprising but nonetheless impressively documented general conclusions:

> FIRST, *a considerable number of Americans, by reason of their color or race, are being denied equal opportunity in housing. A large proportion of colored Americans are living in overcrowded slums or blighted areas in restricted sections of our cities, with little or no access to new housing or suburban areas. . . .*
>
> SECOND, *the housing disabilities of colored Americans are part of a national housing crisis involving a general shortage of low-cost housing. Americans of lower incomes, both colored and white, have few opportunities for decent homes in good neighborhoods. . . .*[30]

In attempting to draw up recommendations to deal with these issues, the Commission could hardly cope with the magnitude and complexities of the interwoven problems that were involved in the housing crisis as a whole. Many of them demanded the most expert and specialized knowledge. It was consequently constrained to limit itself to rather broad and general propositions.

The Report recommended the establishment of biracial commissions on housing for further study and for the investigation of complaints in all cities and states with substantial non-white populations; called upon the President to issue an Executive Order directing all Federal agencies to work toward the goal of equal opportunity in housing; urged the Administrator of the Housing and Home Finance Agency to give "high priority" to such a goal;

29. *Report,* 476; *Liberty and Justice,* 173. Quotation from latter source which makes stronger statement.
30. *Report,* 534–35; *Liberty and Justice,* 180–81.

proposed that the Federal Housing Administration and the Veterans' Administration require builders seeking loans to abide by local anti-discrimination laws; suggested that the Public Housing Authority encourage the selection of sites on open land to avoid the tendency of public housing units to become racially segregated; and, finally, recommended that the Urban Renewal Administration take steps to assume the participation of minority groups in the preparation of all community plans.[31]

There was no explicit dissent to these recommendations. However, Battle, Storey and Carleton—as they had in respect to the section on education—criticized the general spirit underlying treatment of the housing problem. They considered it "argumentative" and felt that much of the material presented was "keyed to integration rather than housing." They warned against the danger of trying to mingle whites and blacks under conditions that would lead to dissension and strife, and further said that if the recommendations addressed to the Federal agencies were fully carried out, the result might well be "delay and in many cases defeat" of broader plans for adequate housing for the people as a whole. A basically conservative view was further indicated in the comment that while government aid for housing was important, it should not be carried too far or be allowed to undermine private enterprise. Finally, the Southerners warned that any local biracial commissions set up to study community needs should take into full consideration the wishes of whites as well as of Negroes.

On the other hand, Hesburgh and Johnson, though in this instance they were not joined by Hannah, made a supplementary statement placing the emphasis on more extended programs of Federal housing aid. They stressed the importance of assistance in the relocation of persons displaced by urban renewal projects to prevent such programs becoming "Negro clearance." Additional low-cost housing on a non-segregated basis, in their view, was one of the nation's greatest needs.[32]

In reviewing the problem of civil rights as a whole in the final chapter of the Report, the Commission stated that through investigations and hearings it had become increasingly convinced of the

31. *Report,* 536–40; *Liberty and Justice,* 182–86.
32. *Report,* 540–43; *Liberty and Justice,* 187–89.

organic nature of the basic issues centering on race. The interrelationship among discriminatory practices in voting, education, and housing made it impossible to think that equal protection of the laws could be maintained by action in one field alone: the overall problem had to be simultaneously attacked on all fronts.

From one point of view the Commission found encouragement in the substantial progress that had been made in strengthening civil rights over the past century. However, it did not believe the pace was nearly fast enough in a revolutionary age which found the colored races of Asia and Africa so swiftly coming into their own. The Commission concluded:

> *Equal opportunity and equal justice under law must be achieved in all sections of American public life with all deliberate speed. . . . The whole problem will not be solved without high vision, serious purpose, and imaginative leadership. . . . The fundamental cause of prejudice is hidden in the minds and hearts of men. . . . America, which has already come closer to equality of opportunity than probably any other country, must succeed where others have failed. It can do this not only by resolving to end discrimination but also by creating through works of faith in freedom a clear and present vision of the City of Man, the one city of free and equal men envisioned by the Constitution.*[33]

This first Report of the Commission admittedly had its ambiguities and contradictions. Many of the statements reflected the difficulties of trying to reach a consensus among members whose views brought into sharp focus the basic conflict between North and South over what equal protection of the laws actually meant. To interpret the differences disclosed in the Report, as did the *U.S. News and World Report,* to mean that the whole investigation "wound up in disagreement"[34] was exaggeration. Equally unrealistic was the view that anything like complete unanimity had been attained among the Commissioners. The Report reflected many compromises and the end result was a moderate, balanced, middle-of-the-road approach to civil rights. In this lay its inherent strength.

"To the future historian," the *American Encyclopedia Annual* recorded for posterity in a burst of unwonted enthusiasm, "the most significant event of the year may well have been the appearance of

33. *Report,* 548–49; *Liberty and Justice,* 193–94.
34. *U.S. News and World Report,* 47, Sept. 21, 1959.

the first report of the United States Commission on Civil Rights."[35]

It is not to detract from the Report's usefulness to suggest this may have been going rather far. What may be said with somewhat more restraint is that through authoritative, factual revelations of the discrimination against Negroes so widely prevalent throughout American society, and strong, unequivocal support for the basic principle of equal protection of the laws, the Commission gave significant impetus to the whole struggle for civil rights.

In its later activities and reports the Commission was not so torn by internal differences, and ultimately its recommendations both became more explicit and commanded unanimous support. Through a stiffening in the attitude of continuing members and the sympathetic views of new members, the Commission was increasingly committed to the basic proposition that discrimination had no place in American life, and that there could not really be two sides on this fundamental issue. In 1959 this bipartisan Federal agency which President Eisenhower appointed to reflect the spectrum of American opinion was still the Commission *on* Civil Rights. Later years were to see it become in effect the Commission *for* Civil Rights.

35. *American Encyclopedia Annual,* 1960.

VI. A NEW MANDATE AND NEW ATTACKS

The Commission submitted its Report with the not unexpected popular reaction of warm approval in the North and severe condemnation in the South. The occasion, however, had elements of high drama in that the timing of the Report's publication coincided with the gathering climax of a long, drawn-out struggle in Congress over the extension of the Commission's life beyond the original two-year term. New civil rights legislation, periodically debated ever since passage of the 1957 Act, was completely bogged down. With Congress on the eve of adjournment, the Commission was fated to expire unless a last-minute rescue operation by northern supporters could save it. In these circumstances the controversial Report exploded like a bombshell. As *Time* reported, the question of extending the Commission's life now became as "hot an issue as civil rights itself."[1]

1. *Time,* 74, Sept. 14, 1959, 26.

Throughout 1959—and well before anyone knew what the Commission might recommend—pressure was steadily rising in favor of new legislation to strengthen the weak provisions of the existing civil rights law. The Administration came to accept the need for further action, however reluctant again to become involved in such a controversial issue, and individual Congressmen introduced a score of varied bills to put more teeth into rights enforcement. All these bills and proposals had one thing in common: extending the Commission's life, either for an additional two years or permanently.

President Eisenhower praised its constructive activities and urged its extension as early as the time of the Alabama hearing. As spokesman of the liberal non-partisan group so responsible for passage of the 1957 Civil Rights Act, Minority Leader Johnson was wholly in favor of renewing the Commission's mandate regardless of whatever else might be done.[2] The South's continued opposition and refusal to cooperate in any way with the Commission strengthened northern support. No more convincing evidence of the importance of the Commission's investigations and hearings could be produced than the uproar they occasioned among segregationists.

The issue first came to a head at hearings before the Senate Judiciary Subcommittee on Constitutional Rights in March, 1959. Southern members, determined to block the Commission's possible renewal, found their position bolstered by rumors of dissension and dissatisfaction within the Commission itself. They inserted in the hearings record a newspaper article stating that four members of the Commission were ready to resign, and quoting Hannah as saying that he hoped to be freed of further responsibility on the ground that "there is no right answer to all sides." Another source attributed to an unidentified member of the Commission the statement that its members generally were "fed to the teeth with futility and frustration." This was all grist to the southern mill; every effort was made to discredit the Commission and all its works.[3]

The testimony of the Commissioners themselves, when called before the subcommittee, served to refute these allegations. They had decided that until publication of their Report they would make

2. *New York Times,* Dec. 11, 1958.
3. *Civil Rights 1959. Hearings Before Subcommittee on Constitutional Rights of Senate Judiciary Committee,* 86th Congress, 1st Session, March 1959, 19–20, 225.

no statements whatsoever relating to pending civil rights legislation or comment in any way on the advisability of extending the
Commission's own life. They also felt it would be presumptuous
to discuss what they might themselves do should the Commission's
life be extended. Storey, however, strongly emphasized in his testimony that no one of them had any idea of quitting before the end
of his term of office. He said also that he had not observed any sense
of frustration within the Commission, and strongly reiterated that
its members were "dedicated to finishing the job we undertook,
which was a two-year job, and beyond that there are no commitments." He introduced supporting evidence on the attitude of his
fellow Commission members, including a telegram from Carleton
in which the latter stated: "We have a useful and important function to perform and I am delighted with the progress already
made."[4]

Hannah took the same position at a comparable hearing before
a subcommittee of the House Judiciary Committee. He personally
thought the Commission's life should be extended, but he was not
prepared officially to recommend it. Playing down the idea of frustration or dissension, he still did not want anything in the record
to indicate a desire on the part of the present Commissioners to
continue in office.[5]

As hearings and congressional debate on the whole civil rights
issue continued, the Commission won increasing support. The
President again spoke out at an address before the national conference of State Advisory Committees held in Washington on June
9. He especially stressed the importance of the Commission's fact-
finding functions but also expressed the view that it was playing a
highly significant role in arousing the national conscience. "Indeed
at times," Eisenhower said, "I think it holds up before us a mirror
so that we may see ourselves, what we are doing and what we are
not doing, and therefore makes it easier for us to correct our omissions."[6]

Still, no action. The Southerners, with a certain logic, considered it precipitate to pass any new law or to discuss the Commission's tenure until submission of the Report that was supposedly

4. *Ibid.*, 242–45.
5. *Civil Rights 1959. Hearings Before Subcommittee No. 5 of House Judiciary
   Committee*, 86th Congress, 1st Session, March 1959, 259.
6. *Public Papers of the Presidents, 1959* (Eisenhower), 448.

to be the basis for further legislation. Quoting an old proverb about the danger of burning one's tongue, Senator Ervin of North Carolina especially wanted to know why such a great rush. The Northerners nevertheless grew impatient of tactics that seemed to be not merely delaying action but postponing it indefinitely.[7]

As the summer drew to a close a very moderate civil rights bill was tied up in the House Rules Committee; another measure extending the Commission's life was deeply buried in the Senate Judiciary Committee. The situation, as the Staff Director reported to the Commission, "was static." With adjournment fever sweeping through Congress, Senators Johnson and Dirksen reached an agreement to give up any further attempts to pass a general bill for the time being but to take the matter up ("if the Lord is willing and I am alive," said Dirksen) early in the next session of Congress. This was all very well but no further legislation left the Civil Rights Commission in limbo. To save its life, senatorial supporters on the eve of congressional adjournment attached a rider to a House-passed mutual security appropriations bill which would provide for its extension and allocate $500,000 for continued investigations.

The southern members of Congress were incensed at this maneuver, and after the Commission issued its Report, confirming all their worst fears of meddling in matters they felt were none of the Federal Government's concern, their fury rose. It was hardly mollified when northern liberals not only strongly endorsed the Report but introduced a number of new bills in both House and Senate incorporating among other proposals its major recommendation for the appointment of Federal voting registrars.

Senator Eastland led off a debate which found almost every southern senator taking the floor to oppose the appropriation bill amendment extending the Commission's life. Following Senator Thurmond's attack on the Report as "radical, vicious, unconstitutional and obnoxious," his colleagues were hardly less restrained in assailing it as "irresponsible," "indefensible," and "ridiculous." In a final burst of impassioned oratory, Senator Talmadge said that it was almost more than he could do "to sustain in Christian charity . . . the resentment which swells within me."[8]

7. *Civil Rights . . . Senate Judiciary Committee,* 253.
8. *Congressional Record,* 86th Congress, 1st Session, Senate, 16878–18024, 19482–508, 19531–45, 19555–67 *passim.*

Such northern senators as Humphrey, Douglas, Morse, Javits, and Keating continued to praise the Report for its moderation and soundness, and they commanded the votes to pass such a relatively moderate measure as a two-year extension of the Commission's life. The wild swinging attacks of the southern senators were wholly futile. Nevertheless, it was a close call with congressional adjournment scheduled for September 14. The Senate passed the disputed amendment to the appropriations bill that final day after a "twelve hour spasm of oratory," the House promptly concurred, and at 4:10 A.M. on the following morning Congress adjourned ("died with a yawn," the *New York Times* said) and it was all over. The final vote providing for the two-year extension of the Commission's life closely paralleled that which created it two years earlier—221 to 81 in the House and 71 to 18 in the Senate.[9]

With its mandate renewed "by the skin of its teeth," the way was finally clear for the Commission to extend its investigations, hold new hearings, and work toward another report that would be due in 1961. Nevertheless, it faced a difficult task in reestablishing a staff which it had begun to phase out because of plaguing uncertainties as to the future; found itself under fresh attack from unexpected quarters; and confronted new problems in its relationship with the Department of Justice. The way was anything but smooth as the revived Commission knuckled down to carry out its prescribed duties.

In spite of the earlier rumors, only one member resigned. Since September, Governor Battle had come to feel that in the light of a position on civil rights so much at odds with that of his colleagues, he could no longer serve usefully. President Eisenhower named as his successor, Robert S. Rankin, the political scientist from Duke University who had earlier joined the staff in an advisory capacity. Both a Democrat and a Southerner, Rankin theoretically maintained the existing balance within the Commission, but he was far more of a moderate than the avowedly segregationist Battle, and accentuated the shift of the Commission as a whole to an increasing commitment to the civil rights cause. The Senate duly

9. *Revolution in Civil Rights*, Washington, 1965, 31; *New York Times*, Sept. 15, 1959, Sept. 16, 1959.

confirmed the new appointment in July but not without opposition on the part of the Southerners, and Eastland was later to attack Rankin as no more than a "stooge" for Hannah.

The staff underwent a very considerable turnover and this led to various changes in the organizational setup. The Commission revised the responsibilities of the various divisions and also their relationship to the State Advisory Committees. It initiated fresh pilot studies to discover new ways of obtaining basic facts and information, and early in 1960 set up a special steering committee to make a thorough analysis of overall plans and "determine where we are going and with what speed."[10]

Hannah was encouraged by these developments and expressed new confidence over what might be achieved through further investigations and reports. He took "comfort and hope," he said in a talk in early December, 1959, "in our lively national conscience which has led us to undertake another searching inquiry into why we have not done better by some of our people at home."[11] Although he saw no final answer to the civil rights problem, he felt the Commission was in a position to make further contributions to its alleviation.

Even as the new plans were being developed, however, the staff found its work unexpectedly interrupted. The Subcommittee on Investigations of the Senate Committee on Government Operations, under the chairmanship of Senator McClellan, initiated an inquiry into Commission operations which involved a personnel audit by Civil Service examiners, a scrutiny of accounts by the General Services Administration, and the summoning of staff members to committee hearings. This led to trouble. Senator McClellan complained to the Commission that his committee did not get the cooperation to which it was entitled and that the "manner and approach of some staff members did not follow proper procedure." On the other hand, the staff witnesses before the Senate committee reported harsh and unfriendly questioning and Hannah indignantly protested against their "abusive treatment."[12]

10. *Staff Activities Report,* Feb. 12, 1960.
11. Talk Before Anti-Defamation League of B'nai B'rith, *New York Times,* Dec. 7, 1959.
12. *New York Times,* March 11, 15, 16, 1960; minutes of 29th Commission meeting, March 20, 1960.

Staff Director Tiffany was the chief object of attack. He was generally held responsible for what the southern members of Congress considered the prejudiced tone of the body of the Commission's Report, and in launching his investigation McClellan was undoubtedly motivated by such considerations. Yet it was also true that Tiffany had not proved to be an entirely fortunate choice as Staff Director, and difficulties developed in his conduct of affairs ranging from allegations of discrimination in the appointment of staff to complaints of poor administration. However, the Senate committee's major charges were that Tiffany sought to block a review of financial data relating to Commission operations; failed to conform to civil service requirements in hiring staff personnel; and had destroyed certain transcripts of the Commission's executive meetings. Hannah instructed him to cooperate fully with the Senate investigators and to give them all available data, but the dragged-out hearings seriously interfered with staff activities and quite naturally had a depressing effect upon morale.[13]

Nothing came immediately from this investigation. Although McClellan repeatedly asked Hannah what he was going to do in respect to what the Senator considered Tiffany's obstructive attitude, the Commission was not prepared to take any action against its Staff Director. Toward the close of the year, however, Tiffany announced his intention to resign, and after preparing a special report to President Eisenhower, formally did so on December 2. The Commission adopted a unanimous resolution praising him for carrying forward an often difficult task with "devotion, intelligence and distinction"; the President in accepting the resignation said, "Your untiring efforts have contributed significantly to the success of the Commission to date."[14]

This was not, however, quite the end of the story. The Senate committee had not as yet issued an official report on its investigation but six months after Tiffany's resignation, on June 21, 1961, it

13. Minutes of 29th Commission meeting, March 20, 1960.
14. Senator McClellan to John A. Hannah, April 17, 1960; Hannah to McClellan, Sept. 21, 1960; McClellan to Hannah, Nov. 30, 1960, in Hannah files; *New York Times*, Dec. 3, 1960; minutes of 36th Commission meeting, Dec. 13–14; Gordon Tiffany, "Report to the President and to the Commission on Civil Rights from the Staff Director, 1958–60," December 20, 1960 (mimeo).

finally released its conclusions. They reaffirmed the charges brought
against Tiffany during the hearings and stated flatly that he possessed "neither the executive ability nor competence" to handle
the important duties with which he had been entrusted. Shortly
afterward McClellan carried the attack to the floor of the Senate
and declared that it was apparent to him "that Mr. Tiffany's subsequent resignation . . . was due to the investigation conducted by
the subcommittee."[15]

Tiffany promptly denied this was the case. Senator Javits, who
was a member of the subcommittee but had not participated in the
hearings, assailed the report as "unusual, useless and unproductive,"
and the Washington *Post* wrote a withering editorial blasting Mc-
Clellan for making Tiffany the target "of a mean and pointless
piece of political back-stabbing." The *Post* suggested that the reason
for such an attack so long after Tiffany's resignation was the Staff
Director's zeal in defense of civil rights. "Senator McClellan's
scandal-mongering," it said, "seems useless as well as vindictive."[16]

While the southern sense of injury and resentment clearly
underlay both the investigation and the belated committee report,
Hannah himself indirectly admitted at one time that the Commission itself was not too happy over Tiffany's conduct of affairs. In
a letter to the latter's successor on February 8, 1961—that is, after
Tiffany resigned but before publication of the Senate subcommittee report—he wrote: "I think it was obvious to you that I did not
enjoy working with our past organization because of its inefficien-
cies and ineptness which made it an unpleasant operation from my
point of view. I am sure, however, that that is all behind us."[17]

In addition to difficulties with an admittedly hostile senatorial
committee, the Commission did not always find the going altogether
happy with a supposedly friendly Administration. Hannah was
repeatedly assured of the full cooperation of the Executive Branch

15. *Incompetence of Staff Director, Commission on Civil Rights—Interim Report of the Committee on Government Operations by the Permanent Subcommittee on Investigation—June 21, 1961, Senate Report 438,* 87th Congress, 1st Session; Staff Activities Report, June 23, 1961.
16. Quoted in *New York Times,* June 24, 1961; Washington *Post,* June 24,
1961.
17. Hannah to Berl I. Bernhard, Feb. 8, 1961, in Hannah files.

of the Government, but the feeling nonetheless persisted among staff members that civil rights was a "White House orphan." More important was friction between the Commission and the Department of Justice. The Commission insisted on a wholly independent status, and yet it had to call upon the Attorney General for enforcement of its subpoena powers and also cooperate with the Justice Department's Civil Rights Division. This made things difficult.[18]

As early as October 21, 1959, the *New York Times* reported that the Commission and Justice had been "quarreling privately and publicly for weeks," and that an unnamed official in the latter organization had said that the best thing for the Commission to do was to go out of office. The Deputy Attorney General disavowed such a critical attitude. He publicly stated that the Commission was doing an "excellent job." The Justice Department was giving careful consideration to its report in the conviction that it had been drawn up by "sincere, able persons."[19]

The liaison between the two agencies subsequently improved in some respects, but further clashes proved unavoidable. The basic issue was conflict between the tendency of the Department of Justice to move slowly. ("They don't mean go slow," commented Thurgood Marshall, the future Supreme Court Justice who was at this time NAACP's leading lawyer, "they mean don't go."), and the desire of the Commission for more vigorous measures. Justice felt that the Commission sometimes acted irresponsibly and interfered with its own legal efforts to enforce existing legislation; the Commission believed Justice to be timid and overcautious in bringing voting rights suits. These differences became more pronounced during the Kennedy Administration, but from the first full understanding and complete cooperation between the two organizations were lacking.

As over against internal difficulties and the delicacy of relations with the Department of Justice, a quite different development strengthened the Commission's hands. The constitutionality of certain aspects of the Civil Rights Act of 1957 and of the Commission's own procedures had remained in question ever since the court injunction forcing postponement of the voting hearing in

18. See Tiffany, "Report to the President and the Commission on Civil Rights . . ."
19. *New York Times,* Oct. 21, 1959.

Louisiana. After a long process of litigation the Supreme Court in July, 1960, finally upheld the validity of the Civil Rights Act in *United States v. Raines,* and then in *Hannah v. Larche* fully sustained the Commission's procedures.

The principal point at issue in the latter case, directly affecting the Civil Rights Commission, was whether a subpoenaed witness who was accused of violating the law by denying a Negro his civil rights, was himself being denied his rights in being unable by Commission rules to confront or question his accusers. The majority opinion handed down by Chief Justice Warren ruled that Congress authorized the Commission to adopt the procedures in question, and that the lower court in upholding the Louisiana injunction erred in the conclusion that such procedures were a denial of due process of law.

The Chief Justice pointed out that the Civil Rights Commission did not issue orders, adjudicate, indict, punish, or impose legal sanctions; it could not take any affirmative action affecting an individual's legal rights. Its only function was to find facts that could be subsequently used as a basis for legislative or executive action. "Thus, the purely investigative nature of the Commission's proceedings, the burden that the claimed rights would place upon those proceedings, and the traditional procedure of investigating agencies in general," his opinion averred, "leads us to conclude that the Commission's Rules of Procedure comport with the requirements of due process. . . ."[20]

The decision was nevertheless hard law. Frankfurter accepted it but submitted an individual opinion; Harlan joined Clark in another separate statement; and, most significantly, Douglas and Black sharply dissented.

The two most liberal members of the Supreme Court, whose deep attachment to civil rights was unquestioned, saw a very great danger in giving the Commission the powers implicit in its rules of procedure. While such hearings as those in Alabama might not lead to indictments, Douglas and Black felt that in reality they constituted a trial in which the whole nation sat as jury. "Farming out pieces of trial to investigative agencies," the dissenters declared, "is fragmentizing the kind of trial the Constitution authorizes. It

20. *Hannah v. Larche,* 363 U.S. 420 (June, 1960), 441.

prejudices the ultimate trial itself . . . it leads to government in-
quisition." They believed the lower court's original injunction
against the Louisiana hearings should be upheld. "Worthy . . . as
the ends are which the Civil Rights Commission advances in these
cases," Douglas and Black declared, ". . . the particular means are
unconstitutional."[21]

The majority opinion of course held, and so reenforced, the
Commission planned to resume the Louisiana voting hearing and
to hold such others as might further serve to bring out the denial
of the right to vote to qualified Negroes.

By this time things were generally under control and the
Commission fully launched on the expanded program gradually
worked out following the renewal of its congressional mandate.
Investigations were moving ahead on a broad front and it was decided to extend them beyond the initial issues of voting, education
and housing to include employment and the administration of
justice. Staff studies were under way in these new fields as well
as continued surveys in more familiar areas.

During its second term of office, the Commission ultimately
held general hearings covering the entire spectrum of civil rights
in Los Angeles and San Francisco, and then in Detroit; staged educational conferences both in 1960 and 1961 comparable to the
initial meeting in Nashville; and conducted a study of discriminatory practices in institutions of higher learning which led to a
special report in January, 1961. The staff also launched a so-called
Black Belt survey relating to discrimination against Negroes in
sixteen selected southern counties, and investigated living conditions of Indians in the Southwest.

The Staff Activities Reports and the minutes of the Commission's monthly meetings throughout this two-year period once again
give a picture of incessant activity. The Commission was constantly
reviewing progress reports from the Staff Director, periodically
went over problems of personnel and assignments to special projects,
worked on budgetary matters and the preparation of the annual
requests for funds to be defended before the appropriate congressional committees, supervised the handling of the individual com-

21. *Ibid.,* 500–1, 508.

plaints continuing to flow in on alleged deprivation of civil rights, and worked to develop closer and more effective relations with the State Advisory Committees. The hearings, especially those on voting in the South, remained the most significant phase of general operations and provided, as in 1958 and 1959, the basic material for forthcoming reports. Although the Commission had more time than when carrying out its first assignments, the area which it was now attempting to cover was so broad that its task was if possible even more challenging.

The Commission was not operating in a vacuum. The whole movement for civil rights was gathering a new momentum; the Negroes were ever more aggressively carrying their revolution into the streets. Before taking up the course of the investigations and hearings themselves, it may be well to consider these background developments in 1960 and 1961 as they affected the Commission's work.

VII. MOUNTING PRESSURES

The gathering force of the civil rights movement was to provide a powerful thrust toward passage of the legislation that bogged down, except for renewal of the Civil Rights Commission, at the close of 1959. When a new law finally passed the next year, however, it proved to be a very limited measure, only slightly strengthening the provisions of the 1957 Act. Civil rights consequently entered importantly into the forthcoming presidential campaign. The question, which for a time remained unanswered, then arose as to whether the Kennedy Administration would meet the issue head-on, or, because of the exigencies of politics, hesitate to take the risks that either direct executive action or insistence on further legislation would inevitably entail.

The year 1960 opened with the beginning of the sit-ins. On February 1 a group of four Negro students from North Carolina

Agricultural and Technical College, in Greensboro, sat down at a dime store luncheon counter reserved for whites and ordered coffee. When they were refused service, they simply stayed on quietly in peaceful protest until the store closed. The movement once started spread throughout the South and to scattered places in the North. Sometimes as a wholly spontaneous move and sometimes organized by CORE (Congress of Racial Equality), or SNCC (the Student Non-violent Coordinating Committee), Negroes invaded segregated restaurants, drug stores, lunch rooms, and the dining facilities of department stores. Angry whites repeatedly heckled them, insulted and spat on them, sometimes beat them up. In many localities the police promptly arrested the Negroes and hauled them off to jail on charges of trespass or disorderly conduct. They remained quiet and peaceful, and indeed courted arrest and imprisonment as a means of dramatizing the discrimination to which they were subjected because of their race and color. "Words cannot express," wrote Martin Luther King, Jr., "the exultation felt by the individual as he finds himself, with hundreds of his fellows, behind prison bars for a cause he knows is just."[1]

The lower courts throughout the South generally upheld the convictions of these demonstrators but the Supreme Court ultimately overruled them on the ground that prosecution of persons seeking service without discrimination at public establishments was a denial of equal protection of the laws. Even before the final court decision, however, the sit-ins had by public pressure forced restaurants, lunch rooms, and many other establishments to desegregate. The campaign, which rapidly spread to include walk-ins, stand-ins, wade-ins, and pray-ins as the Negroes sought to assert their rights in moving picture theaters, libraries, swimming pools, and churches, continued to arouse deep resentment in the South and growing sympathy in the North. The Negro was no longer "the invisible man." He was asserting his rights as an American citizen.

If 1960 was the year of the sit-ins, 1961 was that of the freedom rides. A first group of Negroes and sympathetic whites, organized by CORE, chartered buses for a southern tour to protest the segregated facilities in bus terminals—lunch counters, lounges, and restrooms—which were still maintained in spite of official desegregation

1. Quoted in Arthur M. Schlesinger, Jr., *A Thousand Days,* Boston, 1965, 957.

in interstate transportation itself. Leaving Washington on May 5 with New Orleans their ultimate destination, the original freedom riders encountered no serious difficulties until they entered Alabama. At Anniston a white mob, especially infuriated because "outsiders" were participating in the demonstration, attacked and beat up one busload, and then overturned and burned a second bus. As the freedom riders nonetheless continued toward Montgomery, Governor Patterson, who so strongly opposed the Civil Rights Commission's voting hearing in Alabama, angrily denounced them as "rabble rousers" and in effect encouraged further attacks. "We can't act as nursemaids to agitators," he said. "They'll stay at home when they learn nobody is there to protect them." A mob of one thousand jeering whites bodily assaulted the riders as they reached Montgomery and the police stood idly by without making a move. Here was another crisis finding a state unable—or unwilling—to maintain law and order. President Kennedy ordered six hundred deputy Federal marshals to move in on Montgomery and restore peace. Governor Patterson protested this "invasion," but as the rioting spread he was himself forced to declare martial law and ask for additional help.

As conditions gradually quieted, some twenty-seven of the freedom riders continued by bus, now under armed guard, into Mississippi. On reaching Jackson the local police promptly arrested them but took rigid measures to guard against violence or rioting. On the demonstrators' release from Jackson's jail, they resumed their progress through Mississippi, and their example was now followed by other freedom riders who traversed the South, everywhere insisting that bus terminal facilities be completely desegregated.

The rioting in Montgomery was the most serious racial disturbance up to this time in the postwar era. Even more than earlier incidents, it awoke the North to the persistence of the South's virulent opposition to any lowering of the bars of discrimination. President Kennedy was stirred to affirm in unequivocal terms that everyone who traveled, for whatever reason, was entitled to the full protection of the laws. He instructed the Attorney General to petition the Interstate Commerce Commission immediately to require the desegregation of all facilities in terminals used by buses in interstate travel.[2] The freedom riders, too, had won their battle.

2. *Ibid.*, 936–37.

"White" and "colored" signs began to come down all over the South.*

The segregationists enrolled in the White Citizens Councils and a renascent Ku Klux Klan remained unreconciled and did everything possible to combat the new trend undermining the traditional southern way of life. The Negroes nonetheless were determined to continue their anti-discriminatory campaigns in the face of all opposition. The bleak shadow of racial conflict spread through the South; it was also beginning to overcloud the black ghettos of many northern cities. Still further crises loomed over a darkened horizon.

Against the backdrop of the sit-ins and prospective freedom rides, Congress, as agreed at the close of 1959, took up further civil rights legislation. The battle in both the House and the Senate was a continuation of that so inconclusively fought the previous year and involved all the complexities, political maneuvering, and internal conflicts invariably characterizing civil rights debates. There were three major blocs in Congress: moderates who supported the relatively mild bill the Eisenhower Administration sponsored, a bipartisan group of liberal Northerners who urged a far stronger measure, and Southerners who opposed any new law at all. It became increasingly apparent, however, that the Southerners were now playing their cards far more shrewdly than they had in 1957. They stoutly resisted every attempt by the liberals to strengthen the pending bill, and on the ground that the South was being victimized to provide political dividends for the North, argued persuasively for softening amendments that would moderate racial conflict. Instead of blindly combating any bill at all, that is, the Southerners worked desperately to limit further interference with the South's traditional customs to a law with which they thought they could live.[3]

The Administration bill contained certain of the recommendations of the Civil Rights Commission. One title made it a Federal crime to obstruct or interfere with any court order related to school desegregation; another provided penalties for the perpetrators of

---

* The writer remembers, however, a sign in a desegregated roadside restaurant: "All receipts from colored persons will be donated to the Ku Klux Klan."

3. *Revolution in Civil Rights*, Washington, 1965, 31–36.

the bombing or burning of schools and churches who crossed state lines. On the voting issue, however, the new bill temporized. It called for the preservation of all registration records for twenty-two months (the Commission had recommended five years), and partially accepted the idea of Federal registrars in proposing court-appointed referees to help Negroes register. However, by making the appointment of such referees dependent on civil suits and court injunctions rather than investigation by the Commission, this plan provided no means of escape from the cumbersome processes of litigation. The provisions of the 1957 Act would be somewhat strengthened, but this would still afford very dubious relief for Negroes seeking to vote.

The House passed this bill with reasonable dispatch but the Senate was a different story. The northern liberals favored the stronger Commission plan of voting registrars; the South fought a delaying action with weakening amendments and temporary filibusters. The debate was seemingly endless. At one point Senator Keating offered some statistics: between February 15 and March 10 civil rights arguments had filled over one thousand pages of the *Congressional Record,* the Southerners contributing 785 of the total. New records were established, Keating caustically commented, "in the unrolling of the long, long carpet of verbiage"; and then added in reference to the Southerners: "If they are speaking for posterity we need only continue a little longer and posterity will be in the galleries listening to us."[4]

At long last, on April 8, the issue came to a vote. The Southerners not only beat back every effort of the northern liberals to put sharper teeth into the bill, but succeeded in winning passage of several of their weakening amendments. They naturally voted against the final bill—the tally was 71 to 18—but made no further attempt to filibuster. The House now accepted the changes made in the Senate and President Eisenhower signed the 1960 Civil Rights Act into law on May 6.[5]

In its final draft this measure incorporated the Federal voting referees plan with its complicated legal machinery, most of the other provisions of the original Administration bill in somewhat modified

4. *Congressional Record,* 86th Congress, 2nd Session, Senate, March 10, 1960, 5093–94.
5. *Public Law 86–449; Revolution in Civil Rights,* 34.

form, and, without materially affecting either its duties or responsibilities, spelled out more clearly the powers of the Civil Rights Commission. There was certainly nothing here to persuade the Commission that its own task had been in any way fulfilled. On the contrary, the inherent weakness of the 1960 law emphasized the ever greater need for further investigations, the accumulation of additional facts, if Congress were to be convinced that stronger measures were essential to provide equal protection of the laws for the Negro minority on a realistic basis.

In the light of this ineffectual response to the mounting unrest among the Negroes, the whole issue of civil rights became a major issue in the presidential campaign now getting under way. Republicans and Democrats pledged themselves to prompt action to uphold equality and especially singled out the need to go much further in counteracting discrimination in voting. Without in either case accepting the constitutional amendment proposed by the northern members of the Commission in the 1959 Report, both parties nevertheless reflected the influence of the ideas behind it. The Republicans recommended making a sixth grade education conclusive evidence of literacy; the Democrats called for the complete elimination of all literacy tests. One thing the Commission's investigations had certainly demonstrated beyond question: literacy tests could not be controlled so as to prevent their being used by segregation-minded registrars to bar Negroes from voting.

The civil rights plank of the Democrats, which Kennedy fully supported as a presidential candidate, was the strongest in the history of either major party. In addition to the proposal on voting, it called for Federal assistance to school systems going through the process of desegregation, authorization for the Attorney General to seek injunctions against any deprivation of civil rights, establishment of a Fair Employment Practices Commission, executive action to bring to an end discrimination in Federally financed housing, and permanent status for the Civil Rights Commission.[6]

Such a strong plank led to rebellion in southern ranks, but playing the political game for all it was worth, the Kennedy forces were convinced that the possible defection of southern Democrats would be more than offset by the added votes of northern Negroes.

6. *Revolution in Civil Rights*, 35.

They were right. Only the coming months, however, would determine whether the new Administration would carry out the Democratic platform pledges.

As President Kennedy took office in January, 1961, current reports, as published in *Newsweek,* predicted he would wholly change the Civil Rights Commission "from top to bottom."[7] They proved to be without foundation. The Commissioners submitted their resignations, Hannah writing one correspondent that he would "really like to be relieved of this responsibility," but after a presidential conference on February 7, the White House announced that the Commission would remain as presently established, with Hannah continuing as Chairman, and that it had the President's full confidence.[8]

Hannah presented at this conference a memorandum giving the views of the Commission as to steps which Kennedy, pending further legislation, might take to promote more effective enforcement of equal protection of the laws. The Commission urged the President to issue a proclamation stating that the Administration would practice a policy of non-discrimination in all Government departments, seek the opinion of the Attorney General as to just what the Executive could presently do in respect to withholding Federal funds as a means of enforcing compliance with desegregation in institutions of higher learning, and promptly issue an Executive Order providing for equal opportunity in all housing projects financed or otherwise assisted by the Federal Government. These recommendations, generally conforming to those the Commission had more formally made in its earlier Report, apparently awoke a sympathetic response. The decision to maintain the existing Commission provided substantial evidence that Kennedy approved its program, and Hannah was himself convinced, after his White House discussion on the civil rights problem as a whole, that the President had "real conviction in this area."[9]

Somewhat later, in March, two Commissioners, Carleton and Johnson, resigned for personal reasons in spite of their earlier deci-

7. *Newsweek,* Dec. 26, 1960.
8. John A. Hannah to Edward M. Turner, Feb. 9, 1961, in Hannah files; minutes of 37th Commission meeting, Jan. 7, 1961.
9. Document dated Feb. 7, 1961, in Hannah files.

sion to continue. In their place the President named Erwin N. Griswold, Dean of the Harvard University Law School, and Spottswood W. Robinson, III, Dean of the Howard University Law School. The appointments were immensely significant, indicative both of the general trend of the civil rights movement and of the new Administration's apparently sympathetic attitude toward it. For while the new members maintained the bipartisan character of the Commission and at least in theory the traditional three-to-three division between the North and South, they definitely changed its character. The Commission no longer had any political representatives; its composition was wholly academic and legalistic. Two university presidents, three law deans, and a political scientist made up the new membership. Far more important, it now had a clear majority openly in favor of the liberal civil rights position.

There was no question where Hannah and Hesburgh stood. Their experience made them increasingly aware of the need to meet the Negro demand for equality, and they were fully committed to the civil rights cause on both moral and legal grounds. Dean Griswold came to the Commission with comparable convictions, and would prove to be a forthright advocate for the strongest possible measures to stamp out discrimination. Robinson, the Negro replacement for Johnson, was a native of Virginia and therefore nominally a Southerner. However, he not only had a natural sympathy for racial equality but was directly associated with the civil rights movement as a one-time attorney for his state's branch of the NAACP.

This left only two possible spokesmen for the South—Storey and Rankin. But rather than being avowed segregationists or obdurate defenders of the southern way of life, both men had proved themselves to be very moderate in their views and deeply concerned with the maintenance of the law. The shift in the nature of the Commission that began with the replacement of Battle by Rankin was now so strongly accentuated that the equal division between the northern and southern viewpoints which originally characterized it was clearly a thing of the past. The prospective division on substantive questions dividing North and South was a majority for the North of at least four-to-two. This change was fully recognized. Southerners promptly protested that the Commission was more than ever "getting out of balance," while Negro leaders hopefully declared that "the balance will be tipped in the direction of a more realistic approach."[10]

A further and in some ways even more significant development was the appointment of a new Staff Director to replace Gordon Tiffany. President Kennedy named Berl I. Bernhard, a young lawyer who had been with the Commission since its establishment, taken charge of the Division of Laws, Plans and Research when Johnson became a Commissioner, and then served as Deputy Director and Acting Staff Director. Bernhard was planning to resign but Hannah strongly favored him as the permanent Staff Director because of his fine record as an administrative officer. Indeed, Hannah thought so well of Bernhard that he nominated him for one of the awards annually given by Washington's Junior Chamber of Commerce to the ten outstanding young men in the executive branch of the Government. The other Commissioners, including those who resigned, were no less approving and Bernhard's name went to the President with their unanimous endorsement. Some observers thought that Kennedy might name another candidate, but after the White House Conference on February 7, the President announced that he approved the Commission's recommendation. In view of the key role of the Staff Director, Hannah had in fact made Bernhard's appointment a virtual condition for his own continuance as Chairman.[11]

The appointments of Griswold, Robinson, and Bernhard had of course to be confirmed by the Senate, and southern obstructionism in the Judiciary Committee again caused a long delay. Although the President officially named Bernhard on March 15 and the new Commission members on April 19, the Subcommittee on Constitutional Rights did not begin hearings until June 16. Hannah repeatedly tried to get faster action, and on May 11 had written a sharp letter of protest to President Kennedy. "Until the appointments are confirmed," he candidly pointed out, "the Commission continues to be evenly divided on substantive recommendations."[12]

The President's answer was reassuring in its general support

10. *Congressional Record*, 87th Congress, 1st Session, Senate, July 27, 1961, 12678; Washington *Afro-American*, April 25, 1961.
11. Staff Activities Report, Jan. 7, 1961; minutes of 37th Commission meeting, Jan. 7, 1961.
12. Hannah to President Kennedy, May 11, 1961, in Hannah files.

for the Commission. Its "constructive work," he said, ". . . was never needed more than in this period of racial crisis."[13] Nevertheless, the Senate committee continued to delay and when it finally opened its hearings, the meeting lacked a quorum. "An appropriate time," the Washington *Post* declared in a critical editorial, "for the White House to place several calls to the north wing of the Capitol."[14]

When the hearings were resumed, the attacks on the new appointees were "milder than expected," according to a Staff Activities Report, and the atmosphere more friendly than on earlier occasions.[15] Griswold escaped unscathed, and while Robinson hardly fared so well, Senator Erwin saying that his appointment was "somewhat like having counsel appointed a judge," he was not subjected to any personal abuse. Bernhard made a good appearance and the committee members seemed impressed that he had quite as strong support from the southern members of the Commission as from its northern members. Carleton wrote that his industry, fairness, and objectivity made an "indelible impression" on the Commission, and Battle praised him as an "exceedingly able young man." For his own part, Bernhard declared his intention of maintaining an objective position if confirmed as Staff Director and stated his conviction that civil rights was not a regional but a national problem. With the Southerners casting their adverse ballots rather against the Commission itself than against the new members, the Judiciary Committee on July 7 adopted a favorable report on confirmation by a seven to four vote. Three weeks later, the issue came up on the floor of the Senate.[16]

The Southerners now returned to the fray with greater vigor. Viewing the Commission as a whole, an angry Senator Eastland declared that with the new appointments "adequate and fair representation . . . has now been destroyed." Acknowledging that Hannah was "a good man," he again charged him with knowing "nothing about conditions in the South"; said that Rankin, while nominally representing the southern viewpoint, was in actuality controlled by

13. President Kennedy to Hannah, May 26, 1961, in Hannah files.
14. Washington *Post,* June 17, 1961.
15. Staff Activities Report, June, 1961.
16. *Hearings before the Subcommittee on Constitutional Rights. . . . Senate,* 87th Congress, 1st Session, 11, 16; Washington *Post,* June 17, 1961.

the Chairman "body and soul," and exploded in wrath over the
nomination of Robinson—"this agitator"—who as a Southerner
was the nominal replacement of Governor Carleton. Pointing out
that his Negro predecessor, Dean Johnson, had been one of the
busiest members of the Commission (drawing an allowance for
almost as many working days as all the other members of the Commission combined), Eastland implied that in pressing the case for
civil rights Robinson would follow the same over-eager activist
course.

Other southern senators concentrated their assault on Robinson. While such civil rights adherents as Keating, Javits, and Morse
praised him as "one of the recognized great Negro lawyers of our
time," his critics reiterated that his background and association
with the NAACP showed such bias that there could be no possible
justification for his appointment.

The debate was vehement but brief. An ultimate favorable
vote was never in doubt, but when the Senate finally acted, the
resentment of the Southerners was still very much alive. They ac-
ceded to the appointment of Griswold, and also that of Bernhard,
but voted solidly against Robinson. The final tally on his confirmation was 73 to 17.[17]

Some two weeks later President Kennedy telegraphed Chairman Hannah to say that he was happy that confirmation of the new
members and Staff Director had come in time for the Commission's
joint deliberations on its forthcoming report. "Your work," his
telegram concluded, "was never more needed."[18]

While the reconstitution of the Commission, and especially
the appointment and confirmation of the new Staff Director,
cleared the way for final preparation of the report on which both
staff and members were busily engaged, the question still remained
whether the Commission's life would be renewed beyond the two-
year extension granted during the expiring agonies of the Eighty-
sixth Congress' first session in the autumn of 1959. In his letter in
May assuring Hannah of the Administration's continuing interest,
Kennedy told him that he could "inform the staff of the Commis-

17. *Congressional Record,* 87th Congress, 1st Session, Senate, July 27, 1961,
    12678–866 *passim,* 12678–89, 12694.
18. President Kennedy to Hannah, Aug. 11, 1961, in Hannah files.

sion that we have every reason to believe the Commission's life will be extended." In his August telegram the President reaffirmed his confidence in such an extension. Still, nothing was done.[19]

The Commission became worried. On July 17 Father Hesburgh wrote Harris Wofford, Jr., his former legal assistant, now on the White House staff and assigned to civil rights, that he was deeply concerned about "the Administration's stance on Civil Rights progress versus practical politics." Told of this move, Hannah said that he hoped "it has the desired result." In the meantime, however, the Commission had no alternative, in view of its possible legal expiration, other than to begin to curtail operations. It accepted the resignations of several key workers; it cut down on clerical help. By August the staff was reduced from seventy-one to sixty-one and an additional thirteen resignations were pending.[20]

In spite of the President's support and undoubted sincerity in desiring the Commission's continuance, the fact of the matter was that he was still playing a very careful game on civil rights. Hesburgh's concern over his "stance" was fully justified. Kennedy was leaning backward not to antagonize the Southerners upon whose support, in such a closely divided Congress, he was utterly dependent for enactment of his domestic program. As a candidate he had asked Senator Clark and Representative Celler to draw up a bill embodying the civil rights recommendations of the Democratic platform, including a permanent Commission, but when they introduced such a bill on May 8, he pointedly withheld his support. It was not an Administration measure, Pierre Salinger, the White House Press Secretary, said, and added that "the President does not consider it necessary at this time to enact new civil rights legislation." Moreover, Kennedy failed to take any action to combat public housing discrimination through an Executive Order even though as a presidential candidate he had caustically said that Eisenhower could have done so "by a stroke of the pen."[21]

For all his basic sympathies the President was not as yet really committed to the civil rights movement. Both his principal biographers, Theodore Sorensen in *Kennedy* and Arthur M. Schles-

19. President Kennedy to Hannah, May 26, 1961; President Kennedy to Hannah, Aug 11, 1961, in Hannah files.
20. Father Hesburgh to Harris Wofford, Jr., July 17, 1961; Hannah to Hesburgh, July 20, 1961, in Hannah files.
21. *Revolution in Civil Rights,* 37

inger, Jr., in *A Thousand Days,* make this abundantly clear. His major interest in 1961 lay in other directions, and he was prepared to postpone action on civil rights until his political position was stronger. The question remained one of votes in a deeply divided Congress. Sorensen has written that it was perfectly obvious that no amount of presidential pressure could at this time win enactment of a meaningful civil rights package; Schlesinger has said that the composition of the Eighty-seventh Congress made it clear that any such bill was bound to fail. The President very much wanted to see the Commission's life extended, but even on such a limited measure, the initiative and drive were not to come from the Administration.[22]

The liberal coalition in the Senate which refused to let the Commission die in 1959, again came to its aid, this time through the expedient of amending the State-Justice-Judiciary appropriation bill which had already passed the House. Other private bills were before the Senate to make the Commission permanent or to give it at least a four-year extension, but the bedrock proposal in the appropriations bill amendment, jointly sponsored by Majority Leader Johnson and Minority Leader Dirksen, was a two-year extension with an appropriation of $880,000.[23]

The Commission was building up increasing popular support with the passage of time. It enjoyed, at least in the North, a very good press. The Washington *Post,* commenting in June on the need for its continuation used such phrases as "extremely useful," "vital work," and "urgent need"; later in the summer, as action on the extension seemed very problematical, the St. Louis *Post-Dispatch* and the Milwaukee *Journal* came strongly to its support. The former declared that the new appointees gave "even stronger initiative" to the current program and the Commission should be made permanent, while the latter said that after a "rocky start," the Commission was not only effectively calling attention to the growth of discrimination in American life, but "getting something done about it."[24] Somewhat later Edward P. Morgan added his praise in a broadcast over the ABC network:

22. Theodore Sorensen, *Kennedy,* 470–76; Schlesinger, *A Thousand Days,* 928–31.
23. *Revolution in Civil Rights,* 37.
24. Washington *Post,* June 23, 1961; St. Louis *Post-Dispatch,* Aug. 8, 1961; Milwaukee *Journal,* Aug. 11, 1961.

*The Commission continues to be one of the most remarkable
agencies of the government. Hardly anybody took it seriously when
Congress created it four years ago but after a late and disorganized
start, its investigations of violations of civil rights have been so thoroughly documented and dispassionately done and its findings so revealing that the segregationists have energetically bucked its renewal.*[25]

When the issue of the Commission's tenure first reached the
floor of the Senate on August 29–30, the Northerners made the
most of such evidence of popular approval. They could also cite
the testimony of the Commissioners that uncertainty over the
future greatly impeded their work. In response to an inquiry from
Senator Clark, a strong supporter, Hannah said that while it was
still his general policy not to comment on bills dealing with the
Commission's status, he was prepared to depart from this custom
to the extent of saying that if the Commission were to be continued, it could operate far more effectively if given a longer lease
on life, not less than four years.[26] Still more important, the Administration finally came around to taking a more decided stand than
heretofore deemed advisable, and Representative Celler placed in
the *Congressional Record* a letter from the White House.

"The constructive potential of this agency cannot be fully realized," this letter read, "if its ability to move in long-range fashion
is hampered by the uncertainties of its continued existence." The
Attorney General was further quoted as saying that if Congress did
not consider it feasible to give the Commission permanent status,
anything from four to six years was "highly desirable."[27]

The Senate nevertheless defeated moves to make the Commission permanent or to give it a four-year term by respective
votes of 56 to 36 and 48 to 42. The old liberal coalition then concentrated, as an irreducible minimum, on the two-year term incorporated in the amendment to the State-Justice-Judiciary appropriation bill. "I am willing to give this Commission permanent
status," Senator Saltonstall of Massachusetts said, ". . . but the
only practical solution to the present impasse we have reached at
this session seems to be to adopt the two-year measure." This be-

25. ABC News Release, Oct. 18, 1961.
26. Hannah to Senator Joseph Clark, Aug. 14, 1961, in Hannah files.
27. *Congressional Record,* 87th Congress, 1st Session, 1961, Senate, Aug. 29–30,
    1961, 16252.

came the position of all the Commission's sponsors in the light of the political realities.[28]

The Southerners, not content with blocking every move to make the agency permanent, remained irreconcilable to even a two-year extension. In attacks even more embittered than those they had launched on so many earlier occasions, they assailed the Commission as a "meddling, trouble-making body" which was sowing the "seeds of tyranny." They raked over the coals of the controversial investigation by the McClellan Committee, and even though Tiffany had long since resigned, revived the old charges of his destruction of official records and defiance of a senatorial subcommittee. They were especially virulent in criticizing the new composition of the Commission, going even further than they had when the names of Griswold, Robinson and Bernhard came up for Senate confirmation.

Senator Eastland, becoming almost apoplectic, declared that the Commission no longer had a single spokesman for the South. He reiterated his charge that Rankin did not reflect the philosophy and sentiments of the southern people any more than did Hannah, and he now found Dean Storey infected by the "virus" of northern views. His southern colleagues thoroughly agreed that with its makeup no longer reasonably balanced, the Commission was more inimical to the real interests of the country than ever before. Its "illogical ramblings and babblings of unsound thinking," Senator Thurmond said, might be expected to be far worse in the future than in the past. Could the Commission be impartial with its new membership? "When that question is asked," shouted Senator Robertson of Virginia, "the answer 'No' echoes from Maine to Florida." Replying to the rhetorical query whether any confidence could be placed in the Commission with Robinson replacing Battle, Senator Talmadge said that this was "like making a tomcat custodian of a canary bird."[29]

The Southerners were talking for the record, voicing their sense of outrage. They might be able to command the votes to prevent giving the Commission permanency, but this was a quite different matter from doing away with it altogether. They knew they

28. *Ibid.*, 16399.
29. *Ibid.*, 16207–16366 *passim*.

did not have any more support in their battle against the northern coalition on a limited two-year extension than they had been able to summon up against the original creation of the Commission or against the confirmation of its membership. When the Senate held a final vote on the amendment to the appropriation bill on August 30, the old alignments held. The two-year extension was approved 70 to 19; the House concurred when the bill as a whole was returned to it, and after signature by President Kennedy, the extension became law on September 21. Once again the Commission was saved.

Throughout this fevered debate one thing especially stood out. Both the proponents and opponents of the Commission agreed that its investigations and recommendations were playing an important part in strengthening the civil rights cause. Even though its recommendations were not fully accepted, they helped to point the way toward what could be done. While the Southerners fulminated, not so much over the substantive facts as over their interpretation, the Northerners more quietly made the point that the facts spoke for themselves with a revelation of overt discrimination that could not be tolerated in a democratic society.

VIII. FURTHER FIELD
WORK

During the years 1960–61, marked by the turmoil in the South
as the Negroes pressed their aggressive campaign against discrimination and continued debate and controversy in the world
of politics, the Commission was going steadily ahead with its
own work. The sit-ins and freedom rides, the election of Kennedy, the struggle in Congress over its own existence, did not deter
it from pursuing its prescribed activities. They followed very much
the pattern set during the first term of office. While the changes
in membership and staff, to say nothing of legislative attacks, sometimes hampered current operations, on the whole they proceeded
smoothly. The story of the Commission in this period, with even
greater and more diverse activity on a broadening front, can be
told only through a highly selective process. The transcripts of the
hearings run to thousands of pages; the official biennial Report was
itself nearly fourteen hundred.

A first new development in 1960 was closer cooperation with the Executive Branch. The Commission steadfastly maintained its own independent status but succeeded in developing a more satisfactory relationship with the Civil Rights division of the Department of Justice and more practical ways of collaborating with other governmental departments and agencies in the implementation of policy. While complete understanding between the Commission and Justice still remained an unattainable goal because their respective responsibilities often appeared to conflict, the White House now took a hand in strengthening their collaboration by setting up a new "subcabinet" on civil rights on which the Commission was represented.[1]

In another move along somewhat comparable lines, the Commission endeavored to invigorate the State Advisory Committees, both as a source of information on the state of civil rights throughout the country and as instruments for promoting biracial cooperation in local communities. A new Assistant Staff Director, Cornelius P. Cotton, succeeded by mid-1960 in bringing these committees from "a rather disoriented situation to a peak of interest, organization and productivity that had not been previously achieved." A year later the Commission published an account of their individual operations in a massive volume—687 pages—which was titled *The 50 States Report*.[2] The record was diverse and uneven. Without effective leadership some of the committees accomplished very little, but in other cases interested and dedicated members carried through far-ranging programs which had a real impact on their communities. On the whole the work of the State Advisory Committees constituted a valuable contribution to the civil rights program.

The most significant activity of the Commission, apart from everything else, remained of course the investigations and hearings that enabled it to carry forward its primary function of fact-finding and provided the material for the findings and recommendations in its second report.

A first project along these lines in 1960, and one which led to an interim report at the opening of the next year, was a special

1. Memorandum in Hannah files.
2. *The 50 States Report, from the Advisory Committees to the Commission on Civil Rights,* Washington, 1961.

inquiry into higher education. When the northern members of the
Commission proposed in 1959 the withdrawal of all Federal aid
to colleges and universities which continued to discriminate against
Negroes, the Southerners objected in principle but also said that
staff studies had not explored the problem sufficiently to justify any
conclusions. The new investigation provided a basis for more carefully documented recommendations, and this time a majority agreed
upon what was in effect a reaffirmation of the northern position
two years earlier.

The interim report—Equal Protection of the Laws in Public
Higher Education—commenced with a historical account of segregation in higher institutions of learning and the consequent establishment of Negro colleges which far from being "separate but
equal," were invariably greatly inferior to the white colleges. It
then reviewed conditions as they had developed following the
Supreme Court decisions which asserted that Negroes were entitled
to enroll in white colleges. A number of states heretofore practicing
complete segregation were moving toward either token or limited
compliance, but those in the Deep South obdurately continued
their resistance to any change.[3]

The report then went on to summarize its findings, stating that
among two hundred eleven public institutions of higher learning
in seventeen southern states, eighty-six still excluded Negroes in
clear violation of the law as interpreted by the Supreme Court.
Nevertheless these institutions received Federal assistance in various forms so that the National Government was, in effect, supporting discrimination through its failure to give any consideration to
the practices of the institutions it aided. This made Washington,
the report said, "a silent partner in the creation and perpetuation
of separate colleges for Negroes." Furthermore, a marked disparity existed in the Federal assistance extended to white colleges or
universities as compared with what was given to the Negro colleges. The Federal Government thus also helped to continue rather
than in any way alleviate a marked inequality in terms of educational facilities.

On the basis of such findings, the Commission made three
recommendations. The first and most important, following the
pattern of the 1959 proposal, was that the President, or if necessary

3. *Equal Protection of the Laws in Public Higher Education, 1960,* Washington, 1961.

Congress, should adopt measures to assure that Federal funds were disbursed only to such publicly controlled institutions as did not discriminate against Negroes. The three northern members accepted this recommendation explicitly. Both Storey and Rankin concurred, though somewhat reluctantly. Storey pointed out that since Congress had not delegated such powers to the Executive, it did not intend they should be exercised; further action on its part would be necessary. While agreeing in principle with the recommendation, Rankin expressed concern that if it were too drastically enforced, it might operate as a punitive measure from which the students themselves would suffer. He was somewhat fearful, that is, of unwise implementation of any such new ruling. But the important point was that these two men did concur, thereby making possible a majority for the recommendation that had not previously been attainable.[4]

Only Governor Carleton, who had not yet offered his resignation, dissented. Repeating the views all three Southerners expressed in 1959, he reiterated his conviction that withholding Federal funds to enforce desegregation was unsound from a political, governmental, and moral viewpoint. "I cannot approve," Carleton said, "the withholding of money, coming as it does from the taxpayers of the several states, as a club to forge any fixed pattern set forth by a Federal agency."[5]

The second recommendation applied more generally to enforcement. In the light of the frustrations and delays that marked every move toward school desegregation since 1954, and the expense of litigation, the Report called upon Congress to authorize the use of three-judge courts in cases involving a substantial factual issue. To this proposal, Storey as well as Carleton dissented. Finally, and without dissent, the Commission recommended that Federal aid be given to the states for programs to assist public school teachers and students handicapped as a result of inferior educational opportunity or training.

As they had also proposed in 1959, the northern members of the Commission would have made the major recommendation upon withholding Federal funds applicable to private as well as public institutions. They argued that funds derived from all the citizens

4. *Ibid.*, 267–69.
5. *Ibid.*, 269.

should not be disbursed in any way that precluded any specific group from benefiting from them. Storey, Carleton, and Rankin opposed this inclusion of private colleges. Convinced that the existing powers under the 1960 Civil Rights Act were not yet fully tested, they objected also to another proposal that would have given the Attorney General the authority to institute civil suits to enforce equal protection in institutions of higher learning.[6]

This report was a careful, factual, comprehensive study. It fully documented conditions that while generally known had never before been so closely examined. In the course of its preparation Hannah expressed the opinion that the report "had the potential of being the best thing the Commission has ever done." Perhaps of even greater significance than the conclusions, however, was the report's revelation of the extent to which a clear majority of the Commissioners, including Storey, were now convinced that more positive steps than reliance on court enforcement of the laws, with all its interminable delay, were essential to combat continuing discrimination. The recommendation to withhold Federal funds as a weapon in the war to sustain equal rights, although limited in this instance to public institutions of higher learning, was an important augury of the future.

In its consideration of the problem of segregation in secondary education, the Commission held two new conferences on Problems of Schools in Transition—in Gatlinburg, Tennessee, on March 21–22, 1960, and at Williamsburg, Virginia, on February 25–26, 1961. It also heard testimony on this topic at general hearings, carried forward further staff studies, and received a number of special reports from the State Advisory Committees.

The second educational conference brought together, as had its predecessor at Nashville in 1959, school superintendents and other officials from states ranging from Maryland to Texas where integration was actually under way.[7] These officials once again submitted in advance written statements, giving statistical breakdowns of what had actually been accomplished; presented additional oral

6. *Ibid.*, 272.
7. *Conference Before the United States Commission on Civil Rights: Education. Second Annual Conference on Problems of Schools in Transition, Gatlinburg, Tenn. March 21–22, 1960,* Washington, 1960.

testimony before the Commission; and then made themselves available for question and discussion by all the conference participants.

The testifying school officials, with the exception of Superintendent Oliver of Nashville, were all new to Commission proceedings. The greater number came from school districts in Maryland, Virginia, Kentucky and North Carolina, but there were also representatives from Missouri, Oklahoma and Texas. A special participant was the director of the Higher Horizons Program which had been instituted in one school in New York to encourage and aid children of limited background, primarily Negroes and Puerto Ricans, in going on to college.

In general, the testimony at Gatlinburg was much the same as that at Nashville. School officials told of desegregation plans, some voluntary and others the result of court orders, which provided for pupil assignment on the basis of residential zones but with the possibility of transfer as controlled by local school boards. In a few instances integration was immediately applicable to all grades; more often it still started with the first grade. Faculty integration lagged grievously and the handful of Negro children in previously all-white schools usually did not participate in intramural activities. On the other hand, violence or the threat of violence was rarer than when the school officials reported in 1959.

The Superintendent at Paducah, Kentucky, described what he said was a successful policy leading to maintenance of two types of schools—white-staffed and Negro-staffed—with the parents able to choose which type of school they wished their children to attend. No white children enrolled in the colored-staffed schools, but between 1956 and 1959 the number of Negro children in the white-staffed schools rose from 23 to 129, representing in the latter year eleven percent of the city's Negro pupils.[8]

In Kansas City, Missouri, the School Board initiated a program of total integration; that is, one involving all grades, immediately after the Supreme Court decision in 1954. Among one hundred schools in that city, some forty were successfully integrated. The local superintendent felt that things were going well but he heavily stressed, as did other conference participants, the inextric-

8. *Ibid.*, 53–68.

able involvement of the school problem with segregation in housing. Kansas City consequently provided an escape valve, in areas where tension might be extreme, by maintaining a transfer policy which permitted students to move from one school to another if the latter was not overcrowded.[9]

In his testimony as to what was happening in Nashville, Super-intendent Oliver reported that the plan for desegregating the schools explained at the 1959 conference was proceeding without any racial incidents. Some forty-two Negro children were attending school with white children—nine in the third grade, eighteen in the second, and fifteen in the first. While this was only thirteen percent of those eligible for attendance at white schools, it was a matter of absolute free choice. The Negro children did about the same quality of work as their white classmates, Oliver testified, and they were achieving normal progress. At the same time, children eligible for transfer out of integrated schools continued to exercise the right to do so; in the case of Negroes 275 out of 317, and in that of whites, all those out of a possible ninety.

Referring to Oliver's deep anxiety the previous year over the popular reaction in Nashville—still a generally segregated city—to this plan of gradual school integration, Hannah asked whether the Superintendent now felt that he was "over the hump." "I was afraid, tense and disturbed last year," Oliver answered. "I feel much more relaxed at the present time."[10]

The Superintendent of Schools in Charlottesville, Virginia, described the hesitant beginnings of desegregation in a state that originally adopted a program of massive resistance which called for the closing of any integrated school. In 1955 a group of Negro parents had petitioned the Board of Education to desegregate Char-lottesville's school system. It refused to do so but a year later the Federal District Court instructed the Board not to deny the admission of any child to any school on the basis of race or color. After a number of unsuccessful appeals from the ruling, two colored students were assigned to one school and ten to another. In accordance with the existing Virginia law, the Governor promptly closed the two schools. However, in January 1959, the Supreme Court declared the state statute unconstitutional, and that autumn

9. *Ibid.,* 8–10.
10. *Ibid.,* 155–56, 158.

the Negro children began studying in the two reopened schools.

Approximately four hundred fifty white students, about a quarter of the total, promptly withdrew and were then awarded tuition grants by the State to enable them to enter private white schools. Otherwise the integration of the two public schools proceeded without further trouble. The Charlottesville Superintendent believed that such a dual system which at once provided for desegregation but also made possible tuition grants to students wanting to transfer was the right answer for Virginia. He believed that it would continue to receive community support.[11]

Frank H. Stallings, an associate professor of education at the University of Louisville, submitted a rather different report bearing on quite another aspect of desegregation. Discussing the academic achievement of school children, white and colored, he testified that the transitional integration program did not appear to have any adverse effects for children of either race, and that it gradually led to substantial achievement gains among the Negroes. In his opinion, integration significantly increased motivation among the colored children even when they remained in segregated schools. The feeling that at any time they might be moved to an integrated school and possible competition with white children served as a spur to their efforts to do good schoolwork.[12]

In bringing this conference to an end, Hannah said that he was encouraged to see the calmness with which school integration could be discussed in comparison with the emotions aroused only one year earlier. He stressed very strongly, however, that it remained a continuing problem. He reminded his audience that the country was still a long, long way from compliance with the Supreme Court's decision that segregated facilities could never be reconciled with equality.

The third education conference, held at Williamsburg in 1961, took up the same basic questions and followed the same general format as that at Gatlinburg.[13] It had, however, broader scope and, at the same time, concentrated heavily on certain very specific

11. *Ibid.,* 99–104.
12. *Ibid.,* 137–43.
13. *Conference Before the United States Commission on Civil Rights: Education. Third Annual Conference on Problems of Schools in Transition, Williamsburg, Virginia, Feb. 25–6, 1961,* Washington, 1961.

problems. Departing from previous practice in dealing only with school systems already embarked on desegregation programs, the Commission heard representatives of the irreconcilable school system in Prince Edward County, Virginia; spokesmen for HOPE —Help Our Public Education—an organization in Atlanta engaged in a campaign reflected in its title; and a member of SOS—Save Our Schools—which had the same objectives in New Orleans. The conference in addition discussed the administration of pupil placement laws, the effect of closed public schools on the community and on education, and programs to alleviate the handicaps of Negro pupils transferred from segregated schools.

The testimony of the officials from the Board of Education in Prince Edward County dealt with a widely publicized situation which had led to the complete closing of that county's public schools rather than compliance with court orders to desegregate. After the Supreme Court outlawed the massive resistance program in Virginia, other counties and cities, such as Charlottesville, started upon at least token integration in accordance with this decree. Not so Prince Edward County. It withdrew all support for public schools and the community then created a special foundation with authority to establish a system of private schools for white children and to raise funds for their support in the form of special tuition grants. At the time of the conference, 1325 white children were enrolled in these schools, but with the public schools closed, the county's 1700 Negro children were getting no education whatsoever.

The chairman of the county school board, W. Edward Smith, testified that the lack of educational opportunity for Negro children was solely due to their parents' refusal to accept a program for private Negro schools, with tuition grants, comparable to that for private white schools. The county would have been willing to set up a system of black schools with the financial support of the white community, he said, but the Negroes would not cooperate. Moreover Smith maintained that their attitude was due to pressure from the NAACP and other outside organizations rather than to the desire of the Prince Edward County Negroes themselves. Questioned sharply on this, he defended the existing program. The people of Prince Edward County, Smith asserted, remained adamantly opposed to any form of integration, but they really wanted to provide as good education for Negroes as for whites.[14]

14. *Ibid.,* 83–106.

The spokesman for HOPE was Mrs. Mary Reese Green. She told how she had helped to bring together a citizens' committee to try to keep the schools open in Atlanta amid a most tangled legal conflict. When the courts ordered integration in the city's school system, the Georgia legislature promptly passed a law closing any school that complied with such a decree. SOS campaigned to bring about repeal of the state law, and in what it called Operation Last Chance, tried somehow to reconcile the state conflict with the Federal courts. It finally succeeded in persuading the Georgia legislature to repeal the school-closing law, which Governor Vandiver conceded was an albatross about the state's neck, and provision was then made for pupil-placement, local option and tuition grants designed to provide at least token compliance with court desegregation rulings. However tentative, here was at least a first breakthrough in the Deep South.[15]

The most dramatic story told at the conference was that of Mrs. N. H. Sand, the representative of the New Orleans committee, SOS. Under circumstances very similar to those in Atlanta, the courts ordered a beginning of desegregation and in what Mrs. Sand called "five days of hysteria," the Louisiana legislature passed twenty-one bills aimed at preventing any such move. Amid the greatest confusion of purpose—legislative enactments at odds with Federal court rulings, state educational authorities working at cross-purposes with the local school board—the people of New Orleans hardly knew what was happening. Finally two schools specifically ordered to desegregate attempted to do so, and in calm, unemotional terms Mrs. Sand described what then took place.

United States marshals conducted three little colored girls to the first school and another to the second. Rioting in protest against their admission broke out immediately with mobs of screaming women surrounding the two schools. The segregationists hoped to intimidate the white parents from sending their children to the schools where they would have to associate with the Negro children, force the closing of the two schools, and thus successfully defy court orders.

As the only insistent public voice in favor of open schools in New Orleans, SOS undertook to drive white mothers and children back and forth to the desegregated schools. It was almost hopeless.

15. *Ibid.*, 42–45.

"After the ferry service had been operating a week," Mrs. Sand said, "threats of personal violence to children, parents and drivers reached such a peak that U.S. marshals were called in to take the children to school." White enrollment in one school fell to ten; in the other it dwindled away altogether. During the holidays SOS tried to encourage a return to the schools but met a tragically negative response. Mrs. Sand quoted some of the comments from parents:

I feel as if I'm living under Communist rule. If I send my boy down a street to his own school, my husband will lose his job. What has happened to our freedoms? . . .
I would be fired if I sent my children back. I've got a family to feed. I can't risk it.

At the end of the school year only fifteen white pupils were enrolled at the school with one Negro girl, and at the other, the three Negro girls were still completely alone. As the Commission was later to say with reference to New Orleans in another of its masterpieces of understatement:

"Obviously the problem remains unsolved."[16]

The first of the general hearings, held in Los Angeles and San Francisco at the close of January, 1960, reflected the desire of the Civil Rights Commission to emphasize the interrelationship among all aspects of discrimination and also to demonstrate that it was an acute problem not only in the South but throughout the country.[17]

The opening session in Los Angeles found an even more varied array of witnesses than appeared at other Commission hearings. They were prepared to discuss discrimination in all its phases, as affecting Mexican Americans as well as Negro Americans. The hearing, preceded by the customary pilot studies and investigations, was of course a fact-finding operation. As Vice-Chairman Storey, who was in the chair, stated at the opening, "We do not hold these

16. *Ibid.*, 51–55; *Education—1961. United States Commission on Civil Rights Report*, Vol. 2, 43.
17. *Hearings Before the United States Commission on Civil Rights, Los Angeles, California, Jan. 25–6, 1960, and San Francisco, California, Jan. 27–8, 1960*, Washington, 1960.

hearings to find fault or point a finger." Among those attending were the Attorney General of California, the Mayor of Los Angeles, that city's Chief of Police, and businessmen, real estate brokers, life insurance officers, and representatives of various committees concerned with human relations and civil rights.

It was highly revealing, as in the case of the hearing in New York in 1959, that so many witnesses testified that housing was at the roots of the civil rights problem. In Los Angeles, with a colored population between 500,000 and 700,000, an expanding pattern of segregation created a block of Negro ghettos wholly surrounded by "lily-white suburbia." This situation, it was agreed, restricted education, encouraged discrimination in law enforcement, and adversely affected employment opportunities. While there was no overt discrimination against their voting, Negroes in Los Angeles suffered every other evil flowing from racial prejudice.

Attorney General Mosk reported on California's efforts to uphold civil rights, but admitted that progress was very slow in providing those safeguards whose absence "permitted, if not encouraged, the translation of racial prejudices into overt community discrimination." He cited many examples of the harassment colored people suffered on trying to move into a white community such as, the arrival at the Negro's home of an ambulance or a hearse, assorted telegrams and other messages, and the delivery of unordered building materials. He urged that to aid the Negroes in finding homes, Federal agencies should require affirmative covenants against discrimination: law could not resolve the problem but it could help point the way.[18]

The Commission heard much further evidence on housing, with several sociologists discussing the consequences of segregation on community life; listened to testimony on the related problems of public education; and for the first time, took up the underlying economic issue of Negro unemployment. Spokesmen for large employing firms, the NAACP, labor unions, and other interested organizations participated in the latter discussions. The Civil Liberties Union took the lead in presenting evidence on the administration—or maladministration—of justice, with documentary reports on what it alleged were the discriminatory practices of the

18. *Ibid.*, 3, 30–34.

Los Angeles police in dealing with both Negroes and Mexican Americans. Its representatives stated that reported instances of police brutality were in the ratio of fifty to one as between Negroes and Mexican Americans on the one hand, and whites on the other. He felt that the police were no more than reflecting community feeling; Negroes were naturally suspect. Whatever departmental regulations might stipulate, prejudice invariably led to widespread denial of the non-whites' legitimate rights.

William H. Parker, the Los Angeles police chief, offered statistics alleging that Negroes were far more prone to crime than were the whites, with a record of arrests eleven times greater, and he defended his department against all charges of practicing discrimination. He was proud of Los Angeles. In spite of overcrowding, widespread ignorance and poverty, and a high crime rate in the Negro ghettos, no serious outbreaks of racial violence (the rioting at Watts was still five years in the future!) had occurred. This seemed "utterly remarkable" to Chief Parker and he appeared to accept it with comfortable complacency. Indeed he felt the police were doing an excellent job in forestalling any rioting and getting very little credit for it. "I think the greatest dislocated minority in America today," Parker said, "are the police. . . . No one is concerned about their civil rights."[19]

Spokesmen of the Community Service Organization described discrimination against Mexican Americans. Wholly apart from their difficulties over housing, which could be quite as great as those of Negroes, and prejudice in the administration of justice, Mexican Americans also faced outright discrimination at the polls. This testimony brought the Commission back to its first concern as it heard how the Mexican Americans were often challenged when they tried to vote and disqualified unless they could satisfactorily recite—in English—the Preamble to the Constitution. As a consequence they had little political representation of any sort. One of their spokesmen who was actually a city councilor—the only one in a century, he said—cited among other instances of political discrimination the painful fact that not a single person of Mexican ancestry had ever served on a California grand jury.[20]

19. *Ibid.*, 320–34.
20. *Ibid.*, 305–18.

The discussion of the status of Negroes and Mexican Americans in Los Angeles went beyond specific circumstances relating to housing, unemployment, education, and the administration of justice to consider still broader issues arising from the clash of white and non-white. Los Angeles, bursting apart with an explosive population growth, kept its rapidly increasing minority groups imprisoned in congested ghettos from which there was apparently no escape. The problem, stressed also at the housing hearings in New York, was how these dislocated minorities could ever adjust satisfactorily to urban life.

When the Commission moved from Los Angeles to San Francisco on January 27–28 to hear another group of witnesses on conditions in the Bay area, it was given a number of reassuring official statements on equal protection of the laws and sharply conflicting evidence by civil rights spokesmen of continuing discrimination. Both Governor Brown, who while not appearing in person submitted a statement, and Mayor Christopher, who spoke from the floor, nevertheless made it clear that they were well aware of the problems involved.

The Governor emphasized the importance of the Fair Employment Practices Act which California adopted in 1959, and the significance of its Civil Rights Act and Fair Housing Act. He nonetheless acknowledged that integration was only a partially realized ideal and agreed with other witnesses that the worst aspect of discrimination was in housing. It inevitably imposed a pattern of segregation on schools, churches, playgrounds, and political clubs. In California as elsewhere, Governor Brown said, the large cities "are commencing to reap the grim harvest" of past policies and only a beginning had been made to meet the mounting crisis.[21]

Mayor Christopher dwelt on problems of housing and education for minority groups, but with a complacency comparable to that of the Los Angeles Police Chief said that "we in San Francisco have never had any incidents that could be called 'racial incidents.' " He appeared to believe that the greatest weapon against discrimination was moral suasion, with political leaders assuming a major responsibility. He gave one example. When Willie Mays found it

21. *Ibid.*, 631–35.

seemingly impossible to buy a certain house he wanted, he (the Mayor) publicly invited Mays to stay with him as a guest until he was able to get settled. "Well, I don't know if this shamed the party or not," Mayor Christopher concluded, "but the fact of the matter is that a few days later the house was sold to Mr. Mays."[22]

San Francisco's Police Chief, Thomas J. Cahill, gave somewhat comparable statistics on the incidence of crime as those produced at the Los Angeles hearing. He reported that whites, constituting 86.3 percent of the city's population, accounted for 58.6 percent of the arrests, while the figures for Negroes were 6.8 percent of the population and 35.2 percent of the arrests. In spite of this glaring differential, he maintained that his department made every effort to deal fairly with the problem of law enforcement as affecting minority groups. He agreed with Mayor Christopher that even though San Francisco was a very cosmopolitan city, a basic harmony prevailed among its diverse ethnic groups. "We have had no real serious racial problem," he said, "either from a standpoint of law enforcement or from a standpoint of just living among ourselves."[23]

A good deal less happy testimony was presented on the housing problem: conditions which led to *de facto* school segregation in the depressed Negro sections, and carefully veiled but almost universal discrimination in the new suburban developments. A common technique in the suburbs, various witnesses said, was the formation of improvement associations to which every prospective home owner had to belong. Their membership committees could obviously bar all non-whites. Questioning Frank Quinn, the Director of the Council for Civic Unity who testified on housing segregation among not only Negroes but Japanese and Chinese, Commissioner Storey asked the old question as to whether such groups did not prefer to live by themselves even though conditions might be very crowded. "I do not think, sir," Quinn said, "I could go along with the implication that people prefer to live under these conditions without improving them."[24]

Dr. Luigi Laurenti, an economist, injected a new note into the housing discussion when he challenged the widely accepted proposition that the movement of non-whites into a white housing area

22. *Ibid.,* 473–74.
23. *Ibid.,* 754–59.
24. *Ibid.,* 555.

depressed property values. His research in three cities—San Francisco, Oakland, and Philadelphia—showed no material change in the value of housing when Negroes moved into white areas. However, the question that Earl W. Schwulst posed at the New York housing hearing still remained: did not fears of such property depreciation often provide a self-fulfilling prophecy? Dr. Laurenti expressed the hope that if the implications of his findings became better known, it would with time become possible to move toward a single housing market regardless of race.[25]

The Commission heard its first testimony from a Japanese American. Haruo Ishimaru, associated with the Japanese American Citizens League, reported that Japanese Americans did not experience any discrimination in either voting or employment, but that they very definitely did so in housing. He both generalized on this topic and cited concrete cases. "I would like to point out," Ishimaru further said, "that this problem is more than merely a domestic one. It is imperative to understand that what might be considered an isolated and unimportant problem of discrimination in one of our communities in America can be magnified by people in other countries." This point was strongly endorsed by Hannah, who on many occasions brought out the challenge to democracy in a troubled world of making good its promise of racial equality.[26]

An Indian spokesman, Erin Forrest, a Modoc, and President of the California Intertribal Council, told of discrimination against his people, especially in the public schools, and also touched upon other involved problems confronting the Indian in American society. Discussing segregated schooling, he ironically told of the difficulties Indian parents experienced in explaining this discrimination to their children, "because in their own language, there is no such word."[27]

Though a great deal more testimony was presented on every aspect of the civil rights problem in San Francisco, no consensus emerged as to exact conditions or what should be done about them. Many witnesses urged, as at all the Commission hearings, that the Federal Government should assume a greater responsibility in the field of housing. At the same time, they maintained that in the final analysis discrimination could be abated only through public educa-

25. *Ibid.*, 512–18.
26. *Ibid.*, 780.
27. *Ibid.*, 786.

tion which stressed its moral implications. The most discouraging statement came from the Executive Director of the Council for Civic Unity. "I feel, however," he said after expressing his deep affection for San Francisco, "that we are going backward very fast, and we don't know it, in the whole Bay area."[28]

The Commission attached a great deal of importance to the hearing in Detroit in mid-December, 1960. Here was a northern city with a large Negro population which had made serious efforts to meet the problems of racial conflict. The Commission members attended in full strength, with Chairman Hannah presiding; the sworn testimony of the many witnesses was supplemented by statements submitted by persons for whom it had been impossible to find time on the program, and the hearing attracted widespread public attention. It dealt with many of the issues which were thoroughly discussed on earlier occasions. A great deal of repetition was inevitable, and at times the testimony became confused and conflicting. The Commissioners' continued attention to so much of what they had in essence heard before was an impressive tribute to their patience, stamina and sense of duty.[29]

Walter Reuther, President of the Auto Workers Union, made one fresh and significant statement on the key issue of employment:

Discrimination begins . . . long before the Negro approaches the hiring stage. In most cases it begins when he is born into a family enjoying about half the annual income of the average white family. . . .

In most cases . . . the Negro child is born into a black ghetto, a slum or near slum of overcrowded, inadequate housing. All too frequently he goes to a school that by any standard is inferior to that attended by the average white child in the same city. All too frequently he drops out of school too soon—either because his family needs whatever money he can earn or because he knows that, even if he continues through high school or college, his opportunities of getting employment of as high a level and rewarded with as much pay as a white person with the same educational accomplishments are very limited.[30]

While all such problems received their due share of attention at Detroit, a special emphasis was placed at this hearing on the

28. *Ibid.*, 558.
29. *Hearings Before the United States Commission on Civil Rights: Detroit, Michigan, Dec. 14–15, 1960*, Washington, 1961.
30. *Ibid.*, 58.

administration of justice. This led to several direct clashes in testimony. A number of complainants charged discrimination and brutality on the part of police dealing with Negroes. On the other hand, Police Commissioner Herbert W. Hart sharply denied all such allegations.

These contradictory statements led Father Hesburgh to complain at one point that the Commission was "being whipsawed between different sets of witnesses and hardly knew what to believe." He felt that it was imperative, above all else, that something be done to establish better communication between the whites and Negroes in Detroit so that some understanding could be reached on just what was happening in the city. Police Commissioner Hart agreed that better communications were essential in any effort to resolve racial problems, but he continued to insist that there was no unjustified violence on the part of his police force in dealing with minorities.

"Well, I hope something can be done," Hesburgh said with evident weariness, "because we feel rather futile at the end of one of these afternoons. I think we like to believe that everyone under oath is telling the truth." A better understanding should somehow be worked out, he advised, among responsible persons equally concerned with the maintenance of law and order. The Commission could get a valuable perspective on the national approach to civil rights from its local hearings, but such an issue as the administration of justice had to be worked out on the community level. "I hope," he concluded, "we have been able to contribute something just by listening to both sides."[31]

What brought this controversy to a head were the statements of several individual Negroes. They claimed that it was a general practice of the police to stop and search Negroes on the streets regardless of any evidence of wrongdoing, and that in many instances they beat up alleged suspects without warrant or provocation. When Commissioner Hart casually dismissed one of these complaints as "an uninformed misstatement," the audience reacted so noisily that Hannah, vigorously rapping for order, said he would tolerate no further demonstrations.

One witness suggested the need for a police review board to

31. *Ibid.*, 402–3.

deal with all complaints and to investigate charges of brutality. Hart saw no need for such a board, strongly opposed its possible creation, and defended existing policies in the recruitment and promotion of Negro policemen. "Our department," he stated, "has taken many progressive steps in the matter of maintaining its leadership in the field of human relations and community relations."[32]

This issue of police brutality, which also came up at the Los Angeles hearing, was one that could not be minimized. The Commission was learning how deeply it affected the attitudes of the Negroes in the big-city ghettos and was building up racial tensions that beneath the surface were already gathering an explosive force. Needless to say the deteriorating relations between law enforcement officials and the Negro community, as revealed in the Commission's investigations and reports but so largely ignored or forgotten at the time, were to have their spreading repercussions—especially in New York, Chicago, Los Angeles, and Detroit itself. The growing danger that the issue of civil rights in the North might well come to overshadow the more overt forms of discrimination in the South, with even greater threats of racial strife, was this early clearly demonstrated.

This concern over the breakdown of equal protection of the laws in the North was more prescient of the future than the general public realized in 1960–61. While holding its hearings in Los Angeles, San Francisco and Detroit, the Commission was not, however, neglecting its major responsibility for examining voting practices in the South. In addition to continuing staff investigations of the sworn complaints reaching headquarters, with their referral in many cases to the Department of Justice, the Commission resumed in May, 1961, the postponed Louisiana voting hearing.[33] The Supreme Court decision overturning the injunction that had brought it to a halt in 1959 opened the way to a new session. The going was not yet easy. Requests for a further postponement on the part of the Louisiana officials and continued difficulties in obtaining evidence from the parish registrars, forced another recess before the

32. *Ibid.*, 397.
33. *Hearings Before the United States Commission on Civil Rights—Voting, New Orleans, Louisiana, Sept. 27–28, 1960, and May 5–6, 1961.* Washington, 1961.

hearing could at long last really get under way and be carried
through to completion.

The Commission knew a good deal about conditions in Louisiana as a result of the staff reports in 1959, and further studies were
made before the rescheduled hearing opened on May 5. They
documented the reported activities of the Joint Legislative Committee and the White Citizens Councils in sponsoring the "segregation law package" which was frankly designed "to provide ways and
means whereby our existing social order shall be preserved." So far
as voting went, this meant continued efforts to purge the rolls
where Negroes were registered and to block any new registrations.
The sworn testimony of the Negro witnesses, as well as that of the
voting officials from eleven parishes, amply substantiated the success of this aggressive anti-Negro campaign.

The methods employed were very much the same as those
used in Alabama. The Negroes had in the first instance great trouble
in even finding the registrar, were then subjected to interminable
delays in trying to register, had to be identified by already registered
voters, and were asked to interpret, in a manner that the registrar
found satisfactory, the meaning of the Constitution. Once again
they could be, and were, rejected if the registrar was not satisfied
with any one of their answers or made a single mistake on the
registration forms.

In those parishes where no Negroes were registered, the identi-
fication requirement was almost insuperable. The Reverend John
Henry Scott, a lifelong resident of East Caroll Parish, eloquently
testified about his fruitless efforts to secure the right of suffrage
for himself and a group of other Negroes. At one time he thought
he had assurances of aid from a white voter, only to have the latter
admit that "it wouldn't be any use because it was strictly made up
not to register any Negroes." When a second Negro tried to encourage Scott by saying he had other white friends who were sure to
help him because they were all Christians, Scott answered from sad
experience: "But Christians and this registration business is different. Nobody's a Christian when it comes to identifying you."[34]

He concluded his testimony:

*I just go on, go on because I feel like I am right, and I know where
I am going. I know what I am talking about, and I don't care what*

34. *Ibid.*, 18–19.

*happens. Whatever happens, I got to go to Heaven, and if I go for my
people or for the right to vote I would be perfectly satisfied, so that's
the way I feel about it.*[35]

When a hopeful registrant succeeded in obtaining one
"voucher," he would be told that he needed two. When he finally
found someone else to help him, the answer would be that this
person had already identified another applicant, and the registrar
ruled that a voter could only vouch for one person within twelve
months. The system was virtually foolproof.

In the matter of mistakes, Jewell Wade, a young Negro veteran, testified that after filling in his form, the registrar returned
it as unsatisfactory because there was one error. He could not find
the mistake on going over the form, but the registrar still insisted
it was there. As Wade got up to leave he asked:

Ma'am, would you do one thing for me?
What is that?
Will you tell me the mistake I made?
Oh, sure; you underlined 'Mr.' when you should have circled it.

The Registrar in question contradicted this testimony. Wade
had actually made two mistakes, she said: misspelling "October"
and "Democratic." But she was unwilling to produce his card as
evidence, frankly admitting that she rejected a registration applicant if there was but one misspelling.[36]

The registrar of Webster Parish testified that she did not
always give the constitutional test. When pressed as to how she
made this decision, she answered that she did not know, but if the
applicant had been registering for several years, she usually dis-
pensed with the test. The Commission counsel interrogated her
further:

MR. ISBELL: *In other words, if you know them—*
MRS. CLEMENT: *Yes.*
MR. ISBELL: *You are more likely to dispense with the constitutional test?*
MRS. CLEMENT: *Yes.*
MR. ISBELL: *You say you know a larger proportion of the whites than
the colored people—*
MRS. CLEMENT: *Yes.*

35. *Ibid.*, 23.
36. *Ibid.*, 135, 346–47, 349.

The consequences of this attitude were rather clearly suggested.[37]

This same registrar had on occasion other tactics than asking a prospective registrant to read and interpret something from the Constitution. A Negro named Joe Kirk was registered from 1944 to 1957, but on four subsequent attempts to register he failed. The registrar rejected him three times because of his being unable to interpret the Constitution to her satisfaction, but the fourth time for a quite different reason. Kirk's testimony read:

MR. KIRK: ... *The first question she asked, did I have any illegitimate children. I said, 'Not as I knows of. If I has, I hasn't been accused of.' She says, 'You are a damned liar.'*
VICE-CHAIRMAN STOREY: *Said what?*
MR. KIRK: *'You are a damned liar.' I just smiled; I could still give the smile. Then she said, 'I know you are going to tell a lie at the first place.' Then she asked the question, 'What were disfranchise mean?' I said, 'Just like I am now, this is disfranchise from voting.' She said, 'That doesn't suit me.'*

Asked about this testimony, Mrs. Clement said she couldn't remember any such conversation—then added: "But I could have said it. I could have said it to someone."[38]

So it went. Witness after witness testifying how they repeatedly tried to register—or reregister—only to be turned down for the most casual, trumped-up reasons. Following their new instructions to purge the rolls of Negro voters, the registrars were indeed proving to be highly efficient. Most of them at least indirectly admitted that their procedures were definitely designed to keep Negroes off the voting lists. One refused to answer questions as to how she carried out her duties on the constitutional ground that her answers might tend to incriminate her.

The Louisiana hearing was another milestone—that in Alabama was a first—in revealing through individual sworn testimony what so many rural counties in the South, particularly those with Negroes in a majority, were doing to maintain what they called the purity of the ballot. The voting statistics that the Commission was amassing, especially those in the Black Belt, demonstrated the same thing, but statistics could never convey the sense of rank in-

37. *Ibid.,* 304.
38. *Ibid.,* 115–16, 309.

justice so movingly as did the recounting of actual personal experiences. These earnest Negroes, some of them well educated, others barely literate, coming before the Commission to show how completely inoperative were all the existing safeguards for equal protection of the laws, provided an object lesson in discrimination that had a great impact on the Commission, and eventually on the Congress and the nation. The Louisiana hearing once again indisputably revealed, as had the Alabama hearing, that literacy tests, interpretation of the Constitution, and filling out registration forms were used not to ensure an intelligent and responsible electorate, but as a means to bar one class of potential voters, the Negroes, from the exercise of their rights.

Through these investigations, conferences, field surveys, and public hearings, supplemented by the studies and reports of the State Advisory Committees, the Civil Rights Commission had by mid-1961 assembled a great mass of additional material on which to base a new report to Congress and the President. The data were organized and checked with even more elaborate care than in 1959, and innumerable revisions made of prospective findings and recommendations in the major areas of study. In July, Staff Director Bernhard submitted a complete draft of the whole Report for the consideration of the Commission members. They met in East Lansing, Michigan the next month for a final conference. Some differences and disagreements still existed but they were ironed out more easily than ever before.

The Commission decided to adopt a somewhat different format than that of the first Report: five separate volumes, each running about two hundred fifty pages, respectively taking up voting, education, employment, housing, and justice, with a supplementary booklet of pertinent extracts from the Report as a whole. It further planned to print a total of ten thousand copies (somewhat more than the run in 1959) for distribution among the news media, government officials, libraries, and other interested organizations and individuals. If the first and statutory responsibility of the Commission was to present its findings and recommendations to the President and Congress, a wide distribution would give the Report further educational value among the general public.[39]

39. Staff Activities Reports; minutes of Commission meetings.

IX. THE SECOND REPORT— 1961

The gains have been considerable. As the second term of this Commission draws to a close, it can report that more persons than ever before are exercising more fully their rights as citizens of the United States. . . . The gap between the promise of liberty and its fulfillment is narrower today than it has ever been.

Yet a gap remains.[1]

So the Commission stated in the introduction to its 1961 Report, submitted on September 9, and then went on to summarize the civil rights balance sheet. President Kennedy had come out

1. *1961 United States Commission on Civil Rights Report:* Vol. 1, *Voting;* Vol. 2, *Education;* Vol. 3, *Employment;* Vol. 4, *Housing;* Vol. 5, *Justice;* Washington, 1961; *Civil Rights—Excerpts from the 1961 United States Commission on Civil Rights Report,* Washington, 1961. Quotation from *Voting,* 1.

strongly, as his predecessor failed to do, in support of the Supreme Court decisions on school integration, and while he had as yet made no move on discrimination in public housing, he had established the President's Committee on Equal Employment Opportunity. The Justice Department was continuing to bring suits under the existing laws to promote voting registration. Throughout the country, primarily as a result of the Negro demonstrations, momentum was growing in favor of new legislation to meet the clear-cut need for more effective rights enforcement.

On the other side of the ledger, the Commission reported that in some one hundred counties in eight southern states Negroes were still prevented by overt discrimination or the fear of physical or economic reprisals from exercising their right to vote. Three states—Alabama, Mississippi and South Carolina—had not desegregated a single school or college. Unemployment among the Negroes remained twice as high as among whites, the housing market was widely restricted on the basis of race, and unlawful police violence remained not a regional but a national shame.[2]

After substantiating and documenting conditions in those areas where civil rights were still so precarious, and stressing the extent to which Federal policies so often contributed to discrimination, the Commission made its recommendations. Once again they were generally moderate in both substance and tone, but this time in contrast with the recommendations of 1959, they were for the most part unanimous or commanded—as on the voting issue— a clear majority.

Except in the southern states, which true to form dismissed the Report, in the words of one newspaper, as "another attempt by professional do-gooders to smear the South," the press was approving. The tributes paid the Commission more often singled out its findings than its sometimes controversial recommendations. The Boston *Globe*, indeed, said the report was "highly explosive." However, the Washington *Post* described it unreservedly as "careful, well-documented, thought-provoking," and the *New Republic* said it was "a brilliant and immensely significant document."[3]

2. *Voting*, 5–6.
3. Editorial clippings from Commission files; Washington *Post*, Sept. 11, 1961; *New Republic*, Oct. 2, 1961.

In a first section on deprivation of the right to vote, the Report dealt almost exclusively with the southern states where virtually all the 383 sworn complaints received by the Commission originated. The staff had investigated these complaints and made its special survey of conditions in the Black Belt with close examination of selected counties in five states. After briefly discussing conditions throughout the South, including Mississippi even though it had not proved possible to hold a public hearing in that state, the Report gave a full retelling of what it called "The Louisiana Story." It then made a careful analysis, based on extensive investigations, of the whole course of Federal litigation in seeking to enforce constitutional guarantees of the right to vote. The Department of Justice had initiated suits in fifteen counties and the Report went into them fully.

While the major and most publicized finding was the widespread and overt discrimination in one hundred southern counties, the Report further revealed that in those parts of the South where Negroes constituted a substantial part of the population, a general average of less than ten percent of the non-whites eligible to vote were actually registered. Even more disgraceful, in twenty-three such counties scattered through five southern states, not a single Negro was enrolled on the voting lists.

The Commission recognized that there had hardly been time for full utilization of the additional voting safeguards written into the Civil Rights Act of 1960. In the light of the difficulties the Department of Justice still experienced in instituting suits to combat continued discrimination, however, the prospects under the provisions of the new law did not appear any more promising than under the provisions of the Act of 1957. Litigation was an expensive, time-consuming process. The Commission was fully convinced that existing legislation could not provide adequate remedies to meet an unsupportable situation. "Much remains to be done," the Report stated with exemplary moderation, "before the right to vote is secured against discrimination in every part of the nation."[4]

The recommendations to assure that something further was indeed done marked an interesting shift from the position taken in 1959. Whereas the Commission that year most importantly

4. *Voting*, 111, 135–38.

called, by a five-to-one majority vote, for establishment of a system of Federal registrars to administer state qualifications wherever there was a pattern of discrimination, it now endorsed by a four-to-two vote the broader proposals that the Northerners on the Commission had made two years earlier. This shift was in part due to the modified version of the Federal registrars scheme written into the Civil Rights Act of 1960, but a good deal more to the reenforced conviction within the Commission as a whole that the flagrant misuse of literacy tests could not in any way be controlled.

The Commission majority consequently recommended that Congress adopt the necessary measures to provide that the right of all citizens to vote in Federal or state elections should not be denied or abridged for any cause except inability to meet reasonable age or length of residence requirements, legal confinement, or conviction of a felony. No longer feeling a constitutional amendment necessary, the Commission in 1961 called upon Congress to outlaw literacy tests or any comparable voting restriction which would enable registrars to discriminate against Negroes.

The dissenters, as might be expected, were Storey and Rankin. The former reaffirmed his conviction that every citizen should be allowed to vote, but he still refused to accept the need of a proposal so sweeping that it would basically alter existing Federal-state relationships. He felt such a move unnecessary because alternatives existed and the test of current laws still lay in the vigor with which they might be enforced. Moreover, Storey maintained, the arbitrary discontinuance of all literacy tests could in fact destroy the security and purity of the ballot. Rankin agreed in a concurring statement with these objections to the majority recommendations, and he emphasized his own belief that if additional legislation were necessary on the voting issue, it should be carefully kept within accepted constitutional bounds. He did not deem it wise, Rankin said, "to upset the balance of our Federal system to reach a result which can be achieved through less drastic means."

At the same time the Commission without any dissent made a second recommendation which constituted a more generally acceptable substitute for doing away with all voting qualifications and conformed to the underlying intent of the party proposals in the 1960 presidential campaign. Congress was urged to enact legislation providing that in all states where a "literacy," "understand-

ing," or "interpretation" test was applied to determine an elector's
qualifications, the completion of at least six grades of formal education should be held sufficient to meet all requirements. No less
cognizant than their northern colleagues of the abuse of literacy
tests, the two Southerners were willing to accept this proposal as
less materially affecting Federal-state relations.[5]

Little popular support developed for the more extreme Commission recommendation. Even the generally favorable Washington *Post* thought it "not very impressive," and the *New Republic*
questioned so "simplistic" a solution to the voting problem. Other
newspapers in the North (to say nothing of the expected sense of
outrage in the South) were a good deal more critical. They felt that
the complete elimination of all literacy or educational tests was a
far more extreme remedy than was justified. Even the staunchest
adherents of civil rights were unwilling to go as far as the Commission majority.[6]

On the other hand, the Commission's exposure of continued
discrimination in the southern states and the inadequacy of existing laws reenforced the general feeling that further legislation was
essential. A great deal of sympathy and support was expressed for
the idea of making a sixth grade education a substitute for a literacy test, and this proposal in time became a major feature of the
Kennedy Administration's new civil rights program. This topic
necessarily will be discussed later. It might, however, be said at
this point that when Congress finally got around to doing something about the problem with passage of the Civil Rights Act of
1964 and the Voting Rights Act of 1965, it first adopted the sixth
grade substitute for literacy tests, and then accepted the Commission's earlier proposal for Federal registrars wherever there was
found to be a pattern of discrimination in processing voting registration.

This was for the future. In the meantime, the Commission
unanimously made some further minor recommendations on
voting. It called upon Congress to prohibit any action or inaction
which threatened to deprive a citizen of his vote; to direct the

5. *Ibid.,* 139–41.
6. Commission files; Washington *Post,* Sept. 11, 1961; *New Republic,* Oct. 2,
    1961; New York *Herald Tribune,* Sept. 11, 1961; *Christian Science Monitor,*
    Sept. 12, 1961.

Bureau of the Census to make a nationwide compilation of statistics that would include a count of persons of voting age in every state by race, color, and national origin, and the number actually registered; and to consider the advisability of requiring that all voting districts should be substantially equal in population. The first two recommendations were largely repetitious of those made in 1959; the third would soon be taken out of the hands of Congress through decision by the Supreme Court.[7]

The Commission had no idea that a guarantee of the right to vote would assure southern Negroes of the full enjoyment of all their rights. This was made clear in the presentation of compelling evidence that in parts of the South where non-whites did vote, they were still subject to discrimination in many ways. The Commission nevertheless felt that voting was of primary importance, and that no right could be clearer from a constitutional viewpoint.

The Report's section on education was based on more thorough study than had been possible in 1959, embracing as it did the material garnered from the two educational conferences, the general hearings in northern cities, and various special surveys. It did not add up, as the testimony at the conferences suggested, to a very encouraging picture. The Commission generally found that the pace of integration was still faltering rather than speeding up in the southern states, and that a pattern of de facto segregation was becoming more and more evident in northern cities. "The Nation's progress in removing the stultifying effects of segregation in the public elementary and secondary schools—North, South, East and West," the Report concluded, "—is slow indeed."[8]

Once again nothing new was discoverable in such broad generalizations, or, from the point of view of those concerned with equality in education, anything very radical in the choice of the descriptive adjective "stultifying." However, the irrefutable factual background for what was happening in public education since the Commission first examined the problem in 1959 was of very real value.

The Report discussed at length the integrationist programs,

7. *Voting*, 141–42.
8. *1961. . . . Report, Education*, 173.

some of them described by the witnesses at Gatlinburg and Williamsburg, in those states where segregation was legal prior to the Supreme Court decision of 1954. It told how Virginia moved from massive resistance to freedom of choice, fortified by tuition grants for students choosing all-white private schools. It went into the practical consequences of revised residential zoning, the workability of pupil assignment plans and transfer policies, and the relative importance of a grade-a-year and total integration. The consequences of voluntary and court-enforced programs were also reviewed. With different states following different policies, to say nothing of the experiences of individual school districts, the tangled skeins of educational policy could hardly be unraveled with complete success. The picture remained confused.

What stood out most clearly, eagerly seized upon by the newspapers in their stories on the Report, was one particular set of summarized statistics. Among the 2,836 biracial school districts in the seventeen states which traditionally practiced segregation, only about one-quarter (775) had taken any steps whatsoever toward integration. This was no better than 1959; progress appeared at a standstill. Moreover but seven percent of the Negro children in those districts nominally complying with the Supreme Court decisions were actually attending schools with white students.[9]

The Report did not go nearly as thoroughly into what was happening in the North. It examined a number of cases in which the courts, having decreed that segregated schools could not be justified because of residential patterns, called for the reconsideration of zoning lines. It considered the problems of pupil assignment on the basis of race and drew attention to the gerrymandering of school districts in some northern states which largely negated efforts to maintain bona fide biracial schools. In spite of the evidence of segregation in the North, as illustrated in the testimony of the witnesses in the general hearings on the West Coast and in Detroit, the unrelenting resistance of the Deep South to any educational integration at all commanded far more attention. The distinction of four southern states in not having desegregated a single school stood out as a much more glaring violation of what was theoretically the law of the land than anything happening in the North.

9. *Ibid.*, 176–77.

In drawing together its conclusions, and emphasizing the virtual breakdown of schools in some parts of the South, the Report stressed the imperative need for strengthening the educational system as a whole. This need was related to the international situation and the challenge of what was taking place in Russia. The Commission quoted a statement by Howard Mumford Jones:

It becomes even more difficult to conceive of retreating from public education into private education, anarchic education, or no education at all when one thinks of the cold war. Doubtless the educational philosopher should rise above considerations of international tension as a determinant force in shaping the schools. But it is nonetheless true that the principal rival of the United States, the Soviet Union, shapes its education on public lines and on public lines only.[10]

Against the background of such findings, it was hardly surprising that the Commission arrived at the unanimous conclusion that further Federal action was imperative to speed up desegregation and provide assistance for those school districts struggling to comply with the law. Nothing in the Civil Rights Acts of 1957 and 1960 was materially helping the nation to achieve its educational goals. Resistance to integration in the Deep South was hardly dented; instances of wholehearted compliance in other states remained few and far between. The difficulties were admittedly tremendous and obviously no easy answer was at hand as to what could be done to eliminate segregation and at the same time provide for all American children the improved education the times demanded. The Commission nevertheless sought to point the way with no less than twelve specific recommendations for action by the Congress.

Two of them were no more than a reiteration of recommendations made in 1959: authorization for the Civil Rights Commission to serve as informational clearing house and maintain an advisory and conciliation service; and an annual census to determine the ethnic classification of pupils in all public schools. Three reaffirmed those in the Report on Public Higher Education calling for the withdrawal of Federal aid where discrimination was still practiced in public colleges and universities; the expediting of judicial processes to provide admission of Negroes to other publicly controlled educational institutions; and Federal sponsorship of a program to

10. *Ibid.,* 176.

help teachers and students handicapped by inferior training or educational opportunity.

Other proposals asked Congress to authorize a Federal agency to provide technical or financial aid to local school systems attempting to solve the problems of desegregation, make provision for loans to such school systems where the customary state or local financial support was withdrawn, and direct the Attorney General to afford protection to school officials, parents, and children where a school was trying to carry out a desegregationist program. The Commission also recommended that the President direct the Department of Defense to conduct a survey of what was happening in regard to the education of the children of military personnel, making arrangements where necessary for non-discriminatory on-base schools; and to take the necessary steps for withholding Federal funds from libraries not serving equally all members of the community.

Little objection could be found to these moderate recommendations. The real meat of the report on education, however, lay in two others, actually first on the list, which went far beyond anything yet proposed.

Congress should adopt legislation, the Commission now advocated, making it the duty of every school board still maintaining segregation to file a desegregation plan with a designated Federal agency within six months, and authorizing the Attorney General to take appropriate action to enforce the implementation of such a plan. And this proposal for a legislative fiat to bolster compliance with the Supreme Court decisions was then supplemented by a suggested formula whereby Congress would rigidly limit educational grants-in-aid in those states which still continued to maintain segregation in their elementary or secondary schools.

These two Commission recommendations were very complicated and difficult to administer, but it was highly significant that one was unanimously endorsed and the other upheld by a vote of five to one. Commissioner Rankin accepted the proposal for filing and enforcing desegregation plans, but he dissented to any limitation on grants-in-aid from states still practicing segregation. His point was that the other recommendations were designed to encourage desegregation without harming education, but this proposal might make the children suffer from the sins of their elders. Believing any limitation on financial support to be both unnecessary and potentially punitive, he would have none of it. However, no one else joined in his dissent.[11]

In taking up discrimination in employment, the Civil Rights Commission was hardly breaking new ground.[12] The overall picture of the difficulties Negroes encountered in getting and holding jobs was a very familiar one, thoroughly documented in surveys by many other agencies, governmental and private. In the most simple terms, unemployment during the years of economic recession at the close of the 1950's was twice as high among Negroes as among whites, and this unhappy circumstance continued even as the country's economy gradually righted itself. "The two-to-one ratio," Daniel Patrick Moynihan, one-time Assistant Secretary of Labor, would write in 1965, "is now frozen into the economy." The veteran Negro labor leader, A. Philip Randolph, declared that in the light of the continuing scarcity of unskilled jobs, "black workers face a virtually unsolvable problem."[13]

Both its mandate, generally restricted to the appraising of Federal policies, and the limitations of time, necessarily narrowed the scope of the Commission's investigations in this important area. Its concern was Federally controlled areas of employment and what the National Government was doing, or should be doing, in implementing a stated policy against discrimination.

President Kennedy declared on March 6, 1961, when issuing his Executive Order establishing the President's Committee on Equal Employment Opportunity:

I have dedicated my Administration to the cause of equal opportunity in employment by the Government or its contractors. The Vice-President, the Secretary of Labor, and the other members of the committee share my dedication. I have no doubt that the vigorous enforcement of this order will mean the end of such discrimination.[14]

The Civil Rights Commission was not so sanguine. It found that the Executive Order actually had very limited application and did not importantly help members of minority groups who did not

11. *Ibid.*, 181–85.
12. *1961. . . . Report, Employment,* 1–2.
13. Quoted from Foster Rhea Dulles, *Labor in America,* rev. ed., New York, 1966, 401.
14. Quoted in *Employment,* 5.

have equal opportunity in obtaining training or in applying for jobs. A great majority of Negro workers throughout the country were unskilled. In direct or indirect Government employment, as in private industry, their compelling need was a chance to gain the new skills which would place them in a better competitive position with whites.

In studying this problem, the Commission staff had conducted field investigations and also sent out questionnaires and queries to all Federal agencies. A great amount of data was collected relating to three cities: Detroit as representative of the North, Baltimore of the border states, and Atlanta of the South; and in respect to all Federally related employment, including that on projects involving grants-in-aid, government loans, and other forms of Federal aid.

After an introduction discussing New Deal activity, the creation of the Fair Employment Practice Commission, and the postwar period (characterized as one of "infirmity of purpose—limited advance"), the Report proceeded through a series of chapters providing the basis for the Commission's findings and recommendations. These chapters discussed the Government's role as a direct employer, including both civilian personnel and members of the armed forces, and then the Government as the creator of employment through construction contracts or grants-in-aid for schools, hospitals, highways, airports, public housing, and slum clearance. They took up training and placement, with consideration of vocational education, apprenticeship programs, and state employment services. A final chapter considered the impact of the unions on employment and the extent to which many of them, especially in the building trades, still persisted in discriminatory membership policies.

What did the mass of evidence so carefully assembled add up to? The Commission's conclusion did not present too clear a picture and it is impossible to summarize satisfactorily the twenty-nine separate findings. Broadly generalizing, they showed that the policies of the Federal Government, theoretically directed toward equal opportunity in employment, were inconsistent and contradictory; often subordinated to state policies in case of any conflict, and by no stretch of the imagination, could they be considered successful in terms of declared national policy. There was no uniformity in requiring non-discrimination in either construction contracts or in grants-in-aid; by making job opportunities a condition for admission to vocational classes, the Department of Health, Education and Welfare actually perpetuated discrimination, and the Government often supported programs that militated against Negroes in the employment offices of southern states.

The Commission further found that while the Armed Forces Reserves were theoretically subject to an Executive Order providing for equality, units in some states completely excluded Negroes; nothing had been done to require the desegregation of National Guard units, and not since 1955 had the Department of Defense made any report on the actual status of integration in any branch of the armed forces.

In respect to the unions and discrimination, involving the Federal Government through labor legislation, the Report stated that membership and job referral practices seriously hampered non-discrimination policies as related to government construction work; existing apprenticeship rules often led to the exclusion of Negroes, and the National Labor Relations Board was not exerting such powers as it had to combat discrimination in initial employment.[15]

The obstacles to equal employment set forth in this Report underscored conditions which in their broader manifestations, that is, extending beyond the immediate impact of governmental policy, handicapped the Negro in economic terms more than any other aspect of the discrimination to which he was subjected throughout American society. Employment was obviously a vital need. To a man without a job the right to vote meant very little. Nor could he pay for housing, whether or not it was integrated; or decently bring up his children, no matter what schooling might be theoretically open to them.

The Commission's proposals to remedy such conditions, adopted unanimously, did not go very far. The first and most important was that Congress give the existing Committee on Equal Employment Opportunity, or some similar agency, the statutory authority to encourage and enforce a policy of equality in all direct Government employment, including the armed forces; in all Federally assisted training and recruitment programs; and in the membership of labor unions dealing with employers who were operating

15. *Ibid.*, 157–61.

under Federal contracts. Additional recommendations, spelling out in somewhat more detail how employment discrimination might be otherwise combated, called upon Congress to expand apprenticeship and retraining programs, subsidize additional employment and placement services, and take other steps to make jobs available on a rigidly non-discriminatory basis.[16]

These recommendations impinged upon aspects of the general unemployment problem going beyond discrimination. Their immediate value lay in the emphasis they placed upon the need to utilize more effectively the nation's manpower by trying to upgrade Negro labor through expanded training programs.

The Commission's consideration of housing was in large part a recapitulation of the findings and recommendations made two years earlier. The witnesses at the general hearings in Los Angeles, San Francisco and Detroit had emphatically confirmed the proposition that housing segregation was the evil from which so many other denials of rights inevitably flowed. Quoting the 1959 Report to the effect that a very considerable number of Americans were deprived of equal opportunity in obtaining homes because of their color or race, and that such housing disabilities were part of a national crisis involving a general shortage of low-cost housing, the Commission stated bluntly that these two basic facts "remain as urgent today as they were in 1959."[17]

The Report showed that the Federal Government was still doing little or nothing to meet the problems inherent in the Negro ghettos of the North. The President had not issued the Executive Order directing Federal agencies to work toward the goal of equal opportunity in housing which the Commission recommended in 1959 and to which Kennedy pledged himself during the 1960 campaign. The government agencies supervising banks, mortgage companies and insurance companies, although the agency heads agreed that outright discrimination was improper, appeared helpless to control the practices which were sustaining segregated housing.

The indictment in more detail was a severe one. The Federal Housing Administration and the Veterans Administration had not

16. *Ibid.*, 161–64.
17. *1961 . . . Report, Housing*, 145.

taken any definite steps to see that the benefits they offered were
made available without regard to race. While the Public Housing
Administration was doing something toward improving the physical
surroundings of the non-white population, its continuing policy
of leaving decisions as to building sites and other matters to local
authorities, directly encouraged *de facto* segregation as well as
ghetto-like isolation. The Urban Renewal Administration was
making new housing available for Negroes of the middle-income
group, but operation of its program tended to diminish rather
than increase the total housing inventory of the non-white population.

The Commission summarized:

> *Of the many Federal agencies concerned with housing and home
> mortgage credit, none has attempted to exert more than a semblance
> of its authority to secure equal access to the housing benefits it admin-
> isters, nor to ensure equal treatment from the mortgage lenders it sup-
> ports and supervises. Many have taken no action whatsoever in this
> connection. And neither the President nor Congress has yet provided
> the necessary leadership.*[18]

The Commission strongly urged the President, as it had in
1959, to issue the long delayed Executive Order stating the national
objective of equal housing opportunities and calling upon all
government agencies to shape their policies toward this goal.
The report then made two sustaining recommendations more
far-reaching and more specific. The first proposed that the Federal Housing Administration and the Veterans Administration
be directed to take steps on a nationwide basis to prevent any discrimination in the sale or leasing of housing built with their aid.
The second asked for either executive or congressional action to
require financial institutions subject to Federal supervision to conduct their mortgage loan business on a completely non-discrimi-
nating basis.[19]

The two southern members of the Commission were not very
happy over this latter recommendation. In a closely argued dissent,
Storey acknowledged his agreement with the Commission's objectives but stated his opposition to any further Federal interven-

18. *Ibid.*, 145.
19. *Ibid.*, 150–51.

tion in the affairs or policies of private financial institutions. Rankin concurred in part and dissented in part. He was willing to accept further controls over the mortgage practices of banks which were members of the Federal Home Loan Bank System, but he was fearful of the "wholesale" intervention of Federal authority.[20]

Four additional recommendations dealt with the urban renewal and highway programs sponsored or aided by the Federal Government. The Commission in effect asked that in the execution of all such projects, the President or Congress require that local communities, through specific clauses in contracts with both public authorities and private developers, provide that all persons displaced, regardless of race, creed or color, have access to decent, safe, and sanitary housing.

Time, in its story on the Commission's Report, especially singled out "the chilling text" of the volume titled *Justice.*[21] An exposé citing chapter and verse of police brutality north and south, this volume dealt with civil rights on a broader canvas than racial discrimination. It nevertheless repeatedly showed that Negroes were far more often the victims of such brutality than whites. An analysis of complaints received by the Department of Justice showed that non-whites were involved in thirty-five percent of the reported cases even though they constituted only ten percent of the population. The Commission hoped, the Report stated, that even though criminal justice might in most respects be administered on a non-discriminatory basis, a pinpointing of selected instances where Negroes were allegedly singled out for violent mistreatment might contribute to the correction of "these remaining incongruities."[22]

Drawing upon the accounts of witnesses at the hearings in Los Angeles, San Francisco and Detroit, as well as court records and newspaper stories in other parts of the country, the Report had a sorry story to tell through its harrowing accounts of Negroes badly beaten up, seriously injured, and even killed in the course of being arrested and interrogated. It described cases in which the

20. *Ibid.,* 151–53.
21. *Time,* Nov. 24, 1961.
22. *1961. . . . Report, Justice,* 27.

police stood aside while white mobs were on the rampage, failing to take any action when Negro men, women and children were badly hurt or even killed. As a consequence, Negroes all too often feared the police and felt completely hopeless in trying to secure protection.

The Report gave specific details on eleven cases of police brutality directed against Negroes. One story, quoted from the Detroit *Free Press,* involved a sixteen-year-old Negro boy named Steel. After telling of his arrest for hitting a policeman with a chair during some sort of fracas, the newspaper account continued:

> *Steel was brought into the police garage in a scout car, closely followed by three other cars filled with police.*
>
> *He sat in the back seat of the car. His face showed pain. There was a patrolman sitting next to him.*
>
> *As the car halted, the patrolman left the car and yanked Steel from it by the neck. Another patrolman raced up.*
>
> *'Is this him?' he shouted. Then he threw a fist into Steel's face.*
>
> *A second patrolman pushed that assailant aside and sank his fist into Steel's stomach.*
>
> *Steel fell to the garage floor, moaning. . . .*
>
> *The newsmen stood outside the open door of the garage. One of the policemen saw them and shouted: 'Lower that door!' But all were too busy slugging Steel, now prone on the floor.*
>
> *They dragged him to the side and the onlookers could see only patrolmen kicking and slugging at him.*
>
> *'Lower that door!' shouted one again.*
>
> *Two detectives had entered the other side of the garage and strode grimly across to the newsmen. Their expressions softened as they reached them.*
>
> *'Gentlemen cops don't solve crimes,' one of the detectives said.*
>
> *The patrolmen picked Steel up and rushed him into the station. The detectives turned and walked away.*[23]

Another case of brutality was the fatal beating up of a Negro in Dawson, Georgia for supposedly interfering with the arrest of his father. Stories conflicted as to just what happened. In a subsequent affidavit, however, the victim's widow said that in taking her husband in custody, the police repeatedly hit him with a blackjack, threw him into the police car, kicked him in the groin, and threw sand into his bloody face. The authorities took no discipli-

23. *Ibid.,* 13–14.

nary action against any of the police officers involved, and a year later the local sheriff allegedly said to the widow:

I oughta slap your damn brains out. A nigger like you I feel like slapping them out. You niggers set around here and look at television and go up North and come back and do to white folks here like the niggers up North do, but you ain't gonna do it. I'm gonna carry the South's orders out like it oughta be done.[24]

Then there was the Alabama Negro, a veteran with a wife and three children, who was run off the road while driving home one night by a following car which he did not know was the police. In a sworn statement before the Commission he said:

I got out of my car and an officer came after me and would have struck me with his gun, but I threw my hands up to keep from being struck. I asked what this was all about, and what I had done. He then asked me if I had any whiskey in my car and I told him no. He made me put my hands up on his car, and he began to search me. And while I was standing with my hands up on his car, he shot me in the back, paralyzing me from my waist down. My friend, James Morrow, had gotten out of my car on the same side where we were standing. But a white man in plain clothes who was with the officers, got out and pointed a carbine rifle at him and made him get back into the car. I had fallen on my back in the highway.

I looked up at the officer and asked why he had shot me down like this. He only said, 'Shut up, Nigger.'

The officer involved was the Chief of Police of Helena, Alabama, and after an FBI investigation, a Federal grand jury returned an indictment against him. He claimed self-defense in shooting the Negro and a trial jury acquitted him.[25]

Against the background of these vivid descriptions of police brutality, the Report next considered the weakness of any available means to redress the miscarriage of justice. It found that Federal criminal and civil sanctions for the protection of violated civil rights were inadequate, and that state and local remedies were in many parts of the country wholly lacking. The well-known practice in the administration of justice in southern states of wholly excluding Negroes from jury service in cases involving racially

24. *Ibid.*, 9–11.
25. *Ibid.*, 22.

inspired crimes, was condemned as providing protection for whites and encouraging the most severe treatment of non-whites.

In connection with possible Federal action, the Report stressed the responsibility of the FBI in investigating complaints of police brutality. This admittedly posed a difficult problem and evidence was presented to show that the FBI attached far more importance to maintaining the closest possible cooperation with state enforcement agencies and the goodwill of the local police forces. "It has been reported from time to time," read one Commission statement, "that the Bureau has little enthusiasm for its task of investigating complaints of police brutality."[26]

This discussion of the FBI's role had unexpected repercussions. Staff Director Bernhard made every effort to secure the cooperation of the Department of Justice in obtaining such information as he could on the Bureau's methods, but the statement that the FBI was sometimes reluctant to pursue investigations into police brutality badly strained the always tenuous cooperation between the Commission and Justice. Nor did it greatly help matters when a number of newspapers especially played up this part of the Report, one of them congratulating the Commission because it "dares even to imply some criticism of that sacred cow the FBI."[27]

Perhaps stung by such comments even more than by the Report itself, J. Edgar Hoover sprang to his agency's defense. In an angry, petulant letter to Chairman Hannah he denied that the FBI considered civil rights cases burdensome and declared that anything said to this effect was inaccurate and unfair. "I strongly resent," Hoover said, "any implication that there is any reluctance or lack of enthusiasm in fulfilling our investigative responsibilities in this most important area." He peremptorily demanded—with names—the facts on which the Commission's criticism was based.

Hannah attempted to make a soothing reply: he would ask the staff for more factual material. Five days later Hoover returned to the charge ("I am awaiting the findings"), and when he still did not immediately hear from the Commission, asked for a meeting with Hannah as a matter of great urgency. In the mean-

26. *Ibid.,* 61.
27. *I. F. Stone's Weekly,* Nov. 27, 1961.

time Bernhard conferred with Assistant Attorney General Burke
Marshall over what was becoming an acrimonious controversy. Marshall's advice was that a "poison pen correspondence never leads to
satisfactory results" and that the Commission might just as well drop
the matter, allowing time—though he did not say exactly this—for
Hoover to cool off. On being told Marshall's attitude, Hannah
agreed. In respect to the FBI chief's last note, he instructed Bernhard "to file it and do nothing more at this time."[28]

As for the Justice section as a whole, the Commission followed
its usual procedure in summarizing the findings and then making
recommendations. The first of the latter was that Congress authorize grants-in-aid to state and local governments to assist them in
increasing the professional quality of their police forces. The
second suggested making the penalties of the United States Criminal Code applicable in all cases where a suspect was subjected to
unnecessary force, violence or restraint during arrest or inter-
rogation. The third called for making the local government jointly
liable with the police officer involved for the deprivation of any
rights protected under the Federal Code. And the fourth recommended that the Attorney General be empowered to initiate civil
suits to prevent the exclusion of any person from juries on account
of race, color or national origin.[29]

These recommendations had no immediate impact. Like so
many of those made by the Commission, however, they ultimately
won decisive support and were integrated in a vigorous nationwide campaign to ensure equality in the administration of justice.

Included in this section of the Report was a rather brief and
fragmentary account of the status of the Indian in American society. It first presented some historical material on the old Indian
treaties and their repudiation, the shifts and turns in subsequent
Federal policy, and the various Indian reorganization acts. It
then went into the position of the Indian as a citizen and a Federal
ward, stressing the inherent and ironic anomaly in his present-

28. J. Edgar Hoover to John A. Hannah, Dec. 5, 1961; Hannah to Hoover,
    Dec. 10, 1961; Hoover to Hannah, Dec. 15, 1961; Hoover to Hannah, Jan.
    18, 1962; Hannah to Hoover, Jan. 13, 1962; Hoover to Hannah, Jan. 15,
    1962; Berl I. Bernhard to Hannah, Jan. 17, 1962; Hannah to Bernhard,
    Jan. 22, 1962; in Hannah files.
29. *Justice*, 112–13.

day legal status. Finally, it gave a discouraging description of the Indian's minority role and stressed the discrimination to which he was subjected in so many respects.

Among the general findings were that Indians by and large could vote but suffered the disability of widespread illiteracy; their housing, whether on or off reservations, was usually inadequate; and employment opportunities were as restricted as they were for Negroes. The Commission made no recommendations.[30]

At the close of the volume titled *Justice,* the Civil Rights Commission incorporated a broad, general statement. The delay in attaining the national objective of equality impeded important national programs at home, and abroad subjected the nation to the charge that democracy was not living up to its high promises. No single, limited approach could bring an end to discrimination in American life and there was a mounting need for sustained action on a broader front. The Commission thereupon recommended, in scarcely veiled criticism of inaction at the White House, that "the President utilize his leadership and influence and the prestige of his office in support of equal protection of the laws for all persons within the jurisdiction of the United States in all aspects of civil and political life.[31]

Father Hesburgh added an individual and characteristic note:

> *Personally, I don't care if the United States gets the first man on the moon, if while this is happening on a crash basis, we dawdle along here on our corner of the earth, nursing our prejudices, flouting our magnificent Constitution, ignoring the central moral problem of our times, and appearing hypocrites to all the world.*[32]

30. *Ibid.,* 115–54.
31. *Ibid.,* 165.
32. *Ibid.,* 168.

X. CONTINUING
INVESTIGATIONS

This long and discursive Report fell on what was for a time barren ground. It evoked widespread editorial comment and a number of its recommendations were included in the various civil rights bills which individual congressmen were forever introducing in the House or Senate. Senators Mansfield and Dirksen attached a rider to a minor House-passed bill providing that anyone with a sixth grade education could not be disqualified in any Federal election because of failure to pass a literacy test.[1] The fact remained, however, that President Kennedy was not yet ready to commit himself in trying to force any action on Congress. The *New York Times* reported on January 3, 1962, that he "has let it be known that he will put forward no major civil rights legislation and that he will continue to withhold his signature from the pro-

1. *Revolution in Civil Rights,* 38.

posed executive order prohibiting racial bias in Federal housing."[2]
When southern senators held up the Mansfield-Dirksen bill in
May with a rather casual filibuster, it was quietly allowed to die.

The President, as Arthur Schlesinger has phrased it, still had
"a terrible ambivalence about civil rights." He did not know what
to do. "If we go into a long fight in Congress," he told Martin
Luther King, Jr., "it will bottleneck everything else and still get
no bill." The Negro demand for equal protection of the laws and
an end to discrimination was as insistent as ever. In the North
civil rights advocates were growing increasingly restive and critical
of the Kennedy Administration. But the President was waiting
for a consensus to emerge more clearly in both congressional and
public attitudes. Without being certain of the necessary votes, he
held back from any move which would imperil his own political
position and, he believed, weaken the civil rights movement itself.
As Theodore Sorensen has succinctly described his temporizing:
"The reason was arithmetic."[3]

In contrast with the stalemate on the legislative front, the new
year of 1962 was one of renewed activity for the Civil Rights
Commission. For the first time it found itself free to pursue a
comprehensive and far-reaching investigatory program without
hampering and sometimes frustrating interruptions. With a mandate running at least until the close of 1963, it did not have to
battle for its existence; there were no further legislative inquiries
into operations; the membership remained unchanged with increasing unanimity in the general point of view; and as the new
Staff Director, Bernhard proved to be an exceptionally able and
efficient administrator. In carrying forward its primary function
as fact-finder for civil rights legislation, whatever the immediate
fate of the 1961 recommendations, the Commission steadily
moved ahead.

Although a sharp disagreement with the Department of
Justice developed somewhat later in regard to a voting hearing
which the Commission wanted to hold in Mississippi, collaboration with the Federal Government otherwise seemed to improve.

2. *New York Times,* Jan. 3, 1962.
3. Schlesinger, *A Thousand Days,* 930–31; Sorensen, *Kennedy,* 475.

The feud with the FBI died down and J. Edgar Hoover appointed a liaison officer to work more closely with the Commission staff.[4] In March, Harris Wofford, Jr., the former staff member of the Commission now special assistant to the President on civil rights, was very optimistic. With the membership "no longer split down the middle" and Bernhard in charge of staff activities, Wofford felt the Commission was "becoming a far more active instrument of intelligence and public information."[5]

Further reorganization in the administrative setup created five distinct offices: the Staff Director, the General Counsel, a Program Division, Liaison and Information, and the State Advisory Committees. William L. Taylor, who joined the staff in 1961 after having served as an attorney for the Legal Defense and Education Fund of the NAACP and as Washington legislative representative of Americans for Democratic Action, took charge of Liaison and Information. Peter N. Sussman reorganized the State Advisory Committees. Clarence Clyde Ferguson, a brilliant Negro graduate of the Harvard Law School, became General Counsel—the first of his race to hold such a high position with a Federal agency.

As Staff Director, Bernhard remained the key man in the organization and where he stood in respect to the basic issues with which the Commission was concerned was never in doubt. He believed thoroughly in the importance of its fact-finding role and was prepared to support all major recommendations, as he frequently did before congressional committees, as "not merely desirable but imperative." He further took the stand that on civil rights matters the Commission should serve as "the duly appointed conscience of the Federal Government" and constantly emphasized in his reports the national character of the problem in spite of the urgency of the more overt forms of discrimination practiced in the South. Even this early Bernhard flatly stated that the last battle for equal rights would be joined in the North because discrimination there was more subtle and harder to combat than in the South.[6]

4. Minutes of 48th Commission meeting, Dec. 6, 1962.
5. Harris Wofford, Jr., in *Anti-Defamation League Bulletin,* March 1962, 6.
6. Berl I. Bernhard, Address, Sept. 21, 1962, at Illinois American Negro Emancipation Centennial Celebration, City Hall, Chicago; Schlesinger, *A Thousand Days,* 938.

Sometimes the zeal of staff members, committed by the very nature of their jobs to the civil rights cause, led them to forego the objectivity in assembling material that the Commissioners, for all their own growing involvement, felt should always be maintained. "I admire the energy and enthusiasm of our young staff," Rankin for example wrote Hannah on July 20, 1962, "but I think the Commission can help in the improvement of their judgment."[7]

The immediate occasion for this criticism was a hearing in Memphis a month earlier during which the staff appeared to get a little out of hand. Even before Rankin's letter, Hannah called Bernhard to account for building up too much one-sided testimony. Better leave out some of the material the staff thought necessary, Hannah said, than create the impression that the Commissioners were so much window dressing with the Director and his assistants doing all the questioning of witnesses.[8]

The problem was a very real one. There were inevitable difficulties of communication between the staff and Commission members. The latter were busy men with many other obligations and responsibilities; they met only about once a month on Commission business. Correspondence and telephone calls in trying to reach agreement on projects already under way could never be very satisfactory. The only answer, the Commissioners agreed, was to move very slowly in developing a new program, and even at the expense of delay assemble the evidence more carefully.[9]

A minor but amusing incident reflecting the over-eagerness of the staff involved an item in a report on the Southwest. It stated that in a number of small towns, notably in Arizona, signs reading "No Indians or Dogs Allowed" were set up at park entrances. Senator Goldwater objected violently. Possibly some imaginative staff member had recalled the old canard about similar signs in Shanghai—"No Chinese or Dogs Allowed"—for the report could not be substantiated. Hannah felt obligated to apologize, writing Goldwater of his regret "for any unintended reflection upon the State of Arizona."[10]

7. Robert S. Rankin to John A. Hannah, July 20, 1962, in Hannah files.
8. Hannah to Bernhard, July 27, 1962.
9. Erwin N. Griswold to Hannah, July 20, 1962; Hannah to Howard W. Rogerson, July 17, 1962, in Hannah files.
10. *1961 United States Commission on Civil Rights Report—Justice,* 153; Hannah to Senator Goldwater, Jan. 18, 1962, in Hannah files.

Apart from investigations, the staff spent a good deal of time on routine business. It had to maintain the necessary liaison with White House officials in seeking to implement recommendations made for action by the Executive Branch. Sworn voting complaints had to be checked and, if found sufficiently valid, passed on to the Department of Justice. A lot of work was involved in trying to keep the State Advisory Committees operating effectively. Gathering, cataloging and filing civil rights information remained a continuing and arduous task.

In the matter of complaints, their steady flow into Commission headquarters from all over the country was no more limited to those on voting than in earlier days. They ranged from charges of police brutality to job denials, from irregularities in court proceedings to discrimination in liquor store waiting lines. On one occasion a white man complained that he was threatened with eviction from his apartment because he dated a Negro girl; another time a Negro protested against the name "Nigger Hill" on a Government reservation. Hardly a week passed by without some inmate of a prison or mental institution calling upon the Commissioner for aid. Many complaints were completely incoherent; others as in the past clearly came from cranks.[11]

Both Commission members and the Staff Director periodically appeared before congressional committees to testify on recommendations or defend the annual budget requests. The Liaison and Information Division then drew upon these hearings for news releases as part of its general educational program. The Commission was always publicity-minded; it made every effort to obtain maximum coverage for all civil rights activities and reports.

One special project undertaken in 1962, without conspicuous success, was a lengthy report reviewing the whole history of civil rights.[12] The staff labored mightily in its production; called upon several prominent historians, including John Hope Franklin, for aid; and made every effort to produce a literary as well as historically sound document. The result of all this labor (at an estimated cost of $62,000) was a highly legalistic and rather dull treatise, but its presentation under the title *Freedom to the Free* as a feature of

11. Staff Activities Report, Sept. 10–22, 1962.
12. *Freedom to the Free—Century of Emancipation—1863–1963,* Washington, 1963.

the centennial celebration of the Emancipation Proclamation in January, 1963, at least afforded an occasion for a formal celebration of progress on the civil rights movement. President Kennedy seized the opportunity to praise the Commission highly for "a vital contribution to the completion of the task which Abraham Lincoln began a century ago."[13]

A first important investigation in 1962 was a survey of housing in Washington.[14] Living conditions for Negroes in the nation's capital, who made up a majority of its population, were notoriously substandard, and it was with some trepidation that the Commission planned an open hearing which could hardly fail to be embarrassing to the Federal Government. Nonetheless it decided to go ahead, and the hearing opened in early April with President Kennedy welcoming "this inquiry" by a "bipartisan agency composed of distinguished educators from all sections of the United States." For two days a parade of witnesses gave through their sworn statements a most depressing picture of segregation and poverty in a metropolitan Washington ringed about by the white suburbs of Virginia and Maryland.

The implications of racial discrimination in the Capital as they might affect the non-white envoys from the countries of Asia and the newly created states in Africa came out repeatedly in this hearing. Kennedy singled out the problem in his opening statement; it was always very much in the minds of the Commissioners. "When racial discrimination persists here," the President said, "it sometimes constitutes a personal affront to the diplomats of sovereign nations. . . . Washington should prove an example of our worthiest professions and best practices, both for the nation and the world."[15] The testimony suggested, however, that if it were such an example, a good deal was wrong with American practices!

Some eighty-five percent of the Negroes in the Washington area lived in the District of Columbia as compared with only

13. Minutes of 47th Commission meeting, Nov. 4, 1962; *Public Papers of the Presidents, 1963* (Kennedy), 160.
14. *Housing in Washington—Hearings Before the United States Commission on Civil Rights, Washington, D.C., April 12–13, 1962,* Washington, 1962.
15. *Ibid.,* 12.

twenty-five percent of the whites. The pattern was fixed. Witness after witness told the Commission that there was no escape for Negroes from the consequences of such crowded segregation and that conditions were becoming steadily worse. Even though Wasington now had an integrated school system, segregated housing greatly undermined the value of this reform and continued to have an adverse influence on employment opportunities. "Housing discrimination," a witness stated in describing the close interrelationship of segregationist policies, "is but one of the heads of a hydraheaded monster."[16]

Robert C. Weaver, Administrator of the Housing and Home Finance Agency, himself a Negro and the future Secretary of the Department of Urban Affairs, testified that substantial progress was being made in combating conditions in Washington, but he was the first to acknowledge that a great deal remained to be done. He believed that business leadership—the initiative of real estate developers, large scale builders, and lending institutions—held the key to any significant advance. At once reflecting and helping to mold public opinion, such forces could exert a constructive influence in resolving current problems. However, Weaver felt that the attitude of the real estate and banking interests was actually serving to block any change in existing practices.

Questioned about the role that legislation could play in creating an unrestricted housing market, he expressed a firm conviction in favor of a governmental policy of open occupancy and in the desirability of an executive order from the White House banning discrimination in all Federally assisted housing. The timing for the latter move, he acknowledged, was entirely up to the President. Weaver could not be drawn into any suggestions as to what the Civil Rights Commission might recommend in its report on Washington. "I think it would be a little premature, sir," he mildly answered when Chairman Hannah pressed him on this question, "to make those recommendations now before the evidence is in."[17]

A conflict developed in later testimony, as indeed at every Commission hearing on housing, over the responsibility of real

16. *Ibid.*, 40.
17. *Ibid.*, 33–39.

estate operators and mortgage lenders in imposing a pattern of
discrimination on the community. Spokesmen for the Negroes
testified that the Washington Real Estate Board, on which there
was not a single Negro member, forced a discriminatory policy on
all its members. They said that restrictive covenants, even though
not legally enforceable, were built into real estate contracts in the
suburbs as "gentleman's agreements," and that the realtors in
Washington repeatedly encouraged block-busting campaigns to
depress property values whenever Negroes did succeed in breaking
into formerly all-white neighborhoods. Segregated housing was
in large measure, one witness stated, a result of "covert collusion
of fearful and exclusive-minded property owners, of real estate
dealers, and of lending institutions together."[18]

The real estate interests sought to defend themselves. Their
argument, as on so many other occasions, was that in their operations they were respecting the wishes of the home owners or the
prospective buyers whom they represented. They denied that the
Washington Real Estate Board exerted any pressure whatsoever on
its members, either in favor of or against a policy of open occupancy. George W. DeFranceaux, the President of the Board, took
the position that neither legislation nor presidential executive
orders would be of any real help in meeting the issue of discrimination. "You can drive a horse to the water, but you can't make
him drink," he said with something less than inspired originality,
"—let's face it that way—and until such time as these owners are
ready to accept open occupancy, rules and regulations are not
going to make any material difference." He recognized the existence of a serious problem but his final answer was: "Time is
going to solve it."[19]

Harry P. Bergmann, a Vice-President of the Riggs National
Bank, was no less sanguine over the long-term consequences of
inaction. He felt that if integrated housing were by legal fiat extended to the suburbs, white people ("I mean, don't we have the
freedom of living where we want to and who we want to live
with?") would simply move further away. However, he maintained, with dubious comfort for his audience, that ultimately

18. *Ibid.*, 95.
19. *Ibid.*, 216.

things would work out. Bergmann concluded: "This problem will be resolved but it's not going to be resolved overnight. . . . The next generation, or the generation afterward, will solve the problem, sir."[20]

In the discussion over the international consequences of housing discrimination, G. Mennen Williams, at the time Assistant Secretary of State for African Affairs, and Angier Biddle Duke, the State Department's Chief of Protocol, both took the stand. They very much agreed on the difficulties non-white diplomats often experienced in trying to find homes in Washington. Over and beyond the personal tribulations of the African and Asian envoys, moreover, was their shock in discovering how universal was the discrimination against Negroes in the Capital of supposedly democratic United States. Both State Department officers declared that special attention to the needs of the diplomats in no way resolved the problem from an international point of view. Aiding them as individuals to obtain homes could not cancel out the effect of segregation's existence in forming their attitudes toward the United States.

"This image of the American way of life and this violation of our principles of equality of opportunity," Duke stated decisively, "is something the diplomat will carry with him when he returns to his own native land—and I might say, parenthetically, that that diplomat may turn out to be the next Foreign Minister or Prime Minister of his own country." He thought most foreign leaders accredited to this country believed in the sincerity of our national purpose, but the fact remained that at the present the United States was professing one policy and living by another. No answer was possible to the problem of discrimination, in Duke's opinion, in either the short or long range, "until we have a law which faces up to it in the proper way."[21]

After hearing a great deal of testimony, the Civil Rights Commission decided that instead of waiting to incorporate the findings in the biennial report not due until the close of September, 1963, it would issue a special interim report as soon as possible. The Federal Housing Administration had "done virtually nothing"

20. *Ibid.*, 349–50.
21. *Ibid.*, 139–41.

to meet the issue and the matter was too urgent to be allowed to drift. Sharp differences developed among the Commissioners as to just what they should specifically recommend. Storey and Rankin were very reluctant to endorse any proposals that went beyond calling upon the Federal Housing Administration and the Veterans Administration to follow non-discriminatory policies. By late July, however, the Commissioners were approaching a consensus on the need for more specific governmental regulations. In the final unanimous recommendations to this effect, the two Southerners went no further in expressing their hesitation than to say in a concurring statement that they hoped any such anti-discriminatory regulations would exempt "sales and rentals by individual owners of homes they occupy."

The Report—*Civil Rights U.S.A./Housing in Washington, D.C.*—was issued on September 27.[22] In summarizing the testimony at the hearing, it emphasized "the concerted refusal of members of the housing and home finance industry to deal with minorities seeking to live in certain neighborhoods and communities in the Washington area" and the consequent inability of Negroes to escape from segregation to the surrounding suburbs in Maryland and Virginia. The Commission strongly reaffirmed the recommendations made in 1959 and 1961 for issuance of an executive order providing equal opportunity in Federally assisted housing, and then addressed itself more directly to the Board of Commissioners controlling affairs in the District of Columbia itself.

The Board was called upon to prohibit any discrimination in the sale, rental, or financing of housing accommodations, to suspend or revoke the real estate commissions of any brokers guilty of such discrimination in the conduct of their business, and to declare null and void any racial or religious restrictive covenants. It was urged to aid Negroes seeking homes by making more money available for mortgages and by combating all block-busting techniques. In making such recommendations, the Commission laid heavy stress upon the grave international consequences resulting from discrimination as affecting the non-white diplomats in Washington.

Senator Morse promptly endorsed the Commission's findings.

22. *Civil Rights, U.S.A.—Housing in Washington, D.C.*, Washington, 1962; also news release, Sept. 27, 1962.

In a powerful speech on October 5 he introduced the Report into the *Congressional Record,* together with the legal substantiation of its recommendations drawn up by the Commission's General Counsel. Morse urged the District Commissioners to move promptly, assailed the tactics of the Southerners in seeking delay, and after emphasizing the importance of the issue from a foreign policy viewpoint, stressed the responsibility of the President.[23] As a result of such mounting pressure inspired by the Commission hearing, the Board of Commissioners agreed to issue a regulation prohibiting housing discrimination throughout the District of Columbia.[24]

Following through the policy which led in 1960–61 to general hearings on the West Coast and in Detroit, the Commission held comparable urban hearings in several additional cities.

The first of these was in Phoenix, Arizona, in February, 1962, and represented something of a departure for the Commission. The city's location in the Southwest, a total population of under 500,000, and relatively small minority groups not only of Negroes but of Mexican Americans and Indians, made for conditions quite different from those in New York or Chicago, Los Angeles or San Francisco. The hearing, nevertheless, took up the usual issues involving civil rights, with statements and questioning, and a final panel discussion.[25]

Generally speaking, Phoenix was shown to have had a good record of voluntary desegregation, as attested not only by the city officials but by other witnesses as well, and its problems were revealed as far less serious than those of the large cities in the North. At the same time, spokesmen for the Negroes presented a good deal of critical testimony. Acknowledging what had been achieved in recent years, they nevertheless drew attention to continued discrimination as particularly affecting housing, *de facto* school desegregation, and employment. This was "the other side of the coin,"

23. *Congressional Record,* 87th Congress, 2nd Session, Senate, Oct. 5, 1962, 21343–50.
24. *Civil Rights—Report of the Commission on Civil Rights '63,* Washington, 1963, 260.
25. *Hearings Before the United States Commission on Civil Rights, Phoenix, Arizona, Feb. 3, 1962,* Washington, 1962.

Father Hesburgh said after hearing the first Negro witnesses, and noted that the Commission found such contradictions in every community where it held a hearing.[26]

The Negroes in Phoenix lived "on the other side of the tracks" where housing was substandard and highly congested, the schools generally inferior, and job opportunities very limited. This was an old and very familiar story, but significant in that such conditions existed in Phoenix as well as in larger cities North and South. The white community leaders were not unaware of the Negro slums and the problems they engendered, but they were somewhat complacent. They felt that segregation was gradually breaking down and that further voluntary efforts would speed the process without the need for any governmental intervention.

The panel discussion which explored these differences of opinion was pitched on a rather low key. The emotional undertones were not as pronounced as at other hearings. Nevertheless it was clear that a lack of communication between the white and Negro communities continued to impede progress. The Commission members, as they had on so many previous occasions, urged the importance of everything possible being done to bring representatives of the two races together.

Getting away from the overshadowing Negro problem, testimony was also presented on the position of Mexican Americans and Indians in Phoenix. While the attitude of the whites was not overtly discriminatory, the children of these minority groups suffered educationally, and as a consequence the adults were severely handicapped in the labor market. Mrs. Grace Gil-Olivarez, a radio broadcaster (after protesting how absurd it was to ask a woman to talk about any subject and then limit her to six minutes!), blamed the continued difficulties of the Mexican Americans on both their own lack of leadership and a residue of prejudice on the part of some "Anglos."

We are really here to stay, so, wouldn't it be a lot simpler, and to everybody's advantage, to learn a little about us and to accept the fact that we are of Mexican heritage and, as such, are prone to be slightly different, but definitely not dangerous? We speak Spanish because we learned it at home, and not because we are plotting against anybody.

26. *Ibid.*, 51.

I sure hope this small group of prejudiced Anglos learn to know us, and start out by finding out what race we belong to.[27]

The testimony of Joe Sanders, school teacher, on the status of the Indians was very brief. He did not go much further than to say that while the Indian off reservation did not suffer from overt discrimination, he very much needed better orientation programs to help adjust him to "civilian life."[28]

The Memphis hearing, where the staff members took matters pretty much in their own hands, dealt with conditions in a southern city with 200,000 Negroes, or nearly one-third of the total population.[29] Segregation was historically the rule, and Memphis was only very slowly beginning to adjust itself to new times and new conditions. In these circumstances the atmosphere was hostile to intrusion of a northern investigating commission. The local press was very critical of the methods whereby unfavorable evidence was inserted in the official record and of Staff Director Bernhard's questioning of white witnesses with what was felt to be the approach of a prosecuting attorney rather than that of a wholly objective investigator. But the evidence was not wholly one-sided. It showed that substantial progress was being made against discriminatory policies in some phases of life in Memphis even though in others the Negroes were as far from gaining equality as they had perhaps ever been.

One area new to the Commission was its investigation into public health facilities. The testimony of the City Commissioner and that of the Administrator of the City of Memphis Hospitals was at times contradictory, and Bernhard bore down heavily on them to bring out the actual facts as to the hospital services available for Negroes. They revealed that one 128-bed city-owned hospital was open for paying Negro patients, and the only other local facilities for the 200,000 colored people were a municipal hospital for indigent and part-paying patients, an unaccredited "Negro hospital" with forty-eight beds, and an Eye, Ear, Throat and Nose hospital with twenty beds. Only whites were admitted to the three

27. *Ibid.*, 87–94.
28. *Ibid.*, 95–98
29. *Hearings Before the United States Commission on Civil Rights, Memphis, Tennessee, June 25–26, 1962*, Washington, 1962.

large church-related hospitals which had a total of 2,082 beds. The number of Negro physicians in Memphis was actually on the decline since those graduating from a local Negro medical school were unable to send patients to the white hospitals or to attend them there. The University of Tennessee Medical School controlled all staff appointments at these hospitals. Its Dean testified that the school currently had only one Negro student, newly admitted; he hoped he would soon be able to accept one more. The lines of segregation in health facilities remained virtually intact; moreover, the separate services for whites and Negroes were anything but equal.[30]

The Memphis hearing took up law enforcement. Claude A. Armour, Commissioner of Fire and Police, gave extensive evidence, especially in regard to the policy followed two years earlier during the local sit-ins, and he made a strong case for his department's equal enforcement of the laws. A good many arrests were made during the sit-ins on charges of trespass, loitering or disorderly conduct, but Armour testified that every effort was made to treat whites and Negroes equally without regard to color. He also reported that he had 112 colored employees, including four detectives and twenty-one patrolmen, in his department. When Bernhard's questioning on this point seemed to suggest that this number was very small for a total police force of 675 men, the Commissioner promptly broke in, amid laughter, to say: I know what you are driving at and I'll answer it before you ask." He knew this was a small number and he wanted more Negroes in his department, but in spite of every effort at recruitment, he could not get qualified men.

While the Negro witnesses were not always as certain about equal police treatment, one of them, a lawyer, sustained Armour's claim that he followed a fair and moderate policy during the sit-ins. The police roughly addressed some of the demonstrating students when the arrests were made, this Negro testified, but "none of them had been touched, physically touched." However, this same witness introduced the fact that in spite of the large Negro population in Memphis, there were only ten colored lawyers. They were not admitted to the local bar association, and the environment was hardly favorable for establishment of a successful practice.[31]

Testifying in the field of education, the President of the local

30. *Ibid.*, 7–81.
31. *Ibid.*, 83–122.

branch of the NAACP insisted that in spite of everything that might be said, the Memphis school system was still in effect segregated. He did not believe the School Board had the slightest idea of going beyond the merest nominal compliance with court orders. William D. Galbreath, the Board's President, admitted that it had placed only thirteen Negro students in formerly all-white schools and that this did not represent very rapid progress, but he defended so slow a pace in the light of the history and customs of Memphis. In his opinion it was "almost miraculous" that even this degree of integration was achieved without serious trouble. Galbreath frankly stated:

> I think it should be said that the board of education is not primarily interested in promoting segregation or desegregation. We're interested in operating the best possible school system for all the people of Memphis. The views of the board members are the composite views of moderation.[32]

After further testimony in the educational field, involving comparative figures on the status of students, curriculum matters, and the rate of dropouts in white and Negro schools, the Commission turned to problems of employment. Witnesses from Federal and state employment agencies, employing firms, labor unions, and the Urban League, all took the stand.

A continuing pattern of segregation was very clear in employment opportunities, and Staff Director Bernhard again often seemed to be the prosecuting attorney determined to bring this out. Under his sharp questioning several witnesses admitted restrictions in existing vocational training, lack of opportunity for Negroes in apprenticeship programs, and the operation of segregated employment agencies. One exchange between the Staff Director and a representative of the Labor Department was significant:

MR. BERNHARD: *What steps have you taken to make the Negro community aware of the President's policy concerning fair employment?*
MR. TOMLIN: *I have not made any effort to make the Negro community aware of the President's policy concerning fair employment.*[33]

32. *Ibid.,* 133.
33. *Ibid.,* 195.

Representatives of several large companies frankly stated that their employment policies were based upon "compatibility," and in the more skilled jobs and clerical work, this definitely meant the exclusion of Negroes. A representative of the Southern Bell Telephone and Telegraph Company, asked whether the absence of Negroes among operators, mechanical workers, and clerical staff was due to the assumption that they could not perform these services, was very outspoken: "No, sir. That's based on the assumption that local tradition and customs had not changed to the point that we feel it is the thing to do in our company at this time."

The southern members of the Commission, as well as those from the North, pressed this issue. The invariable answer from the employer representatives was the continued need, as one of them phrased it, "for having compatibility not only within the work group itself, but with the customers which we're dealing with."[34]

Another angle of this problem was segregation in the local unions, especially widespread in the building trades. In those unions where there was a mixed membership, whites were overwhelmingly in the ascendancy among skilled craftsmen, while Negroes made up the bulk of unskilled workers. The latter, for example, constituted ninety-eight percent of the membership in the hod carriers' union.

The segregationist pattern, as might be expected, was virtually universal in the field of housing. The Director of the Housing Authority made no bones about saying that if a Negro applied for housing accommodations, he would be automatically assigned to a Negro project. When Bernhard asked him if the Federal Government was not thus in fact providing public housing on a segregated basis, he agreed that this was so but felt it might be stated somewhat differently:

> I think the Federal Government would probably like to have it said in this fashion: that they insist that any city that is the recipient of Federal funds—that such city make adequate provision for all races, and then whether or not it's segregated is a matter of local conditions.

Negro witnesses said that governmental authorities in Memphis were following a policy that was actually increasing housing segregation and in some cases even obstructing the building of homes for Negroes.

34. *Ibid.*, 327, 332–33.

The hearing concluded—it had been at times a stormy one—with Vice-Chairman Storey seeking to defend the Commission in the face of the highly critical local press comment. (At one point the Memphis *Commercial Appeal* suggested the Commissioners were no more than listening to their "hired help" produce testimony directed toward preconceived conclusions.) The Commission was only interested in facts, not bias, prejudice or half-truths, Storey said; it was composed of both Northerners and Southerners, and was prepared to perform its responsibility of properly evaluating all the facts submitted. He congratulated Memphis for creating an atmosphere favorable to obedience to the law and for the avoidance of violence in seeking to cope with the problems of integration.[35]

The final public hearing in 1962 was that in Newark in early September.[36] Organized along the customary topical lines, the witnesses, some forty-eight of them, represented all elements in the community. A building trades panel, with participants drawn from among contractors and union representatives, a special discussion of apprenticeship training, and a further panel on the administration of justice, were somewhat novel features. In the field of education, the Commission not only considered conditions in Newark, but those in such other New Jersey communities as Orange, Plainfield, and Montclair.

These sessions particularly illustrated the extent to which discrimination still existed in a northern state with strong anti-discrimination laws. "While this legislation has clearly eradicated many inequalities of opportunity," Commissioner Robinson, who presided over the hearing, stated, "the laws have also made denials of equal protection more subtle and sophisticated, and hence more difficult to pin-point and correct." He pointed out that the hearing revealed that "suburban communities, unlike central cities, are making little or no headway toward making possible equality of opportunity, for all cities within metropolitan areas."[37]

The testimony and discussion on employment brought out a

35. *Ibid.*, 355, 358, 388, 429.
36. *Hearings Before the United States Commission on Civil Rights, Newark, New Jersey, Sept. 11–12, 1962,* Washington, 1962.
37. *Ibid.,* 500.

number of important points: the continued discrimination in apprenticeship training, the lack of qualified Negroes applying for jobs with companies which were making every effort to hire them, and the discrimination against Negroes in labor unions. And in spite of substantial progress, employer professions of non-discriminatory policies were not always observed in practice.

This contradiction was also evident in housing. The Executive Director of the Newark Housing Authority, submitting a great mass of statistical data, testified that not a single project in the city was segregated and representatives of the real estate fraternity vigorously denied all charges of discrimination. A spokesman for the NAACP, however, said that the Negro population of Newark, some thirty-seven percent of the total, was densely crowded in one small section of the city and that this was directly due to the policy of the real estate interest.[38]

This Negro witness felt that housing discrimination was the central issue in the whole field of civil rights and he attributed a growing national recognition of this fact largely to the work of the Civil Rights Commission and the State Advisory Committees. He further agreed with the Commission's own view that the most important thing to be immediately done was for the President to issue the still delayed executive order barring discrimination in all Federally assisted housing.

The discussions on education at the Newark hearing underscored, as did every hearing and investigation in the North, the broad and in some instances increasing extent of *de facto* school segregation. The testimony was repetitious of what the Commission had heard many times before. Nevertheless it again provided a great body of facts stressing the complexities of this issue and the need for a new climate of opinion, quite as much in the North as in the South, before any really satisfactory progress toward integrated schooling could be made.[39]

One interesting comment toward the end of the hearings was that of the Executive Director of the Mayor's Commission on Group Relations. He said that he had been very skeptical when first approached by the Commission as to the value of its fact-finding for he believed popular attitudes toward discrimination far more im-

38. *Ibid.,* 106–62.
39. *Ibid.,* 226–444.

portant. "This afternoon, after two days of your hearings," he testified, "I'm ready to eat crow. I believe that your witnesses and the testimony which they have given before this Commission is conclusive proof that facts are, indeed, necessary before attitudes can be changed."[40] In conclusion Rankin and Griswold, as members of the Commission, returned the compliment to Newark. They affirmed their conviction that the community was realistically grappling with the whole problem of civil rights and that Newark was clearly trying to do the right thing.

Education was always a matter of prime concern. Over and beyond the information obtained at the general hearings, the Commission consequently again went farther afield in gathering material on the course of desegregation. A fourth annual conference on schools in transition was held, this time in Washington. While it conformed generally in form and substance to the earlier educational conferences, the Commission paid more attention to what was taking place in northern cities and to their experience in trying to break down long existing patterns of *de facto* segregation.[41]

The staff supplemented the direct testimony of school officials at this meeting with information on selected individual school systems throughout the country. These surveys led to the publication in 1962 of one special staff report providing an over-view of desegregation in the South, with more detailed studies of Kentucky, North Carolina, Tennessee, and Virginia; and another report on what was happening in the North and West, with special accounts of schools in Philadelphia; Chicago; St. Louis; Highland Park, Michigan; and New Rochelle, New York.[42]

Although once more demonstrating the iron wall of resistance to desegregation in the South and the snail-like pace of token

40. *Ibid.,* 484
41. *Conference Before the United States Commission on Civil Rights—Education. Fourth Annual Conference on Problems of Schools in Transition, Washington, D.C., May 3–4, 1962,* Washington, 1962.
42. Under general heading, *Civil Rights, U.S.A.,* the Commission published among other staff reports: *Public Schools in Southern States 1962; Public Schools North and West 1962; Public Schools North and West 1963, Camden and Environs; Public Schools North and West 1963, Oakland; Public Schools North and West, 1963, Buffalo;* and *Public Schools Southern States, 1963, Texas.*

integration in the border states, the published reports even more significantly stressed the troubles of the North. Evidence was presented of demonstrations and sit-ins in northern New Jersey, most notably Englewood, where Negro parents resented the assignment of their children to all-Negro schools; of picketing in suburban Philadelphia; of strikes in Boston with Negro high school students staying out of school to attend workshops in neighborhood churches with instruction in civil rights; and of a protest movement in St. Louis where two thousand colored children marched with banners proclaiming "Freedom Now" and "Don't Teach Segregation."

The problems of the North centered about the definition of what might constitute "racial imbalance" in predominantly white or Negro schools which were not actually segregated. This involved all the legal and administrative complexities of residential zoning, pupil assignment, and transfer policies which naturally differed among the school districts of both metropolitan and suburban areas. In some cases school boards would allow the transfer of white pupils but not of Negro pupils, thus strengthening segregation, and even when open enrollment plans were instituted, the inability of predominantly white schools to accommodate additional pupils often meant that little change occurred in existing student distribution.

A good deal of evidence showed that both state boards of education and many local school districts were conscientiously trying to overcome these handicaps to effective integration. For example, the open enrollment plan in New York, which went so far as to provide transportation for students electing to attend schools outside their neighborhood, enabled a considerable number of Negroes and Puerto Ricans to transfer to predominantly white schools. It was nevertheless apparent that all such programs were greatly limited by circumstances beyond the control of school authorities.

This was a vicious circle: how could discrimination in other areas be broken down until better schooling enabled Negroes to improve their economic and social status? How could they obtain better schooling within the confines of the black ghettos? And going beyond the immediate problems of segregation and racial imbalance, were the still deeper and more pervasive issues of urban blight that affected both poor whites and Negroes.

Wherever it turned, the Civil Rights Commission was laying

bare the evils that beset a society which had not yet realized anything like the full potential of a democracy founded on the principle of equality.

All this in 1962. The Commission's overall task of investigation and fact-finding continued the next year. It held another general hearing in Indianapolis along the lines of those in Phoenix, Memphis and Newark; conducted further surveys in housing and employment, and the staff's educational studies were extended to Camden, New Jersey; Oakland, California; Buffalo, New York; and once again the South with an in-depth report on public schools in Texas. However, the greater part of the material that was to go into the next biennial report, due at the close of September, 1963, was already assembled.

In the meantime, the Administration and Congress were still marking time. As 1962 drew to a close, Martin Luther King declared that the year was one in which "civil rights was displaced as the dominant issue in domestic politics. . . . The issue no longer commanded the conscience of the nation."[43] Toward the end of September, however, an incident in Mississippi awoke the President and the country to a new realization that the Federal Government could not ignore the South's challenge to equal enforcement of the laws with impunity.

This incident was a direct challenge to Federal authority— somewhat comparable to that President Eisenhower faced in Little Rock five years earlier. Governor Barnett of Mississippi, in direct violation of court orders, undertook to block the admission of James Meredith, a Negro student, to "Ole Miss." The university officials, however reluctantly, were ready to comply with the court decree, but the belligerent governor stood his ground: "We will not surrender to the evil and illegal forces of tyranny." When Meredith attempted to enroll on September 20, with students parading about the campus singing "Glory, Glory, Segregation," Barnett took personal charge and blandly refused to accept his registration.

Acting through his Attorney General, President Kennedy immediately made ready to intervene. In the face of such arrogant flouting of a court order, he had no more choice than President

43. Quoted in Schlesinger, *A Thousand Days*, 950.

Eisenhower in 1957, even though the governor of a state was even more directly involved. Frantic efforts were made to effect some sort of a compromise enabling Barnett to back down without forcing a crisis, with long telephone calls between Washington and the Mississippi capital at Jackson, but no agreement could be reached. An explosive situation was rapidly getting out of hand as segregationists from all over Mississippi streamed into Oxford. Attorney General Kennedy obtained a further court order citing Barnett for contempt in defying an injunction against further interference with Meredith's admission to the university. The chips were down, but with popular support for his defiant position, the Governor gave no signs of giving way. As September drew to an end, President Kennedy federalized the National Guard and gave orders for regular troops to stand by.

The threat of violence mounted steadily but then at the last moment, asserting he surrendered to superior force, Barnett agreed to Meredith's being flown to Oxford on a Sunday (October 1) and quietly enrolled under the protection of Federal marshals. The President went on the air that same evening to announce over a nationwide television network what was happening and called upon the students of Ole Miss to remain calm. Even as he was speaking, however, a mob surrounded the university administration building where the Federal marshals were stationed under the direction of Deputy Attorney General Katzenbach. Taunting and cursing the marshals with shouts of "kill the nigger-loving bastards," hurling bricks and bottles, the ranks of the rioters, now swollen to some 2,500 students, townsmen and visitors, surged toward the administration building. Shots rang out from the mob, the beseiged marshals countered with tear gas. Before the Federalized guardsmen and regulars reached the scene—the latter hurriedly summoned from Memphis and flown in by helicopter—two persons were killed in the rioting and several hundred, including a third of the marshals, were injured.[44]

Newspapers throughout the country, and indeed throughout the world, headlined rebellion in Mississippi. The state's militant defiance of the Federal Government was a first sensation, and even greater was the decisive action taken by the President. Kennedy

44. *Ibid.,* 940–47; Sorensen, *Kennedy,* 483–88.

showed that when his hand was forced—no matter how slow he had previously been to act—he could respond with cold determination. The crisis in Oxford was brought under control. With the continued protection of Federal marshals, Meredith bravely stayed on at Ole Miss to graduate in 1963. But the incident underscored both the racial tension that existed throughout the South and the impossibility of the Federal Government avoiding involvement.

Whether or not this was the actual catalyst, Kennedy was persuaded the time had come to make his first concrete move in forwarding civil rights on the national scene. At long last he decided to issue the Executive Order on non-discriminatory housing which the Civil Rights Commission so urgently recommended both in 1961 and in its special report the next year on housing in Washington. Various reasons accounted for the long delay, including controversy over a projected Department of Urban Affairs, but on November 20, 1962, the President announced the order's promulgation, declaring that "it is sound, public, constitutional policy and we have done it." The Executive Order did not go as far as the Commission recommended. It was limited to housing built with the aid of mortgages insured by the Federal Housing Administration or the Veterans Administration; it did not include housing built with the aid of conventional mortgages granted by other Federally assisted financial institutions. Nevertheless this forthright move was highly significant and the press generally hailed it as an "ice-breaker" in the campaign against segregation.[45]

The housing order, moreover, was a harbinger of things to come. As the pace of the civil rights movement began to quicken, both the President and Congress made further moves in response to such popular pressure. The new year proved to be an epochal turning point in the whole struggle for racial equality.

45. *Report. . . .'63*, 95; *Sorensen*, 480–82.

XI. YEAR OF
CRISIS

The year 1963 was one of crisis affecting every phase of the civil rights movement. It opened with President Kennedy prepared to push through new legislation; it closed tragically with his assassination before Congress had acted. The interval witnessed further nationwide protests with Negroes ever more militantly carrying their revolution into the streets; furious controversy and debate in Congress; and so far as the Civil Rights Commission itself was concerned, a dramatic, controversial report on Mississippi and another struggle over its continuation.

With the advent of a new Congress, following the mid-term elections of 1962, the President felt that his hand was sufficiently strengthened to seek the further guarantees of equal protection for Negroes from which he had so long held back. But something deeper than the calculations of political power affected his attitude. As his experience in the confrontation with Governor Barnett of Mississippi was supplemented by further evidence of the recalcitrance of the South, and other developments demonstrated the growing counter-force of the Negroes' insistent demand for "Freedom Now," his old ambivalence about civil rights gave way to a determination to face the issue squarely. Kennedy's basic sympathy with the Negroes' position became a deep conviction that equality must be fully upheld. He was willing to take the risks that he had heretofore avoided, not only because it was politically safer, but because, in the words of Theodore Sorensen, he was now "deeply and fervently committed to the cause of human rights as a moral necessity."[1]

His first legislative proposals to Congress, on Febraury 28, were still relatively moderate ones. They included the proposal that a sixth grade education should be accepted by voting registrars as presumptive evidence of literacy; Federal assistance for schools seeking to implement a policy of desegregation; and extension of the life of the Civil Rights Commission. These were moves the Commission favored, but they fell far short of its stronger recommendations on voting and education and ignored almost everything else in the 1961 Report.

In his sponsorship of the Commission, Kennedy proposed that its functions be broadened so that it might serve as a national clearing house to provide information, advice, and technical assistance to any agency, public or private, requesting its services. He recommended that its life be extended, not permanently for that would be "a pessimistic prediction that our problems will never be solved," but for at least four more years.[2]

This was all very well. But without anything in the program to speed up the processes of school integration, to combat discrimination in housing and employment, or to guarantee the access to public accommodations which was the major objective of the sit-ins and freedom rides, the Negroes were bitterly disappointed and northern civil rights advocates hardly less so. The President's proposals simply did not live up to the promise of his accompanying

1. Sorensen, *Kennedy*, 470.
2. *Revolution in Civil Rights*, 39; *Public Papers of the Presidents, 1963* (Kennedy), 221-30.

message which eloquently declared that discrimination in every phase of American life must go.

The members of the Civil Rights Commission shared this sense of disappointment. In a meeting with the President before his message to Congress, they urged the strongest possible civil rights bill. In respect to their own functions they suggested, as first developed in a memorandum from Staff Director Bernhard, that the Commission be given "the facility" to assist the Executive Branch in implementing non-discrimination policies, to establish a mediation service, and to enforce equal protection of the laws in the extension of Federal benefits. "We conclude unanimously," stated a memorandum left with the President on February 12, "that the Commission should not be continued if its functions are limited to those presently incorporated in its statute and if it is subject to renewal for only two years."[3]

While the President expressed his sympathy for such recommendations, the Administration did not make any effort to explore further the idea of making the Commission an enforcement rather than a predominantly study-oriented agency. An exchange of letters among Hannah, Hesburgh and Griswold in March revealed a continued sense of frustration, growing perhaps even more out of the attitude of the Department of Justice than that of the President himself. The three men agreed that in spite of the President's support, the future seemed very uncertain. "I would be inclined to resign now," Hannah wrote Hesburgh on March 22, "if it would serve a useful purpose to indicate the ineffective role in which we are cast by the Attorney General and others."[4]

In the meantime, however, Senator Hart of Michigan, with twenty-eight co-sponsors, was prepared to introduce a bill in Congress incorporating the Administration's moderate proposals for broadening the Commission's functions and extending its life for four years. On the ground that even if this were not all it wanted, a four-year continuation was "sufficient assurance of continuity," the Commission decided to cooperate in this move. Hannah drew up a possible draft for the proposed new bill which was transmitted to Vice-President Johnson and through him to Senator Hart. The

3. Minutes of the 49th Commission meeting, Feb. 12, 1963.
4. John A. Hannah to Father Hesburgh, March 22, 1963, in Hannah files.

Commission members and Staff Director were ready to support this measure and to work for its passage.[5]

As individual congressmen introduced additional bills implementing other phases of the President's new civil rights program, the Commission was willing to testify in their behalf as well. There were none of the hesitations that marked its members' original appearances before congressional committees. On June 6 the Chairman even went far beyond the immediate issue of the day in an eloquent plea before the Senate Subcommittee on Constitutional Rights in behalf of the whole civil rights cause.

A revolutionary change was taking place in race relations, Hannah told the committee, and the turmoil in which the country found itself involved was not at all surprising. Even though violence should never be condoned, "we should understand why some feel they are driven to it." He had himself learned a great deal about civil rights during the past six years and also worried a lot about the problem.

> *Philosophically, a slow, tedious advance toward equality in education, employment, housing and justice may be best, but the individual Negro cannot afford to be philosophical. He has but one lifetime; who can blame him for wanting to enjoy his rights within that lifetime. . . . If, when the current struggle is over, we have been driven into opposite camps and are left with a legacy of hate, fear and mistrust, nobody will be victor.*

The demonstrations were bound to continue, the Commission's Chairman concluded, but if Congress and the American people resolutely lived up to their obligations, he remained hopeful for the long future.[6]

The Hannah who a few years earlier was described as "by no means a zealot" for civil rights and said himself, "there is no right answer to all sides," had come a long way. He was now constantly

5. Berl I. Bernhard, "Role of the United States Commission on Civil Rights," *Law in Transition,* 23, Summer, 1963; *Hearings Before Subcommittee on Constitutional Rights . . . Senate,* 88th Congress, 1st Session, May 21, 22, 23 and June 5, 6, 12, 1963, 137–63; *Report 914, Subcommittee No. 5 of House Committee on the Judiciary, May 16, 1963; Congressional Record,* March 19, 1963, Senate, 4226–27, 4229.
6. *Hearings Before Senate Subcommittee,* 232; *New York Times,* June 7, 1963

to emphasize in statements and public addresses this idea that the Negro had only one life to live; he would repeatedly stress the inherent justice, after so many generations of neglect, in the ringing cry for "Freedom Now."

Congress continued hearings on the new legislative proposals throughout the spring, but the usual political clashes between Northerners and Southerners blocked any real progress. No action was taken to prolong the Commission's life. However, events were building up tremendous pressure against further delay or procrastination. The civil rights movement was gaining a new impetus. A sense of urgency was in the air. The President was soon to go before Congress with a far broader program than the one submitted in February and call more emphatically for prompt and vigorous action.

The Civil Rights Commission made a first contribution to this growing sense of urgency. Breaking all precedent, it issued on April 16 a special interim Report on conditions in Mississippi.[7] The Commission was convinced that open racial conflict dangerously threatened this most conservative of all southern states, and that the issue presented by Mississippi's defiant attitude in so aggressively maintaining segregationist policies could be resolved only through some form of Federal intervention. While the President rejected the Commission's recommendations, the tenor of the Report created something of a sensation and added new fuel to the fires that in the spring of 1963 were sweeping through the whole civil rights movement.

This special Report grew out of a deepening feud between the Civil Rights Commission and the Department of Justice over a voting hearing that the Commission had long wanted to hold in Mississippi. Three times the Commission planned hearings; three times Justice forced their postponement. The dispute was again the natural one over tactics between what was essentially an investigative and advisory agency, and an agency charged with law enforcement. The Commission wanted to expose conditions in Mississippi to encourage Federal intervention and was not primarily concerned over the possible consequences of its hearings on any

7. *Interim Report of the United States Commission on Civil Rights,* April 16, 1963 (mimeo).

legal proceedings in which the Department of Justice might be engaged.

That this "smouldering dispute," as one newspaper described it at the time, went deeper than affairs in Mississippi and worried the Administration is attested by Theodore Sorenson. The Mississippi situation was not the only one, he wrote rather caustically in his account of the civil rights movement, "in which the freewheeling Civil Rights Commission proved to be a somewhat uncomfortable ally in this struggle."[8]

When the Commission, at a meeting in December 1962, for the third time scheduled a Mississippi hearing for early the next year, Attorney General Kennedy forcefully objected. His grounds were that it might prejudice the criminal contempt proceedings that his department was currently bringing against Governor Barnett for his interference with James Meredith's admission to Ole Miss. On December 15 he wrote Hannah that the Justice Department "might be severely hampered" by the proposed hearing. The Commission agreed under such pressure to forego its plans for the time being, but as Hannah answered the Attorney General on January 2, 1963, "we must state in all candor that this decision is difficult for us."[9]

The issue did not die, however. The Commission received a report from the State Advisory Committee in Mississippi which further documented a mounting wave of violence against Negroes and civil rights workers. A number of homes, including that of the Committee's Vice-Chairman, had been bombed. The Mississippi Council of Federated Organizations, representing the NAACP, CORE, and other groups, castigated the Commission in a series of telegrams for failing to live up to its obligations and abjectly submitting to the Department of Justice in postponing the Mississippi hearing.[10]

On March 21 the question of the relationship between the Commission and Justice Department came up at a White House press conference when an interviewer asked President Kennedy whether the Commission should have given way to the Attorney General. The President answered: "No, that is a judgment the Civil

8. New York *Post*, April 18, 1963; Sorensen, *Kennedy*, 488.
9. Attorney General Kennedy to Hannah, Dec. 6, 1962; Hannah to Kennedy, Jan. 2, 1963, in Hannah files.
10. Commissions files

Rights Commission should—any time, any hearing they feel advances the cause or meets their responsibility which has been entrusted to them by the law, then they should go ahead and hold it."[11]

In spite of the President's statement, the Attorney General did not budge. Referring to the proceedings against Governor Barnett, he said: "While this case is pending, I continue to hold the view that a public hearing in Mississippi by the Civil Rights Commission would not be appropriate." The Commission felt itself boxed. It could not flaunt the Attorney General and as Griswold later wrote, "thought it advisable to obey his command." Smarting under the criticism they were receiving from civil rights organizations, the Commissioners, however, decided that the responsibility for not holding the hearing should "get back to the Administration where it belonged." The least they could do was to inform the public of conditions in Mississippi and what they felt should be done about them.[12]

At a tense meeting in Indianapolis on March 29, the Commissioners consequently considered a preliminary report on Mississippi which the staff had drawn up and debated how it might be revised and published. They agreed that the report should on the one hand include a bill of particulars regarding the recent civil rights incidents in Mississippi, illustrating that state's "flagrant disobedience of the law of the land," and on the other, provide an account of the aid that state was nevertheless receiving from the Federal Government. It should also be made clear, Rankin proposed, that a report was being issued under such unusual circumstances "with the hope of avoiding possible insurrection and armed conflict within the State of Mississippi."

Hannah instructed the staff to revise its draft report along these lines, with additional checking of the essential data, and at a second meeting the next morning the Commissioners unanimously endorsed this rather hurried revision. They also decided that the Chairman would first present the Report informally to the President, but if he did not officially release it within seventy-two hours, the Commission would make it public.[13]

11. *Public Papers of the Presidents, 1963* (Kennedy), 279.
12. *Interim Report,* 1; Barbara Carter, "The Role of the Civil Rights Commission," *Reporter,* 29, July 4, 1963, 10–14; *Harvard Law Review,* April 18, 1963.
13. Minutes of the 50th Commission meeting, March 29–30, 1963.

Hannah, accompanied by Staff Director Bernhard, met with Kennedy. The President, quite evidently unhappy on reading the text, asked whether the Commissioners were in unanimous agreement and whether they were adamant about publishing the Report. The answer to both questions was affirmative. Kennedy then went over the document again and told Hannah and Bernhard:

I still don't like it. If the Commissioners have made up their minds, I presume they will issue the report anyway. I think they are off the track on this one, but I wouldn't try to suppress it. That would be wrong —couldn't do it anyway. It is independent, has a right to be heard, but I do wish you could get them to reconsider.[14]

There was no reconsideration; the Report was officially released on April 16. The Commission immediately found itself involved in a storm of controversy going far beyond anything it had previously experienced.

The Report, which was very brief, first gave a devastating picture of conditions in Mississippi from which the Commission had received one hundred voting complaints since October: "citizens of the United States have been shot, set upon by vicious dogs, beaten and otherwise terrorized because they sought to vote." It described the assaults which had been made upon civil rights workers, including ministers and students, and the bombing of the Vice-Chairman of the State Advisory Committee's home. It declared that "even children at the brink of starvation had been deprived of assistance by the callous and discriminatory acts of Mississippi officials administering Federal funds."

The other side of the picture, the Report then went on to say, was that the Federal Government was continuing to provide massive economic assistance to Mississippi even as the state placed itself in direct defiance of the Constitution and of court orders. The people of Mississippi and of the other states should know that whereas the Federal Government received in 1962 from all sources in Mississippi only $270 million, it paid out in grants and contracts to the state and local governments over $650 million regardless of the discriminatory expenditure of these funds. One glaring example the Report singled out was a two million dollar grant for building

14. Schlesinger, *A Thousand Days,* 953.

a jet airport to serve Jackson even though the approved plans called for segregated eating and restroom facilities.

What made the Report so controversial, however, were the recommendations. The Civil Rights Commission proposed, first, that Congress and the President "consider seriously" whether legislation was not appropriate to assure that Federal funds should not be made available to any state which continued to refuse to abide by the Constitution and laws of the United States; and, second, with its shafts aimed more directly at the particular state involved, that the President "explore" his authority "to withhold Federal funds from the State of Mississippi until the State of Mississippi demonstrates its compliance with the Constitution and laws of the United States."[15]

As headlined and reported in newspapers throughout the country, the words "seriously consider" and "explore" were forgotten. The press generally announced that the Civil Rights Commission urged immediate action to cut off all Federal funds from Mississippi and in effect was prepared to read her out of the Union for her discriminatory treatment of Negroes.

The two Mississippi senators were outraged. Eastland called the Report "a monstrous libel"; Stennis assailed it as a "meddling of busybodies." Southern newspapers fulminated over "this outrageous recommendation" and "the dictatorial extreme to which fanatic impatience would go to implement its own dogma." The Louisville *Courier-Journal* was an exception. The American people, it editorialized, were entitled to assurance that their tax money "is not being used to perpetuate Mississippi's brand of apartheid." Otherwise the southern voice of condemnation was loud and insistent.[16]

Negro leaders and other civil rights advocates welcomed the Report. Roy Wilkins, Executive Secretary of the NAACP, endorsed the Commission's stand in a letter to the *New York Times:* Walter Reuther, of the A.F. of L.–C.I.O., praised its "courageous and forthright position." Among members of the Senate, Javits of New York said the Commission had placed the basic issue squarely before the

15. *Interim Report,* 1–5.
16. Barbara Carter in *Reporter,* quoting Richmond *News Leader,* April 19, 1963; Richmond *Times-Dispatch,* April 22, 1963; Nashville *Banner,* April 23, 1963; Louisville *Courier-Journal,* April 20, 1963.

country; Hart of Michigan agreed that once again it had proved itself to be the conscience of the nation; and Keating of New York and Kuchel of California urged acceptance of its recommendations.[17]

Among northern newspapers and magazines, however, a far more general opinion, as summed up by *Time,* was that the Commission "showed poor forethought and considerable irresponsibility" in its recommendations. Even those periodicals sympathetic with the civil rights cause and quite ready to agree that something should be done about Mississippi, felt that the Commission had come up with "the wrong answer." David Lawrence in *U.S. News and World Report* spoke of "brazen charges" and "cruel and unusual punishment." "What an emotional accusation!" he wrote. "And this comes from a Commission composed of men who are not only trained in the law but regarded as leaders in the academic world of today." Other editorial writers almost universally agreed that any blanket withdrawal of Federal funds from Mississippi, as they interpreted the Report's recommendations, was wrong in principle and unworkable in practice.[18] The *New York Times,* with its usual air of authority, took this censorious attitude in a long editorial on April 19: cutting off Federal aid to Mississippi would offend the accepted concept of sound Federal-state relations and bear most onerously on those poor citizens, inevitably including the great mass of Negroes, whom such a move was designedly to aid. "We can think of no suggestion," the *Times* said flatly, "less calculated to promote civilized race relations or to cool the inflamed passions that erupted in the Civil War." In his column adjoining the editorial, James Reston wrote that any idea of trying to read Mississippi out of the Union in retaliation for her sins was thoroughly misguided. He thought it more advisable to develop a program which would treat that state as an "underdeveloped nation."[19]

Although no national magazine was a stronger advocate of civil rights than the *New Republic,* it was greatly disturbed by the implications of the Mississippi Report. "Every impulse of sympathy

17. *New York Times,* April 29, 1963; Hannah to Walter Reuther, April 22, 1963, in Hannah files; Washington *Post,* April 19, 1963.
18. *Time,* 81, April 26, 1963; *U.S. News and World Report,* 54, April 29, 1963.
19. *New York Times,* April 19, 1963.

rises for the Civil Rights Commission," this liberal journal said, but even though there was something "persuasively personal" in its members' reaction to conditions in Mississippi, "the impulse of the heart, however, is constrained by the doubts of the head." But while the *New Republic* could not accept the proposed moves against Mississippi, it strongly warned against casually dismissing the Commission's requests. "The President may refuse what they ask," the editorial concluded, "but none of us can refuse the urgency which has impelled them to ask it. The President has a proper distrust of fanatics; but he will be in peril to his duty to all Americans if he dismisses as fanatics any group of moderate men whom the sight of reality has driven to immoderation."[20]

In the meantime Kennedy made known his reactions to the Commission's recommendations in a conciliatory personal letter to the Chairman and an abrupt, critical statement for the press. Writing Hannah on April 19, the President defended the position of the Department of Justice, outlined the steps being taken by the Administration to deal with the situation in Mississippi, acknowledged the propriety of the Commission expressing its "deeply held" views, and concluded by saying that while cutting off funds from Mississippi raised "difficult and far-reaching considerations," the proposal would be "promptly and carefully reviewed within the Executive Branch." That same day, however, answering questions following a talk before the American Society of Newspaper Editors, he indicated that his decision was made. The President did not have the power "to cut off aid in a general way as proposed by the Civil Rights Commission," he stated, and, furthermore, he thought "it would probably be unwise to give the President . . . that kind of power." There should be no further extension of Federal aid for specific projects which either encouraged or permitted racial discrimination, but arbitrarily to end all assistance to Mississippi as a disciplinary measure was something else again—"I couldn't accept that view."[21]

He reaffirmed his position at a press conference five days later: any blanket withdrawal of Federal funds from a single state was unwise. However, when asked whether he had any idea of withholding funds from the Civil Rights Commission because of the

20. *New Republic*, 148, April 27, 1963.
21. *Public Papers of the Presidents, 1963* (Kennedy), 333–35.

extreme position it had taken, he answered succinctly: "No, I don't. No."[22]

As the controversy raged on in the press, the Commission staunchly stood its ground. Its members felt that the recommendations were widely misinterpreted for they asked only that the President explore his possible authority to act. A writer in the *National Observer* on April 22 described Hannah as being "unperturbed" over all the excitement, and quoted him as saying simply, "we are trying to do what we think is right."[23] Staff Director Bernhard later told another reporter that all the Commission actually contemplated was a program-by-program review of Federal aid projects in Mississippi as "leverage for bargaining" which might "stimulate the business community to cooperate." It had no idea of punitive measures.

The fullest contemporary account of this episode in the Commission's history is found in an article by Barbara Carter in the *Reporter* for July 4, 1963, which very clearly depicts the rivalry and feuding between the Commission and the Department of Justice. "They're very unhappy over there," Miss Carter quoted Deputy Attorney General Katzenbach as saying of the Commission. "They say things are not going fast enough." He admitted this indeed might be the case, but emphasized the difficulties in speeding things up, especially in Mississippi, and expressed the view that the Commission's attitude was "somewhat of a do-it-yourself approach. It is not calculated to induce cooperation." When Dean Griswold was asked in turn about relations with Justice, he answered rather mildly, "I would like it if greater cooperation could be developed between us."

Miss Carter further quoted Griswold as defending the Mississippi Report and being very critical of the President's reaction. He felt that he should have more understanding of what the Commission was really trying to do. "When Kennedy dismissed our Report," Griswold declared, "he said he had no powers, which wasn't accurate. Moreover, it creates a negative attitude and encourages people not to comply."

The *Reporter* article highly praised the Commission:

22. *Ibid.*, 347–49.
23. *National Observer*, April 22, 1963, quoted by Barbara Carter in *Reporter*, July 4, 1963.

In six years the Commission has gained broad and valuable experience in analyzing civil rights, not only in voting, but in education, housing, employment, and the administration of justice. A number of its recommendations have provided the basis for congressional action or have been put into effect by Executive Order. As the President has said, the Commission is now in a position to provide even more useful service to the nation.[24]

In retrospect some justification may be found for the criticism of the Commission Report in that it was put together too hastily and reflected too openly the sense of frustration and resentment growing out of the opposition of the Department of Justice to the proposed Mississippi hearing. The text easily lent itself to the interpretation, even though a false one, that the Commission was intemperately proposing an immediate cutoff of *all* Federal aid to Mississippi. Newspapers had to have headlines. Although no warrant existed for dismissing the Report as "silly" or "absurd," and even less for characterizing its authors as "tub-thumpers" and "Fascistic," the Commission left itself open to attack by not expressing more moderately and more clearly just what it had in mind.[25]

More important than the controversy over the Commission recommendations and their possible validity was the shock effect of the Report's disclosures of Mississippi's violations of equal protection of the laws and of the extent to which they were condoned, and even encouraged, by the Federal Government through grants-in-aid and other forms of assistance to state programs. Nothing could have more clearly demonstrated the inadequacy of existing civil rights legislation. Whatever else may be said of the Mississippi Report, it helped to shatter any existing complacency over progress in the South. It drove home the imperative need for further congressional moves if the Negroes were in fact to win the right to vote and otherwise enjoy equality before the law.

The spotlight which the Civil Rights Commission for a time focused on Mississippi, soon swung back to Alabama. Under the leadership of Martin Luther King, Jr., the Negroes of Birmingham launched a new drive to end discrimination in shops, restaurants,

24. Carter, 10–14.
25. Staff Activities Report, April 19, 1963.

and employment. This campaign met determined resistance on the part of the municipal authorities, with injunctions and arrests, and racial tension steadily mounted. King himself went to prison for a time, from which he wrote his famous "Letter from Birmingham Jail," but this hardly served to halt the demonstrations. They came to a climax on May 2 and 3 when thousands of Negroes, including school children, took to the streets to demand justice.

Birmingham's Police Commissioner, the already notorious "Bull" Connor, swung into action. He ordered his men to break up the demonstrations at all costs and they turned on the Negroes with fire hoses and police dogs. The next morning newspapers around the world described the scene—and printed the photographs —of men, women, and children being driven back by the high-pressure hoses, clubbed and beaten, beset by the lunging police dogs. This shocking spectacle had an immense impact on the national mood. President Kennedy was later to say that "Bull" Connor had "done more for civil rights than almost anybody else!"[26]

A truce of sorts was patched up in Birmingham following this clash, but with Governor Wallace stating he would not be a party to any "compromises on the issues of segregation," it was short-lived. Trouble broke out again when whites bombed a number of houses and hotels in the Negro district, including the home of Dr. King's brother. With new rioting in the streets, President Kennedy threatened to send Federal troops to the city, and the local author-ities were forced to take more equitable measures in upholding law and order. Only very slowly did racial tensions die down with the restoration of something like calm.

Birmingham, however, was only the most dramatic of the civil rights disturbances of this critical year. In April, a white postman on a protest walk from Tennessee to Mississippi was found dead of bullet wounds in northeast Alabama; early in June the state Chairman of the Mississippi branch of the NAACP, Medgar Evers, was killed in front of his home in Jackson. Demonstrations and riot-ing occurred in Nashville, Tennessee and Greensboro, North Carolina; in Albany, Georgia and Selma, Alabama. Several hundred demonstrations in all took place, and the police made something like fourteen thousand arrests in the states of the old Confederacy.

26. Schlesinger, *A Thousand Days*, 971; Sorensen, *Kennedy*, 489.

This same June the still irreconcilable Governor Wallace "stood in the schoolhouse door" to block the enrollment of two Negro students at the University of Alabama—only to retreat somewhat ignominiously when following the pattern of the clash at Ole Miss, President Kennedy sent Federalized troops of the Alabama National Guard to the Tuscaloosa campus.

Things were heating up with the promise of "a long hot summer." Even with both the President and Congress finally responding to these growing pressures, the demonstrations and agitation continued. They reached a remarkable peak in August when Negroes and white sympathizers, a quarter million strong, staged a great March on Washington. Gathering in front of the Lincoln Memorial in an unprecedented demonstration in support of justice and freedom, this tremendous but orderly and restrained crowd heard its leaders insist on the right to "Freedom Now." Stressing the vital importance of peaceful integration, Martin Luther King, Jr. told a rapt audience in unforgettable phrases:

> *I still have a dream. . . . I have a dream that on the red hills of Georgia the sons of former slaves and the sons of former slave-owners will be able to sit together at the table of brotherhood. . . . I have a dream that even the state of Mississippi, a state sweltering with the heat of injustice, will be transformed into an oasis of freedom. . . . I have a dream. . . .*

When the great crowd finally dispersed, the echoes of its impressive singing hung over Washington:

> *We shall overcome, we shall overcome,*
> *We shall overcome, some day,*
> *Oh deep in my heart I do believe,*
> *We shall overcome some day.*[27]

Whatever the exact turning point in the national mood, President Kennedy felt that the time was at hand not only to reemphasize his all-out support for the civil rights movement, but also to broaden the limited legislative proposals he had submitted to Congress in February. Was he acting out of moral conviction? or as Walter Lippmann critically wrote, only because "the Negroes have

27. Schlesinger, 972–73

gone into the streets to face the fire hoses and the dogs and the clubs?" Again to quote Schlesinger and Sorenson, they are agreed that Kennedy had postponed action only through an astute sense of timing. Schlesinger has written that "Birmingham and the Negroes themselves had given him the nation's ear"; and Sorenson has said that in comparison with its previous indifference, the country now "was listening."[28]

President Kennedy, in any event, went on the air in a nationally televised speech on June 11—the immediate occasion was the confrontation with Governor Wallace—to emphasize the immediate need for broader legislation, and eight days later submitted to Congress a new omnibus civil rights bill.

In his public address, he said:

> The fires of frustration and discord are burning in every city, North and South, where legal remedies are not at hand. Redress is sought in the streets, in demonstrations, parades and protests which create tensions and threaten violence—and threaten lives. . . . Now the time has come for this nation to fulfill its promise. . . . We face a moral crisis as a country and as a people. It cannot be met by repressive police action. It cannot be left to increasing demonstrations in the streets. It cannot be quieted by token moves or talk. It is a time to act. . . . Those who do nothing are inviting shame as well as violence. Those who act boldly are recognizing right as well as reality.[29]

The omnibus bill drew its provisions from many sources, ideas already embodied in other proposed measures and the recommendations of the Civil Rights Commission. It again included the substitution of a sixth grade education for literacy tests, authority for the Attorney General to file suits to enforce school integration, a four-year extension of the Civil Rights Commission, and with greater boldness, a provision cutting off Federal aid for any state or local program practicing discrimination. On this latter proposal Kennedy stated, with an oblique reference to the Mississippi Report of the Civil Rights Commission, that while it was not always helpful to withdraw funds unconditionally "as is often proposed," Congress should nevertheless make clear that Federal assistance would be halted for any discriminatory programs, not as punishment to the

28. *Ibid.*, 966; Sorensen, 494.
29. *Revolution in Civil Rights*, 39; Sorensen, 495; Schlesinger, 965.

state but in order to clarify the authority of any administrator of Federal money.

The "symbolic heart" of the omnibus bill, however, was Title II, which was designed to guarantee equal access to public accommodations regardless of race or color. This was far and away the most controversial of any civil rights recommendations so far made to Congress. The program as a whole, the President declared, should command support not merely because it would promote economic efficiency, diplomacy, and domestic tranquility "but, above all, because it is right."[30]

To present this sweeping legislation was by no means to assure its passage even though the mood of the country appeared to be so favorable. What the Administration and the bipartisan civil rights coalition faced in the months ahead was the immense task of building up congressional support that would not only assure a clear-cut majority for the bill, but in the Senate a two-thirds majority. It was virtually certain that the public accommodations section would invite a southern filibuster.

The members of the Civil Rights Commission and the Staff Director were among those called before congressional committees to testify on the bill. They supported it fully. When questioned on the matter of their special concern and competence, that is, the status of the Commission, they emphasized, as they had at earlier hearings, the importance of both broadening its functions and extending its life for at least four years if not making it permanent. In his testimony of July 24, Griswold forcefully stated that civil rights was "the most important issue facing this Congress."

As the bill became subject to the usual political maneuvering to strengthen or soften its impact, the Administration stood firm. The President did not wish to make any drastic changes that would alienate moderates who were already skeptical of its constitutionality, nor would he retreat before southern roadblocks. It soon became evident in these circumstances that no action would be taken before the end of the current term of Congress. The congressional leaders agreed, however, that further consideration of the bill would be taken up promptly at the beginning of 1964.[31]

30. *Public Papers of the Presidents, 1963* (Kennedy), 483–94.
31. *Revolution in Civil Rights,* 39, 41.

This postponement meant that for a third time the life of the Civil Rights Commission was placed in jeopardy. In anticipation of the possible expiration of its legal mandate at the end of September, future planning had to be suspended, as had been the case in both 1959 and 1961. With resignations reducing the Staff from 76 to 56, the gloom was thick in the Washington headquarters.

The Commission built up further popular support during the year. The criticism widespread at the time of the Mississippi Report was muted; newspapers throughout the North favored the agency's continuation. The Washington *Post,* to quote that influential newspaper once again, spoke out strongly in May. The "tough-minded and realistic Commissioners and Staff Director," it said, had "exceptional drive and emotion" and had rendered an "invaluable public service." The Commission was a "trail blazer for those who would completely eradicate from American life every form of discrimination based upon race or ancestry."[32]

Even one southern newspaper spoke of the Commission's usefulness. The Greensboro (N.C.) *Daily News* declared that in spite of the "windmill-tipping blunder" of the Mississippi Report, it had a good record and should not be killed off. Challenging the stubborn opposition of North Carolina's chief congressional spokesman, Senator Ervin, the *Daily News* editorial concluded: "Mercy, senatorial executioners."[33]

The *New York Times* was again highly approving when in September the question of the Commission's extension was very much in the news:

> The Commission and its State Advisory Committees have been useful watchmen over civil rights. Since it began functioning in 1958 it has often been the clearest voice in calling public attention to the unequal application of the laws and to the gross abuses of constitutional guarantees. It is tragic that the delay over its extension, plus the unremoved doubt that it will stay alive at all, has already made such inroads in its ability to conduct its task effectively.[34]

However, nothing happened. "Outwardly worried about its continued existence and inwardly seething over not being given

32. Washington *Post,* May 28, 1963.
33. Greensboro *Daily News,* May 23, 1963.
34. *New York Times,* Sept. 15, 1963.

credit for the job it has done," was one contemporary description of the Commission's unhappy state of mind. Deeply disturbed, Hannah finally called a press conference to insist upon the need for action. With some bitterness he stated that a great many people were willing "to let the Commission go down the drain" without realizing what it had achieved. Time was in fact running out. There appeared to be good reason to fear, as Senator Keating phrased it, that the Commission would be "ignored out of existence."[35]

But once again rescue was at hand. Supporters in the Senate, following the technique employed in earlier crises, attached a rider to a minor bill, already passed by the House, providing for the Commission's extension for one year. The general belief that the four-year term incorporated in the pending omnibus civil rights bill would ultimately be adopted, led to this seemingly quick and easy way to meet the immediate emergency. Even then the South could not let the opportunity escape to renew its attacks on the Commission. One of Louisiana's excited representatives said it was "tearing us apart . . . as the Communists want us to be divided." Senator Russell was content to express his continued opposition more laconically: "Let it die."[36]

The result of voting on the one-year extension was not really in doubt. The Commission had issued its third Report, and the statutory date for it to begin to wind up its affairs had passed, but during the first week of October, Congress endorsed this temporary lease on life. With southern congressmen maintaining their traditional opposition, the count in the Senate was 70 to 15 and that in the House 265 to 80.[37]

Yet the Commission could not be certain of the longer future. For better or worse its fate was tied up with that of the broader civil rights legislation which Congress had put over to the next year for further consideration. Commenting on this state of affairs a sympathetic *New Republic* compared the Commission's checkered life with "The Perils of Pauline." It finally won through for a third time, the *New Republic* said, but "this sequence was one of the cruelest the scenario has yet produced."[38]

35. *Ibid.,* Sept. 26, 1963; Sept. 29, 1963.
36. *Ibid.,* Oct. 8, 1963; *Time,* Oct. 15, 1963.
37. *Revolution in Civil Rights,* 41.
38. *New Republic,* 149, Oct. 12, 1963, 3–4.

XII. THE THIRD REPORT— 1963

The Third Biennial Report of the Commission on Civil Rights was something of an anticlimax against the background of events in 1963.[1] It could hardly have the impact of the Negro demonstrations in Birmingham or the March on Washington; it was not as attention-commanding as the Commission's own explosive document six months earlier on what was happening in Mississippi. True, the Report's release coincided with the sharp struggle in Congress over the extension of the Commission's life, but it in no way affected the outcome of this controversy.

Two aspects of the Report nevertheless stood out conspicuously. Describing the awakening of the country to the urgent necessity for new measures to meet the demands which the Negroes

---

1. *Civil Rights—Report of the United States Commission on Civil Rights '63*, Washington, 1963.

so graphically dramatized through their demonstrations, the Commission explicitly stated that for the first time it was "able to report an atmosphere of genuine hopefulness." The Report itself did not always seem to substantiate this optimism. The Commission declared that the existing conflict created a danger that "white and Negro Americans may be driven even further apart and left again with a legacy of hate, fear, and mistrust." Still, the Commissioners felt that genuine progress was being made in the war against racial discrimination and that the country was finally embarked on a firm course to establish equal protection of the laws.

The second important feature of the Report was its unanimity. Even on the controversial issue of voting safeguards, which always before revealed sharp differences of opinion, the Southerners now joined forces with the Northerners. There were no dissents. The Commissioners as a body were wholly committed to strengthening civil rights in every area where racial discrimination still existed.

In an introduction, significantly entitled "Challenge and Response," the Commission not only emphasized the above points but not surprisingly stressed the need for a more comprehensive effort to resolve the whole civil rights problem. It called for immediate measures to implement its own recommendations on local, state, and Federal levels. "At this time in our history," the introduction concluded with a rhetorical flourish, "we must fulfill the promise of the United States to all this country's citizens, or give up hope for our national greatness. The challenge can be met if the entire Nation faces its responsibilities."[2]

In form and content the body of the Report differed substantially from the Reports of 1959 and 1961. It was very much shorter —a single volume of only 268 pages, without the extensive background material and voluminous statistics that characterized its predecessors. This reduced content was largely due to the influence of Staff Director Bernhard who felt that the earlier reports had been too long and overpadded. The new Report, in his opinion, should be largely limited to conclusions, findings, and recommendations. At a meeting in February, the Commission agreed to this plan, and six months later, after the usual consultations, changes,

2. *Ibid.*, 5.

and revisions in respect to the staff's original draft, unanimously accepted the Report's final version.[3]

It included the customary sections on voting, education, employment, housing, and the administration of justice, and additional chapters on health facilities, urban areas, and the status of the Negro in the armed forces. Following this substantive material were a review of the operations of the State Advisory Committees, a list of all Commission publications, and, a more unusual innovation, an appendix analyzing executive and congressional response to the Commission's previous proposals.

The new recommendations generally followed familiar lines. They brought together those made on voting in 1959 and 1961 in somewhat different form, and in such fields as education, employment, and justice were even more repetitious. Nothing was recommended on housing. New proposals were made in the fresh fields of investigation relating to health facilities, urban areas, and the armed services. The previous Commission recommendations were in many instances still being discussed in Congress, and the major task at this time appeared to be their reenforcement. What the Commission wanted to do was once again to stress, less emotionally, the cold, hard facts that underlay the current demonstrations and thereby strengthen the hands of congressional proponents of a stiff, new civil rights law.

In making its recommendations on voting in 1961, the Commission had recognized that the ballot would not resolve all the problems of the Negro in the South. It now said again that "the right to vote alone cannot break the vicious circle in which Negro Americans have so long been trapped." But this was one civil right, it reiterated, over which there could legally be no dispute—the constitutional guarantees were explicit—and one which was an essential first step in alleviating the second-class citizenship of the South's hundreds of thousands of disenfranchised voters.

The analysis of current progress on the voting issue to which the Report then proceeded was dismaying. Six years after passage of the first Civil Rights Act, only the slightest gains were recorded in the voting strength of southern Negroes. In those one hundred

3. Minutes of 49th Commission meeting, Feb. 12, 1963; 51st meeting, Aug. 6–8, 1963.

counties in eight states where the 1961 Report showed such widespread denial of the right to vote, the proportion of eligible Negroes allowed to register had risen only from 5 percent to 8.3 percent. The total was 55,711 out of a possible 668,082. And these statistics no more told the whole story than had those of 1961 for such gains as had been made remained scattered and uneven. Among those counties of Alabama whose Negro witnesses at the 1959 hearing told such moving stories of their inability to register, Macon County showed considerable improvement. However, no Negroes at all were as yet registered in Lowndes or Wilcox. The conditions in Louisiana were worse. In those parishes where the authorities had undertaken to purge the voting rolls, the number of Negroes registered declined from ten to seven percent of those of voting age. The record in Mississippi was even more incredible. In thirty-eight counties examined by staff investigators, the registration of Negroes fell between 1955 and 1962 from 3,251 to 2,267, standing in the latter year at 1.1 percent of the eligible total.[4]

Citing this startling evidence, the Commission could indisputably demonstrate that the 1957 and 1960 Civil Rights Acts, with all their elaborate formulas for litigation and court action, had "not provided a prompt or adequate remedy for widespread discriminatory denials of the right to vote." The Commission did not blame the Department of Justice for failing to enforce existing law. On the contrary, it praised the vigor displayed by Justice in instituting some thirty-six suits to sustain the right to register and vote, and stated flatly that "the frustrations of these efforts to eradicate discriminatory practices is due to factors beyond the control of the Department."

The conclusion was obvious:

All present methods having proved ineffective, and in view of the continued failure of some states to take appropriate steps to solve the problem, the Commission again asks that Congress act to establish uniform voter qualifications in order to enforce the provisions of the 14th and 15th Amendments.[5]

Pulling together its earlier proposals, the Commission rephrased the idea that minimum schooling should be accepted as

4. *Report* . . . *'63*, 16–21, 32–35.
5. *Ibid.*, 28.

an equivalent for a literacy test by simply recommending that the right to vote should not be denied except for prescribed length of residence, other accepted state disabilities, or the failure to complete six grades of formal education. It revived in careful form the further proposal to set up a system of Federal registrars wherever a definite pattern of discrimination existed. And, finally, it recommended that if these steps still proved ineffective, Congress should enact legislation, as provided in the 14th Amendment, to reduce the representation in the House of Representatives of those states where voter qualifications continued to be used as a means to deny the franchise on grounds of race, color, or national origin.

Unlike 1959 with the three-to-three division on the voting proposals, and 1961 where it had been four-to-two, all six Commissioners now unqualifiedly endorsed these recommendations. Storey and Rankin did so somewhat reluctantly; they were still deeply concerned over Federal-state relationships. But they felt they had no alternative. In a concurring statement the two Southerners noted that progress toward achieving equal voting rights was virtually at a standstill in many localities, and consequently "we have concluded sadly, but with firm conviction, that without drastic change in the means to secure suffrage for many of our citizens, disfranchisement will continue to be handed down from father to son."[6]

The Report's section on education stated, as all the evidence so clearly indicated, that most schools in the South continued to be segregated in spite of the nearly decade-old Supreme Court decision, and that *de facto* segregation in the North and West, resulting from the residential concentration of non-whites within the larger cities, was if anything more widespread than before. It was difficult to find in the material presented, from whatever part of the country, any substantial ground for encouragement in the processes of school integration.

So far as the southern and border states were concerned, the statistics were indeed bleak. Among the 3,052 school districts in this general area with both white and Negro students, 979—or 204

6. *Ibid.,* 27–31.

more than reported in 1961—admitted Negroes to formerly all white schools. But 702 of them were in the border states. In the Deep South very little had been done: South Carolina, Alabama, and Mississippi had still to desegregate a single school. The overall figures for the entire area of southern and border states showed that only eight percent of the Negro children attended schools with white children— a gain of one percent since 1961. The Report concluded with a moderation that could hardly be exceeded: "Progress continues to be slow in the South."[7]

A more detailed study of conditions in other parts of the country once more went over the whole problem of "racial imbalance" and the efforts being made to combat it—as reported at the Commission hearings—through the revision of pupil assignment practices, new transfer policies, and open enrollment plans. But it was again and again found that these devices as developed by the most conscientious boards of education actually had little effect on the racial composition of urban schools. The 1963 Report stated:

In spite of all efforts to achieve racially heterogeneous schools, it seems inevitable that many, particularly in the large cities, will retain a large degree of racial imbalance until discrimination in housing and employment are things of the past.[8]

The Commission was hardly in a position to provide answers to these seemingly insoluble problems; its recommendations to Congress did not go beyond earlier proposals to any significant extent. They were indeed reduced to four in this Report, as compared with the dozen made two years earlier. The first two were a reformulation of old proposals: (1) a requirement that school boards promptly adopt plans for integration with provision that if they failed to do so or did not implement them, the Attorney General should be authorized to take legal action; and (2) the extension of technical and financial assistance to school districts attempting to meet the problems resulting from segregation or desegregation. Two additional recommendations were for a somewhat technical change in the urban renewal law which might aid in re-

7. *Ibid.,* 63.
8. *Ibid.,* 59.

ducing racial imbalance in northern cities, and for a White House conference to discuss the whole problem of providing American children with an equal opportunity for an education.[9]

Nothing was more evident, as illustrated both by this Report and the steps subsequently taken by Congress, than that effective provision of adequate and equal educational opportunities for children was a local problem with which individual communities had somehow to cope largely on their own initiative. The role of the Federal Government, although it could grant or withhold financial assistance, was in this area a relatively limited one.

Employment, as in previous reports, was the third topic taken up. The Commission was largely concerned with how the Federal Government—and the states—were discharging their responsibilities in the job-training and job-generating programs initiated to meet the overall problem of unemployment in the face of technical advance and automation. The Report again made it clear that Negroes were the greatest victims of the displacement of men by machines, and that their high unemployment rate was largely due to their lack of special skills. Vocational training was a primary need to enhance the Negroes' opportunities for any sort of employment in a contracting labor market. On the Federal level, the Commission carefully examined the impact of such measures as the National Defense Education Act, the Manpower Development and Training Act, and the Area Redevelopment Act.

Under the first of these laws, with its program for training technicians, Negro enrollment remained at very low levels. The Report said that the prescribed courses were not offered in Negro schools to the same extent as in white schools, and that Negroes were often "counseled out" of such courses when they did exist because of limited job opportunities resulting from both employer and union discrimination. The picture was more favorable for the unemployed undergoing training under the Manpower Development Training Act and the Area Redevelopment Act. In the former program, 18.8 percent of the trainees were Negroes and they were fairly well distributed through all job categories.

The original laws did not contain explicit provisions on

9. *Ibid.,* 69–70.

non-discrimination, but the Department of Health, Education and Welfare, and the Department of Labor, under which they were administered, nevertheless set up procedures to prevent discrimination. "I am proceeding currently," the Report quoted the Secretary of Labor as saying, "to assure complete compliance with these operating rules. . . . It is a prior condition of approval of training programs that the trainees will be selected and referred for training without regard to race, creed, color, or national origin."[10]

The conclusion the Commission drew from the studies made in this general area was that the Federal Government was beginning to administer its job-generating and job-training programs in a manner consistent with the principle of equal opportunity. While Negroes were not well represented in some of the technical and professional courses, their participation was otherwise generally favorable.

The recommendations made in the employment field were primarily directed toward reenforcing existing policies. The Commission called upon the President to direct the Secretary of Health, Education and Welfare to require that all training programs be maintained on a strictly non-discriminatory basis, conduct periodic investigations to see that this was being done, and terminate all Federal aid to state programs in the event of non-compliance. It asked Congress to provide additional funds for special programs in literacy and basic skills that were prerequisite for further vocational courses. And, finally, it recommended that the President direct agencies responsible for administering loan, grant, or aid programs to ensure that the employment they generated be open at all levels to all qualified persons.[11]

While not making any recommendations on housing, the Report fully discussed the antecedents, pronouncement, and implementation of the non-discriminatory Executive Order which the Commission had so strongly urged the President to issue. The order was at this time but a year old and it was acknowledged that only time could tell what the ultimate effect might be. The Com-

10. *Ibid.,* 79.
11. *Ibid.,* 91–92.

mission nevertheless remained critical of the limited scope of the order and felt that steps toward its implementation were proceeding very slowly.

The key to future effectiveness, the Report stated, was the extent to which Federal departments and Federal agencies operating in the housing field were prepared to enforce the order. It noted approvingly the creation of the President's Committee on Equal Opportunity in Housing but pointed out that the Committee's concern would necessarily be general policy rather than day-by-day practice. The Commission consequently declared its intention to continue investigating Federal housing programs to determine the degree to which the agencies concerned were in fact carrying out the President's overall policy.[12]

The Commission once again buttressed earlier reports and generally strengthened prior recommendations in respect to discrimination in the administration of justice. The 1963 Report recapitulated the record of police action in respect to the sit-ins and freedom rides, discussed the role of local human relations agencies in helping to resolve civil rights problems, analyzed state and Federal laws in this area, and summarized material obtained through nationwide questionnaires upon the extent to which Negroes were employed in law enforcement agencies. While the picture which emerged from these studies was somewhat blurred, the distressing facts of discrimination against the Negro were undeniable.

The Commission found that official action in the recent civil rights demonstrations in southern cities, and especially in Birmingham, infringed in many instances upon the rights of free speech and peaceable assembly; that legal remedies for blocking such interference were inadequate with the result that legitimate protest against the deprivation of civil rights was often frustrated; and that Negro lawyers attempting to cope with such issues found themselves subject to reprisals. Recognizing that demonstrations might sometimes go beyond the legitimate boundaries of free speech, the Report stated that those studied had with few exceptions been within the protective guarantees of the First Amendment.

12. *Ibid.*, 95–103.

In the summary of the questionnaire study of Negro employment in law enforcement agencies (answered by a representative sampling but not by all those queried), the Report said that proportionately few Negroes were on the staffs of police departments in the North and West, while in the border states and South no more than token employment existed. State police and highway patrols had almost no Negroes, and employment in county prosecutor offices was extremely limited. While the Department of Justice had increased its Negro employees very considerably since 1960, the number was still very low. In short, law enforcement agencies throughout the country were predominantly staffed by whites. Whatever might or might not be the consequences of this racial disparity in the administration of justice, the Commission was firmly convinced that it deeply affected the attitude of Negroes in their relations with local law authorities and built in a natural antagonism toward the police.

In the recommendations on the administration of justice, the Commission repeated two previously made: local governments should be jointly liable with their police officers for any deprivation of civil rights, and the Federal Government should provide grants-in-aid to raise the quality of local police forces. It further advanced the always controversial proposition that Congress should empower the Attorney General to initiate civil proceedings to prevent any denial of constitutionally guaranteed rights, with trial in Federal courts wherever state laws or the actions of state officials jeopardized such rights.[13]

The section on health facilities was a new departure. It grew in part out of the hearing at Memphis and a later one in Indianapolis, but the information from these sources was supplemented by a questionnaire survey of 398 hospitals in thirty-four states, and an intensive study of the operation of the Hill-Burton Act under which the Federal Government had since 1946 been providing funds for hospital construction. The evidence conclusively proved that throughout the country Negroes did not enjoy access to health facilities on equal terms with whites, and that the Federal Government itself was directly contributing to this discrimination.

The most interesting feature of this part of the Report was

13. *Ibid.,* 107–25.

an analysis of the constitutional contradictions in the Hill-Burton Act. In its provisions for fund granting, the law expressly stipulated that the Surgeon General of the Public Health Service ensure that state plans provided adequate health facilities without discrimination. An exception could be made, however, when separate facilities were set up for different population groups so long as the services were "of like quality." Fourteen states had taken advantage of this latter provision, and since 1946 Federal grants totaling $36,775,994 had been made for the construction or remodeling of eighty-nine segregated medical facilities—seventy-six for whites and thirteen for Negroes.[14]

The constitutionality of the Hill-Burton Act was under challenge at the time the Report was being prepared, and a decision in the Fourth Circuit Court later in 1963 overthrew the separate-but-like quality provision. In the meantime, however, the Commission found that the Hill-Burton Act was being interpreted to allow grant recipients to segregate patients on the basis of race, and to refuse staff privileges to Negro physicians. This clearly constituted a denial of equal protection of the laws, the Report stated, and also adversely affected the maintenance of adequate health standards.

The Commission revealed that the prevailing racial discrimination in hospitals was by no means limited to the South, where it was a universal practice, but existed to a varying degree in every part of the country. While northern hospitals might not refuse to admit Negro patients, they often assigned them to separate wards. So far as such hospitals continued to receive the Hill-Burton grants, the Report repeated, the Federal Government was a partner in their segregationist policies.

The Commission's recommendations quite understandably sought to deal directly with this denial of equality. They called upon the President to direct the Surgeon General and the Secretary of Health, Education and Welfare to refuse grant applications under the discriminatory provision of the Hill-Burton Act and in all other cases where applying hospitals planned to set up duplicate facilities on a segregated basis. The two officials should insist upon adequate assurance that grant recipients specifically provide for

14. *Ibid.*, 130–31.

the non-discriminatory use of all their facilities by both patients and medical practitioners.[15]

The Chapter dealing with urban areas was designed to emphasize the Commission's growing conviction, repeatedly expressed in its members' individual statements, of the interlocking relationship of all aspects of racial discrimination in the nation's cities. The testimony of witnesses in the four representative cities where general hearings were held, the Commission declared, disclosed flagrant denials of civil rights in education, the administration of justice, employment, housing, and access to places of public accommodation. Each form of discrimination affected or directly impinged upon the others.

The substantive material was very brief since much of the pertinent evidence was presented in other parts of the Report. One set of statistics dealing with housing segregation was especially revealing. In Phoenix, ninety-seven percent of the Negro population lived within a radius of one mile of the railroad tracks; approximately eighty-three percent of the Negroes in Newark were concentrated in six restricted neighborhoods, three of which were the most run-down in the city; eighty-nine percent of Indianapolis' Negroes lived in an "inner city" with buildings averaging from seventy-five to one hundred years old; and in Memphis, where ironically traditional housing patterns had not been segregated, a marked trend in that direction was gaining headway. The Report again emphasized how such housing conditions encouraged discrimination in every phase of urban life and fostered all the social evils of the slum.

The Commission expressed the hope that its urban hearings had helped to arouse the communities in which they were held to a broader understanding of the basic problem of civil rights and stressed the need for a greater assumption of responsibility on the local level. In conclusion it recommended that the President seek to encourage this by some form of recognition for those men and women whose civic activities resulted in significant advances in civil rights in their respective communities.[16]

15. *Ibid.*, 143.
16. *Ibid.*, 147–68.

The Report's eighth section, based on staff investigations, traced the course of integration in the armed services during the fifteen-year period elapsing since President Truman's Executive Order calling for such reforms in 1948. It described the difficulties faced in implementing this order, the special problems encountered by the different branches of the armed forces, and the progress made in recruitment and promotion procedures. It discussed current conditions including the treatment of servicemen and their families both on- and off-base, especially in communities where segregation was a traditional custom.[17]

In general, the Commission found that although wide disparities still existed between Negro and white personnel in occupational areas and in ranks, a marked improvement was evident over the years. An exception to this was in the case of the Navy. This branch of the armed services relied less on Negro personnel during the Korean War than during World War II, and little change had taken place since then. Both the Army and the Air Force, on the other hand, were using Negroes in more areas than were open to them in civilian life. A most serious problem, the Report stated, was off-base discrimination. Segregation was almost entirely eliminated on military installations with housing, schools, clubs and recreation facilities fully available to all personnel, regardless of color. However, the Department of Defense was only beginning to assume any responsibility for protecting the interests of military personnel in local communities. When Negroes left the base, they often faced discrimination all along the line. The Report said:

> These practices in housing, education, and public and recreational facilities are galling reminders that second-class citizenship has not been completely eradicated, and have a detrimental impact on military morale and efficiency.[18]

The Commission made six specific recommendations to improve conditions affecting Negro servicemen. Most importantly, it called upon the President to insist that corrective action be taken in the Department of the Navy, to request the Secretary of Defense to reappraise all testing procedures in recruitment and promotion

17. *Ibid.*, 171–224.
18. *Ibid.*, 214.

to assure full utilization of both Negro and white manpower re-
sources, and to see that the Department of Defense followed a fully
affirmative program in dealing with off-base discrimination as it
might affect community service clubs, housing, schools, and public
accommodations.[19]

In reporting on the activities of the State Advisory Committees,
the Commission stressed the importance of their double role in
contributing to its own work and in carrying on throughout the
country their own special hearings and conferences. Since reorganization in the spring of 1962 their membership had grown to
485. It included eleven university presidents, seven academic deans,
ninety-seven attorneys, seventy-eight businessmen, five bishops,
fifty-two other clergymen, thirty-one journalists, nine judges,
twenty labor leaders, five mayors, ten physicians and dentists, and
two Indian tribal leaders.

Their operations remained as diverse as those described in
the 1961 volume, *The 50 States Report*. Nine committees had conducted studies of apprenticeship training showing how very few
Negroes were enrolled in such programs, jointly maintained by
unions and employers, because of their lack of skills and widespread discrimination. Eight examined and reported on housing
with conclusions that reenforced the Commission's own conviction
that it was "the most ubiquitous and deeply rooted civil rights
problem in America." Several others, most notably the committees
in Louisiana, Virginia and Oklahoma, surveyed conditions in their
local school districts.

A newly organized District of Columbia committee, investigating discrimination in local employment, reached conclusions
highly critical of the policies of the Federal Government. The
Florida committee made a study revealing widespread discrimination against Negroes in official employment policy; the Kansas
committee went extensively into the problem of vocational education; and the North Carolina committee took up almost every
aspect of segregation.

After looking into community relations in Los Angeles and
the San Francisco Bay area, the always active California committee

19. *Ibid.*, 215–17.

made an especially significant report. It stated that reasonably effective channels of communication existed between the Negro communities and law enforcement agencies in San Francisco, but that in Los Angeles there was an almost complete lack of rapport. "Negroes in California appeared to feel very strongly," this State Advisory Committee soberly warned, "that race was a factor in police practices and that little or no recourse was available to victims of police abuse." Once more it appeared clear that the seeds were sown—though the warning again went unheeded—for such an eruption as that which took place in Watts two years later.

A considerable number of State Advisory Committee reports were individually published in 1962-63. The titles included "Equal Protection of the Laws in North Carolina," "Reports on Rapid City," "Report on Washington, D.C.: Employment," "Report on Connecticut: Family Relocation under Urban Renewal," "Report on New Jersey," "Report on Arkansas: Education," "Report on California: Police-Minority Group Relations," and "Report on Massachusetts: Housing in Boston."

In briefly summarizing all this, the Commission pointed out that with few exceptions the State Advisory Committees were biracial and often constituted the only such groups in their respective states. Entirely apart from their fact-finding, they provided in many areas where racial antagonism was rising the single means for a direct dialogue between Negroes and whites.[20]

The brevity of the overall Report in comparison with earlier ones, and the repetitious character of so many of the recommendations, accentuated the fact that in what were now the six years of its operations, the Civil Rights Commission had to a great extent fulfilled its original mandate. As early as April, 1963, testifying before a House Subcommittee on Appropriations, Storey said that "the so-called fact-finding days of the Commission are largely in the past."[21]

This is not to say that continuing investigations could not be very useful or that they might not lead to new proposals. But a great deal had been done with specific recommendations on vir-

20. *Ibid.*, 227-43.
21. *Hearings Before House Subcommittee on Appropriations,* 88th Congress, 1st Session, April 11, 1963, 992.

tually every phase of the policies of the Federal Government. The Commission itself emphasized in the appendix to its Report how many earlier recommendations, now so generally reaffirmed, had either been adopted or were currently under discussion in congressional debate.

The pending omnibus bill included the substance of the Commission's major voting proposals and five of its recommendations in the field of education. The Department of Health, Welfare and Education was implementing various Commission suggestions; several Federal agencies were following its lead in developing equal employment opportunities; and the National Government was gradually extending the proposed nondiscriminatory rules in various Federal aid programs. The President's Executive Order on housing was another instance, at least in part, of response to Commission pressure, and the District of Columbia accepted its recommendations in the special report on housing in Washington. One area in which no action was taken and no legislation was as yet under consideration was the administration of justice.[22]

The reception given the Report when it was published at the close of September followed customary lines. Northern newspapers and magazines were almost universally favorable. *Newsweek* and the *U.S. News and World Report* gave it good coverage and especially stressed the "gloomy indictment" of southern barriers to the Negroes' right to vote and the consequent need for congressional legislation to remedy such intolerable conditions. The *New York Times* singled out the Report's unanimity and expression of hopefulness for the future, and stressed its analysis of the voting issue and its advocacy of what the *Times* termed "stiff guarantees." An editorial in the *New Republic* noted that through their closeness to the issue, the members of the Commission had become ever stronger advocates of civil rights. It quoted approvingly a statement by Senator Keating. The Report showed that the Kennedy Administration had done more for civil rights than any of its predecessors, he attested, but even more important, it also "says very clearly that the Administration has not done enough."[23]

Southerners resumed the old battle in Congress. True to form

22. *Report . . . '63,* 247–64.
23. *Newsweek,* 62, Oct. 7, 1963; *U.S. News and World Report,* 55, Oct. 7, 1963; *New York Times,* Oct. 1, 1963; *New Republic,* 149, Oct. 12, 1963.

Senator Russell found the Report "cruel and inhuman," "vicious," "inflammatory and unsound." Emphasizing a general complaint on the part of the South, Hill of Alabama declared that under the guise of collecting information, the Commission's agents "have invaded our communities and have incited agitation and animosity where none existed before they came." On the other hand, northern civil rights advocates in Congress welcomed the support given to their efforts to press forward with the new legislation. As a leader of this bloc in the House, Representative Celler hailed the Report as "the ringing of a bell to shake the torpor of the American conscience."[24]

As its factual summary of the relationship between its recommendations and the forward movement of civil rights showed, the Commission greatly encouraged and materially aided the onslaught against discrimination by Congress and the Executive that would soon come to a climax with the new laws of 1964 and 1965. It sometimes tended to exaggerate its own importance. In that news conference on September 28, 1963, in which Chairman Hannah spoke out so strongly on the danger of the Commission being allowed to "go down the drain," he also said that "every step taken by Congress and the Executive Department in the field of civil rights in the past four years originated with the recommendations of the Commission or depended on the facts it has gathered."[25]

This could of course be disputed and an article in the *Wall Street Journal* on October 18 denied it altogether. The article suggested that the fact that so many of the Commission's recommendations were incorporated in the proposed legislation was "only a coincidence," and said further that "the Commission never has been in the forefront of civil rights advisers to either Congress or the White House, and this won't change."[26]

Over and beyond the claims made by Hannah, however, there was authoritative evidence contradicting the *Wall Street Journal*. In his message to Congress in February, 1963, President Kennedy declared that the Commission's recommendations "have provided the basis for remedial action both by Congress and the Executive

24. *New York Times,* Oct. 1, Oct. 8, 1963.
25. *Ibid.,* Sept. 29, 1963.
26. *Wall Street Journal,* Oct. 18, 1963.

Branch." In subsequent senatorial debate on the further legislative proposals submitted in June, repeated mention was made of the debt owed the Commission. "Much of the civil rights legislation now pending before us," Senator Long of Missouri would state in April, 1964, "is predicated on Commission recommendations." Senator Keating of New York was no less emphatic on this point. "In all candor," he said in the course of the same discussion, "we can say that today, were it not for the work of the Civil Rights Commission, the facts and figures which stand behind the affirmative case for the pending bill might not have been gathered."[27]

27. *Public Papers of the Presidents, 1963* (Kennedy), 226; *Congressional Record,* 88th Congress, 2nd Session, Senate, April 6, 1964, 6779, 6785.

XIII. NEW LEGISLATION;
NEW FUNCTIONS

The congressional deadlock over further civil rights legislation and the ambiguity of its own status found the Civil Rights Commission in a most unhappy frame of mind in the autumn of 1963. Events had seemingly passed it by. Its emergency one-year extension was obviously a stopgap and gave no real assurance for the future. The omnibus civil rights bill fell far short of fulfilling earlier hopes that a new law might transform the Commission into a permanent agency with some sort of enforcement powers, and there was still in any event a dismaying uncertainty as to when Congress would finally take any action. In these circumstances it was little wonder that the Commission was in considerable disarray with both actual and prospective resignations further emphasizing a confused and confusing situation.

Dean Storey, who had served the Commission so faithfully

since its initial establishment, resigned for personal reasons. His wife and son were critically ill and he had stayed on the job during the past year only at the earnest urging of the President and Vice-President. A second loss was Spottswood Robinson who resigned on being appointed to the Federal District Court in the District of Columbia. Kennedy accepted the resignations of both these men in October. Even more important from an administrative point of view, Staff Director Bernhard decided to return to the private practice of law and General Counsel Ferguson also resigned.

In light of the troubled circumstances in which the Commission found itself, Chairman Hannah wrote a rather bluntly phrased letter to President Kennedy on October 10 discussing the pending resignations, the depletion of the staff, and the urgent need for some guidance as to what the Commission should do. He said that he was himself ready to resign and believed that Father Hesburgh, as well as Storey, was also prepared to do so. "Before it can act intelligently," Hannah concluded in respect to the Commission's future, "it needs to know what your desires are."[1]

The President answered this letter reaffirming his confidence in the Commission and expressing the strong hope that Hannah would continue as Chairman. Under such urging Hannah reconsidered his plans (he had, however, already written Storey, "We cannot all run out and leave the ship without some direction"), and following a Commission meeting on October 27 which tried to lay out a tentative future program, he informed Kennedy of his willingness to remain—"at least for the present."[2]

The situation still remained difficult. The Commission now had only four members, busy men with many other commitments; the Staff Director's resignation created a further dilemma. The administrative problem was temporarily resolved with the appointment of Howard W. Rogerson as Acting Staff Director. He had been for some time with the Commission and his experience enabled him to take hold very effectively. At the same time William L. Taylor was appointed General Counsel when Clarence Ferguson left the staff and a number of other changes were made in the administrative setup. The three Assistant Staff Directors were F.

1. John A. Hannah to President Kennedy, Oct. 10, 1963, in Hannah files.
2. President Kennedy to Hannah, Oct. 21; Hannah to Storey, Oct. 14; Hannah to President Kennedy, Oct. 21, 1963, in Hannah files.

Peter Libassi, in charge of Liaison; Victor Wright, as Supervisor of Programs; and Peter M. Sussmann, continuing as Director of the State Advisory Committees. At the October meeting the Commission approved a budget for the current fiscal year and a staff paper on future programming. The latter contemplated studies of state and local reaction to racial unrest, Federal civil rights policies, and the National Government's existing authority to enforce non-discriminatory distribution of Federal aid and to protect civil rights workers.[3]

Some two weeks later Hannah saw the President to inform him of how the Commission planned to carry on and to emphasize how important it was to appoint a permanent Staff Director to replace Bernhard. He found Kennedy fully cooperative. The President expressed an interest, over and beyond the Commission's primary concern with equal protection of the laws for Negroes, in the civil rights of Indians, Mexicans, Puerto Ricans, and Eskimos, and he promised continued support for the Commission pending passage of new legislation. "I came away from our session," Hannah reported, "very much encouraged."[4]

In these improved circumstances, though with the Commission still in a state of suspended animation until Congress acted, there fell the devastating blow that created such great new uncertainties not only for the Commission and the civil rights movement, but for the whole future of a shocked and grieving America. On November 23, President Kennedy was assassinated.

When Lyndon Johnson assumed the Presidency, he at once gave positive assurance that he was ready with all the influence at his command to press forward the civil rights legislation which Kennedy had initiated in June. "No memorial oration or eulogy," he told the Congress in his first message on November 27, "could more eloquently honor President Kennedy's memory than the earliest possible passage of the civil rights bill for which he fought so long."[5]

The members of the Civil Rights Commission—still reduced to four—did not quite know what to do after Kennedy's death. In their behalf Hannah immediately wrote the new President report-

3. Minutes of 52nd Commission meeting, Oct. 27, 1963.
4. Hannah to President Kennedy, Nov. 13, 1963, in Hannah files.
5. *Revolution in Civil Rights*, 41.

ing on the previous correspondence with Kennedy and stating their willingness to continue in office with a "minimum visibility" until Johnson had the opportunity to consider the possible reconstitution of the Commission. There was no immediate reply and Hannah was unable to see the President. While still awaiting word from the White House, the Commissioners agreed at their next meeting "to pick up the ball at this point and carry it forward." Then on January 21, 1964, Johnson definitely informed Hannah that he hoped they would continue in office and develop their future program along the lines outlined in the Kennedy correspondence.[6]

The Commission's February meeting was largely taken up by a lengthy but somewhat dispirited discussion of the future—the inadequacies of the civil rights bill which the House had just passed; the possible relationship between the Commission and a proposed Community Relations Service; and the presently lagging program of the Commission itself. A report submitted by the Acting Staff Director stated that he "sensed some dissatisfaction on the part of the Commission either with the program, or with its implementation, or with both"—and then added frankly, "I am in the 'dissatisfied with both' category." He thought the Commission should directly challenge the Administration on its future—"bring us into the mainstream or abolish us."[7]

In setting forth their own ideas, the Commissioners themselves were equally outspoken. Father Hesburgh deplored the fact, as the minutes of the meeting reported, "that the Commission did not have at this time—as it had in the past—a clear-cut awareness of what it wanted to do." He believed it should become active in such areas as President Johnson's new anti-poverty program. On the other hand, Rankin felt it should deal with the trouble spots in civil rights and seek to make more constructive suggestions on the Government's role. Griswold favored the continuance of its basically educational work. On one point at least a general consensus emerged. No matter in what direction the Commission might move, it faced an increasingly difficult problem in "attempting to remain objective and at the same time participate in the mainstream of administrative activities in the civil rights field."

6. Hannah to President Johnson, Nov. 23, 1963; Jan. 16, 1964; President Johnson to Hannah, Jan. 21, 1964, in Hannah files.
7. Minutes of 54th Commission meeting, Feb. 12, 1964.

Hannah's contribution to this discussion, the minutes suggest, was to try to mitigate the Commission members' feeling of discouragement and to urge a more affirmative attitude. With practically every feature of the new civil rights bill embodying a Commission recommendation, he did not feel they were warranted in being so self-critical. He believed that with the law's passage, the Commission would have further opportunities to continue its constructive contributions to the equal enforcement of the law.[8]

While the Commission tried to move ahead, it could actually do little more than mark time until Congress provided for its extension and the President nominated two new members to replace Robinson and Storey. The nominations came first. In February, the President named Mrs. Frankie M. Freeman, who since 1956 had been the Associate General Counsel of the St. Louis Housing and Land Clearance Authority, to succeed Robinson, and two months later designated Eugene C. Patterson, editor of the Atlantic *Constitution,* as the replacement for Storey. These nominations conformed to the pattern set by Kennedy rather than that of Eisenhower. While maintaining the bipartisan character of the Commission, they strengthened its support for civil rights. As that indefatigable foe, Senator Russell of Georgia, promptly pointed out, the original division within the Commission between northern sympathizers with civil rights and defenders of the southern way of life was now wholly a thing of the past. He expressed his regret that unlike the fair-minded Eisenhower, President Johnson seemingly had no interest in appointing even a single person dedicated to local self-government and Jeffersonian principles of state rights. The Commission was now entirely composed, Russell stated, "of those who not only believe in the unlimited use of Federal power to strike down such few rights as remain to the states, but who also believe that Federal compulsion should be employed to establish social equality between the races in every aspect of American life."[9]

Mrs. Freeman had the distinction not only of being the first woman appointed to the Commission, but was a person, as described by her state's senior senator, possessing "great personal charm" as

8. *Ibid.*
9. *Congressional Record,* 88th Congress, 2nd Session, Senate, March 11, 1964, 4576.

well as "exceptional ability, intellect and initiative." A graduate of Howard University Law School, Mrs. Freeman had practiced law in Missouri and was appointed an Assistant District Attorney before becoming associated with the Housing and Land Clearance Authority in 1956. As a Negro, she could be expected strongly to support civil rights, and this prospect was reenforced by the fact that she was on the executive board of the St. Louis chapter of the NAACP. On her appointment, which she accepted as a "responsibility and a challenge," she told reporters that she had "picketed in the streets for what I believe and I will do it again if the need is there." Her selection was warmly supported by the St. Louis newspapers with the *Post-Dispatch* citing her distinguished career and stating that President Johnson had made "an excellent choice."[10]

Eugene Patterson was a Southerner, but his background and experience were perhaps responsible for his adoption of a position on civil rights that was hardly typical of his region. Forty years old, he was a journalist who had served as a bureau manager for the United Press in both New York and London. Returning to his native Georgia in 1956, he was the Executive Editor of the *Atlanta Journal* before becoming the Editor of the *Constitution*. Coming from neither the academic nor legal world, he represented a new approach to civil rights and as Vice-Chairman in succeeding Storey, he was in a position to exercise great influence in the development of the Commission's educational role.

His realistic attitude toward the Negro demand for equal rights was set forth in an editorial in the Atlanta *Constitution* on January 21, 1964, which may well have accounted for Senator Russell's despair over the omission of any spokesman for the southern way of life in the reconstituted Commission. For while Patterson originally believed that the process of desegregation in the South should be pursued on a wholly voluntary basis, and consequently opposed the public accommodations section of the civil rights bill, he reversed his position in this editorial and asserted his belief that legislative action was the only way to end discrimination. Some time later, in response to Johnson's stand on guaranteeing racial justice, he emphatically stated that the President "especially needs

10. *Hearings Before Subcommittee on Constitutional Rights of the Committee on the Judiciary, Senate,* 88th Congress, 2nd Session, July 28, 1964.

the South's help, not hindrance."[11] This was a change indeed from the period when the South's most prominent representative on the Commission, Governor Battle, so candidly set forth his strong convictions on the social values of segregation.

The appointments of Patterson and Mrs. Freeman had of course to be confirmed by the Senate, and they were subjected to the frustrating delays to which the Judiciary Committee, headed as it still was by Senator Eastland of Mississippi, was so invariably addicted. The Subcommittee on Constitutional Rights did not hold its hearings until July 28, 1964. Contrary to previous experience, however, they were brief and cursory. With the nominees highly praised by the senators from their respective states, the committee members did not even ask them any questions.[12] The approval of the Senate itself was a foregone conclusion even though the southern senators still bitterly felt that the Commission had come to represent but one side of the civil rights issue. Only after considerable further delay, however, were the two appointments officially confirmed: that of Mrs. Freeman on September 15 and of Patterson as Vice-Chairman on October 19.[13]

In the meantime, the issue of civil rights legislation and the status of the Commission were finally settled by passage of the Civil Rights Act of 1964. Its legislative history was even more complicated, more long drawn-out, and more marked by controversy than that of either of its predecessors.[14] This was primarily due to the unrelenting opposition of the South to the bill's far-reaching provisions on public accommodations incorporated in Title II. The lobbying on both sides was intensive, with the Negro organizations and other civil rights groups furiously battling a powerful opposition led by the well-financed Coordinating Committee for Fundamental American Freedoms. The House passed the bill on February 10 and the Senate took it up toward the close of that month after its supporters succeeded in bypassing the hostile Judiciary Committee and putting it directly on the calendar.

11. Quoted in *New York Times,* Jan. 22, 1964; Minutes of 56th Commission meeting, June 26, 1964.
12. *Hearings Before Subcommittee on Constitutional Rights.*
13. *New York Times,* Sept. 16; Oct. 20, 1964.
14. *Revolution in Civil Rights,* 51–70.

Throughout a long spring, however, the usual political maneuvering, the consideration of innumerable amendments, the interplay of Republican and Democratic partisan interests, the rivalry of other political groups, and interminable speeches on the Senate floor blocked any definitive action.

With the Southerners prepared to filibuster indefinitely, the impasse was broken only after eighty-three days of debate when the civil rights advocates forced a historic showdown by calling for cloture. The vote on June 10, with all senators present, was 71 to 29—four more than the necessary two-thirds majority. The Senators from the Deep South, five additional Democrats, and six Republicans made up the opposition. There were some further speeches in the following week under the one-hour rule imposed by the cloture vote, and on June 19—one year to the day after President Kennedy first submitted his proposal to Congress—the Senate finally passed the disputed bill by a vote of 73 to 27.

When it was now returned to the House for acceptance of Senate changes, further parliamentary maneuvering was still required to break through the obstructive tactics of Representative Howard K. Smith, the veteran Chairman of the Rules Committee. His opposition was unwavering. "Already the second invasion of the Southland has begun," this unreconstructed Virginian declared. "Hordes of beatniks, misfits and agitators from the North, with the admitted aid of the Communists, are streaming into the Southland mischief-bent, backed and defended by other hordes of Federal marshals, Federal agents, and Federal power."[15] His obstruction, however, was overcome. On July 2 the House adopted the Senate bill by a vote of 289 to 126, and a few hours later President Johnson signed the Civil Rights Act of 1964.

Its passage meant a monumental advance in comparison with the relatively weak and far less comprehensive measures of 1957 and 1960. The President declared that the new law "is a major step toward equal opportunities for all Americans—a milestone in America's progress toward full justice for all her citizens."[16] Negro leaders (except for Malcolm X who said, "You can't legislate goodwill") were enthusiastic. Dr. Martin Luther King, Jr. declared that

15. *Ibid.*, 69.
16. *Ibid.*, 67.

it would bring "a cool and serene breeze to an already hot summer"; James L. Farmer, the National Director of CORE, said the bill might well prove to be "the single most important act of our Congress in several decades"; and Roy C. Wilkins of the NAACP characterized it as "a giant step forward, not only for Negro citizens but for our country."[17]

Sweeping as was its general scope, the 1964 Act could not of course wholly resolve the problem of civil rights, and its omissions or weaknesses were soon to prove more glaring than was realized at the time. On the primary issue of voting, it required that registration tests be administered in writing and that a sixth grade education be accepted as presumptive evidence of literacy. In leaving enforcement to suits instituted by the Attorney General, however, the right to vote remained subject to the judicial process rather than executive enforcement. This provision fell far short of the Civil Rights Commission's basic recommendation for the appointment of Federal voting registrars wherever there was found to be a pattern of discrimination. Moreover in the field of education the law went in effect no further than to authorize Federal aid for desegregated schools, and it had nothing whatever to say on the problem of discriminatory housing.

On the other hand, it outlawed all discrimination in employment, creating an Equal Employment Opportunity Commission with investigative and conciliatory powers; embodied the Commission's bitterly attacked proposal that Federal assistance should be barred to any state or local program practicing discrimination; and created a new Community Relations Service. Finally, its most important feature, the public accommodations section incorporated in Title II, made it unlawful to deny access to restaurants, lunch counters, soda fountains, theaters, sports arenas, hotels, motels, and lodgings (except owner-occupied units with five or less rooms) to any person because of race, color, or religion. The Attorney General was authorized to bring a civil action to enforce this provision in any instance where he had reasonable cause to believe in a pattern of discrimination.

The section dealing with the Civil Rights Commission did not break very much new ground. It established certain new requirements in respect to the conduct of hearings; as a result of a flurry

17. *Ibid.,* 67–68.

of excitement over a questionnaire sent out by the Utah Advisory Committee, barred any investigation into the practices of fraternal organizations, college fraternities, private clubs, and religious organizations; broadened existing functions with authority to serve as a national clearing house for civil rights and to investigate voting frauds as well as denials of the right to vote; and extended the life of the Commission for four years with a final report required as of January 31, 1968.[18]

These provisions dealing with the Commission were a minor and relatively uncontroversial feature of the new law, but they inspired a renewal of congressional debate over the Commission's usefulness and the merit of its recommendations. The 1963 Report accentuated the continuing resentment of Southerners; they saw all their worst fears confirmed in the further prolongation of the Commission's life. They were agreed that it had abused its powers, was intent on harassing and intimidating local officials in the South, and incited agitation and animosity. Senator Hill declared in familiar vein:

The Commission's recommendations run on and on in the endless pursuit of a government of the bureaucracy and for the bureaucracy. No subject or principle is sacred enough to escape attempted emasculation by these self-appointed captains of our ship of state.[19]

Ellender of Louisiana attacked along comparable lines what he described as "a political animal, trained from birth to be on our good southern people like a bird dog on a covey of quails." "Who could have predicted," he told the Senate, somewhat shifting his metaphors, "that in six short years this brawling infant, brought into the world by political midwifery, would have been recommending the complete subversion of a system of constitutional government developed over a period of almost 200 years of proud and glowing American history?"[20] As on previous occasions, more of the criticism was directed against the staff than against the Commission itself. Senator Russell again declared that in his opinion both investigators and consultants were "generally composed of

18. *Ibid.,* 71–74; *Public Law 88–352*
19. *Congressional Record,* 88th Congress, 2nd Session, Senate, April 13, 1964, 7528.
20. *Ibid.,* March 11, 1964, 4882, 4824.

the most fanatical of the professional race agitators in this land."[21]

Northern senators rallied still once again to the Commission's support. They stressed the importance of its recommendations and the extent to which they were embodied in the pending bill. Senator Scott of Pennsylvania, calling the agency "a symbol of the tremendous struggle to secure equal rights for all Americans," suggested that fundamental factors quite unrelated to the charges that it had been brainwashed accounted for the Commission's growing awareness of the need for further action in the civil rights field. He was especially concerned with the limiting effect on operations of a temporary mandate. "When Congress stirs," Scott said, "the Commission quakes, when the Department of Justice issues an admonition, the Commission gets the jitters." He declared it was high time the Commission was "taken off the political trading block" and given a reasonable life expectancy.

Senator Long cited the record of the Commission's recommendations in a vigorous speech and emphasized their influence on Congress. Over and beyond this, he expressed his strong personal conviction that the Commission had helped "to reduce tensions and promote calm and reasonable solutions" in the whole civil rights field, and that the State Advisory Committees provided a meeting ground for "the resolution of sectional and political approaches." "I say unequivocally," he concluded, "that the Commission has earned the confidence that Congress entrusted to it."[22]

If the new Civil Rights Act did not settle all legislative problems in respect to equal protection of the laws, no more did it automatically quiet Negro discontent with discrimination which laws did not reach or touched upon only inadequately. The demonstrations of previous summers continued during that of 1964, and while they remained generally peaceful in the South, they were characterized in the North by increasing violence and rioting. This was an ominous development holding out the threat of a new chapter in racial strife. The rallying cry of Black Power had not yet been voiced. The rioting was sporadic. The trouble almost always broke out as a result of some incident involving the treatment of Negroes by white policemen. This would spark a conflict

21. *Ibid.,* March 9, 1964, 4576.
22. *Ibid.,* April 6, 1964, 6779, 6763, 6768, 6754, 6783.

that often opened the way for Negro teen-agers, and sometimes hoodlums, to release their pent-up aggressions by throwing rocks, bottles, and other missiles at the police; looting and plundering white-owned stores; and going on a general rampage. The contrast with the sit-ins, freedom rides, and ordered marches of southern Negroes was very striking. Where southern Negroes were peacefully demanding the right to vote and equal access to public accommodations, the northern Negroes were turbulently protesting against intolerable living conditions in the segregated black ghettos of northern cities.

A first "incident" in the summer of 1964, arousing the entire country, was nevertheless of a quite different order from southern demonstrations or northern riots. Three civil rights workers, two of them white and one a Negro, who were engaged in an educational and voting registration campaign in Mississippi conducted by the Council of Federated Organizations, were reported missing in late June. After a search of some six weeks their bodies were found in a shallow trench near the little town of Philadelphia, Mississippi, with indisputable evidence they had been shot and the Negro brutally beaten before his murder. The FBI, called in for the search and investigation, subsequently arrested twenty-one whites (including the sheriff of Neshoba County) on the Federal charge of having conspired to deprive the murdered men of their civil rights. However, a United States Commissioner threw out the charges against them in a move which the Department of Justice said was "without precedent" and the state authorities took no action whatsoever. Finally, in February, 1965, a Federal jury returned an indictment against eighteen of the accused on the conspiracy charge only to have the presiding judge promptly dismiss it. The nation was scandalized by this dramatic demonstration of how hard—how virtually impossible—it was to obtain justice in the South when the crime involved was one involving an attack by whites, in this case murder, upon Negroes or civil rights workers.[23]

In the meantime, the Negro riots in the North were following the already tragically familiar pattern of some almost happenchance incident, attacks upon the police, and general disorder. Patterson and Elizabeth, in New Jersey; Philadelphia; a Chicago suburb; and then New York, all experienced racial outbreaks. That

23. *Revolution in Civil Rights,* 8.

in New York was far and away the most serious. Following the fatal shooting of a Negro teen-ager by an off-duty white policeman, rioting raged through Harlem for five days in mid-July with serious injuries, though no additional deaths, among both the rioters and the police, and widespread destruction of property. Regardless of the immediate cause, the disorders reflected a somber feeling of Negro unrest—a spirit of rebellion steadily to mount in ensuing years—which nothing in the Civil Rights Acts could directly remedy.[24]

In the light of continued discontent in the South and this rioting in the North, civil rights again entered importantly into national politics and became a critical issue in the 1964 presidential campaign. The Democrats, with the full support of President Johnson, forthrightly pledged themselves to "enforcement" of the new law; the Republicans, under the leadership of Senator Goldwater, somewhat temporized by promising its "execution." While the former party was trying to maintain the support of the Negroes and civil rights advocates, the latter counted on the "white backlash" against Negro rioting to win over conservatives in both the North and South. Where Johnson emphasized in his major speeches the equal protection of the laws, Goldwater dwelt on Federal usurpation of states' rights, the futility of attempts to legislate morality, and the lawlessness of the riots. Many other factors influenced the election results, but these divergent approaches on civil rights undoubtedly helped to swell Johnson's overwhelming victory.[25]

Upon his reelection the President promptly moved to bring together and invigorate the various agencies within the Federal Government dealing with civil rights, and in early December gave to his Vice-President, former Senator Humphrey, a primary responsibility for coordinating their activities. Recognizing the weaknesses in existing legislation in respect to Negro registration in the South, Johnson also prepared new proposals on this important issue. Early in 1965 Congress began consideration of a new voting rights bill.

The passage of the 1964 Act left the Commission in something of a quandary. Its members tended to feel as Father Hesburgh

24. *Ibid.*, 8.
25. *Ibid.*, 68.

had earlier expressed it, that "we have outgrown our former role of developing facts,"[26] and while the new law gave the agency certain additional functions, their scope was far from clear. The necessary reorientation in existing programs proved to be difficult. Reporting at the monthly Commission meeting in July, 1964, Acting Staff Director Rogerson said that the staff was once again "showing signs of frustration." They reflected a feeling that the Commission was no longer "the focus of attention in the civil rights movement" and that in the current circumstances "there is not for us the publicly dramatic role as the conscience of the Nation." Rogerson urged that to compensate for any diminishing of status, the Commission should seek "a refinement, focus, and better direction."[27]

Considerable discussion of this problem took place at this and subsequent meetings very much like the earlier soul-searching in February. On one occasion Patterson proposed that the Commission undertake a full investigation of the outbreaks of violence in northern cities. Perhaps unfortunately the Commission rejected this suggestion as too broad an inquiry for it to handle with a limited staff and other extensive commitments.[28] The general consensus finally reached on future operations, with Chairman Hannah playing his customary role as moderator, was for the Commission to concentrate its energies in carrying out to the best of its abilities both the old and new functions prescribed under existing legislation.[29]

As revised plans took shape and form both members and staff grew more confident that the Commission still had a significant role. The staff worked out ways to cooperate with the Equal Employment Opportunity Commission and the Community Relations Service created by the 1964 Act; made ready to provide technical assistance to other government agencies charged with the law's implementation; and in its own phraseology, began "to structure" a Technical Information Center to enable it to carry out its new clearing-house functions.

In the latter half of 1964, either on staff initiative or in coopera-

26. Father Hesburgh to Edward Rutledge, June 14, 1963.
27. Minutes of 57th Commission meeting, July 22, 1964.
28. Minutes of 58th Commission meeting, Sept. 2, 1964.
29. Minutes of 57th and 58th Commission meetings.

tion with the State Advisory Committees, the Commission sponsored a series of regional conferences or workshops bringing together state and local officials, educators, businessmen, union officials, clergymen, and civil rights workers for general discussion of the new rights law and ways to stimulate its enforcement. Meetings were held in as varied places as Little Rock, Arkansas; Newark, New Jersey; Nashville, Tennessee; and Atlanta, Georgia. The one held in Atlanta in early August, attended by some four hundred people, revealed a new spirit of cooperation in tackling the problems of segregation. "This is the real news of Georgia," the Atlanta *Constitution* commented, "of the South, and of America these days."[30]

The most important conference took place in Washington in January, 1965. With President Johnson sending a message in which he praised the Commission for the "wisdom and foresight" of its recommendations, the meeting was attended by Vice-President Humphrey, the Secretary of Labor, the Secretary of Health, Education and Welfare, and representatives of thirty-five governmental agencies. Hundreds of delegates from civil rights organizations and other interested persons had an opportunity to ask questions and thrash out every phase of the problems created by the new law. In holding such a meeting, *Time* reported, the Commission had "discharged an immensely valuable catalytic function."[31]

The State Advisory Committees were very active throughout 1964 under the new direction of Samuel J. Simmons, who had succeeded Peter Sussmann. They staged a national conference, attended by one hundred fifty delegates, on June 26–28 for a full review and appraisal of Federal policies, and also made additional civil rights surveys which the Commission published. The Iowa committee, after meetings in Des Moines, Sioux City, and Waterloo, reported "massive racial discrimination" which was primarily due to the lack of fair housing laws and the "indifference" of municipal authorities. A survey by the Texas committee showed that while greater progress toward desegregation was reported in Texas than in any other southern state, only 2.3 percent of its Negroes attended interracial schools. A report from New York indicated discrimination in the hospitals in Buffalo and a serious shortage of Negro

30. Files of Civil Rights Commission; Atlanta *Constitution,* Aug. 15, 1964.
31. Staff Activities Reports; Commission files.

physicians in New York City. Other State Advisory Committees held informational meetings in South Carolina, Delaware, West Virginia, and Nevada.[32]

The Commission itself published in August a "Civil Rights Digest" of which more than one hundred thousand copies were distributed, and in October a "Three Months Report on Compliance and Non-Compliance with the Civil Rights Act of 1964." A number of in-depth studies on special problems led to additional publications, of which the most important was "Equal Opportunity in Farm Programs"—published on February 27, 1965.

The staff developed this Report with great care, but when submitted for final consideration at the Commission's meeting in January, it evoked the criticism that so often in the past revealed some divergence of views between the staff and the Commission members. The latter felt that the Farm Report contained too many sweeping generalizations, extreme statements, and unwarranted value judgments—it should be "toned down a bit." Chairman Hannah accepted the need for further improvement, assuaged the ruffled feelings of the staff by saying that on the whole they had done "a superb job," and ultimately succeeded in obtaining unanimous approval for a revised draft.[33]

The Report's conclusions were devastating as applied to Negro farmers in the South. Such Federal agencies as the Agricultural Extension Service, the Soil Conservation Service and the Farmers Home Administration were in almost every instance following "local patterns of racial segregation and discrimination in providing assistance paid by Federal funds." The Report produced unassailable evidence on inequities in the extension of farm loans and limitations on other forms of aid for non-white farmers based on what were described as "low expectations" of the Negro farmers' capabilities. Non-whites were excluded from policy-making positions in the local Federal agencies, subjected to segregationist practices when employed, and granted only limited access to such programs as the 4-H Clubs.

As a result of these findings, the Commission recommended that the President direct the Secretary of Agriculture to end all

32. See *Catalogue of Publications—1964*, Civil Rights Commission, Washington, Oct. 1964, 11–12.
33. Minutes of 62nd Commission meeting, Jan. 6, 1965.

discriminatory practices, encourage equal participation and equal opportunity in all farm programs, and initiate periodic reviews of what was taking place to assure full compliance with the law and with his own rulings.[34]

The immediate official response to this Report, which President Johnson wrote Hannah was "timely and constructive," was a revealing illustration of changed attitudes toward discrimination. Secretary of Agriculture Freeman, in a public statement on its release, accepted its validity; admitted that no one, except those who refused to accept facts, could deny that "there has been discrimination in the administration of the programs"; stated that a massive effort was already under way to make future operations consistent with Administration policy; and pledged himself to do everything possible to remove all remaining vestiges of discrimination. Moreover the President wrote Freeman this same day that the Commission's recommendations deserved prompt attention. "I hope I may receive within thirty days," he said in his letter, "a report on the recommendations of the Commission and the actions taken or contemplated by the Department."[35]

Secretary Freeman rendered such a report on March 26 indicating what had been done. The President responded in a further letter which recognized progress in implementing a policy of equal rights, but asked for another report on the Agriculture Department's additional steps.

The Commission continued to aid other Federal agencies in the implementation of the Civil Rights Act, tried in every way to keep the public alert to what was being done, and encouraged cooperation at the local level in promoting better racial relations. So far as the new clearing-house functions were concerned, the staff remained busy furnishing information to Federal agencies, interested civil rights groups, and other organizations or individuals seeking out their services. A series of clearing-house publications was initiated in January, 1965. They included brief popular pamphlets on such topics as civil rights under Federal programs, equal opportunity in hospitals and health facilities, and equal

34. *Equal Opportunity in Farm Programs, An Appraisal of Services Rendered by Agencies of the United States Department of Agriculture,* Washington, 1965.
35. Commission files.

opportunity in the farm program. They were designed to acquaint members of the public—and especially Negroes—with the rights and opportunities to which they were legally entitled.

These expanded operations called for further administrative reorganization, additional personnel, and a larger budget. The Commission now set up eight offices—those of Staff Director, General Counsel, Business Administration, Information, Federal Programs, Research and Publications, Field Services and Voting Investigations. So far as the budget was concerned, the Commission had been operating ever since its creation on approximately the same annual appropriation granted it originally. With a staff of approximately seventy-six, expenditures for the fiscal year 1964 amounted to $817,000. Immediately after passage of the new Civil Rights Act, President Johnson requested a supplementary appropriation of $295,000, and with personnel increased to about one hundred, total expeditures in fiscal 1965 rose to $1,147,000. The Commission then proposed, at its November, 1964 meeting, a further addition of some thirty new staff positions and a budget increase to $1,766,000—or approximately double the annual figure for its first six years.[36]

The responsibility for defending this larger budget again led to the appearance of Commission members and of the Acting Staff Director before the congressional appropriation committees. Theirs was not an easy task in persuading hostile or skeptical congressmen that the Commission needed more money. The Chairman of the House Appropriations Committee, John J. Rooney of New York, was a civil rights advocate, but a tough man to convince on money matters. At one point during his committee's hearing on March 22, 1965, this colloquy ensued:

MR. HANNAH: *As you know, while the Civil Rights Commission has been controversial from the beginning—*
MR. ROONEY: *Are you telling me?*[37]

Hannah put up a spirited defense of the Commission's past activities and future needs. What the Chairman felt most strongly

36. Minutes of 60th Commission meeting, Nov. 5, 1964; Commission files.
37. *Hearings, House Committee on Appropriations,* 89th Congress, 1st Session, Mar. 22, 1965, 854.

was that its careful and objective fact-finding had made the record of discrimination in American life incontrovertible. "If the Commission has done nothing else," he told the House Committee, "we have taken the whole matter of civil rights out of the area of contention." He felt it had done more. Citing the record, he again put forth the claim that there was nothing in the 1964 Civil Rights Act which had not originated with the Commission, and in considering the proposed new voting law, Congress was incorporating recommendations from the Commission's Reports—"pretty nearly word for word, certainly the intent." Hannah also took particular pride in pointing out that the recommendations in the 1963 Mississippi Report, for which the Commission, in his phrase, was so generally "clobbered" by the newspapers, were the basis for Title VI of the Civil Rights Act halting Federal aid for any state program practicing discrimination.[38]

The Commission did not obtain the full appropriation sought. It was cut to $1,500,000 from the $1,766,000 asked and personnel was consequently held down to some one hundred sixteen jobs. Still, the increase was ample for it to go ahead and plans were laid to seek and justify a much larger appropriation the next year.

In the meantime the Commissioners were grappling with the serious problem of appointment of a new Staff Director. Rogerson efficiently filled this difficult and important post throughout 1964, but he was anxious to return to his own legal practice. The Commission's unanimous recommendation for the job was the General Counsel, William Taylor. At a meeting with the President in July, Hannah submitted his name. Not until late February, 1965, however, did the President officially nominate him and Taylor then served as Staff Director-designate until in August the Senate finally got around to approving his appointment.

The Commission continued its usual practice of carefully reviewing all the work of the staff and its future plans. However, the topic which absorbed more time and attention than any other throughout this period was a revived project for holding the controversial Mississippi voting hearing which had been so often postponed. The Commissioners could not forget this obdurate state. They felt strongly that its continued denial of civil rights to

38. *Ibid.*, 854-55.

Negroes should be placed more authoritatively on the public record. Both Hannah and Father Hesburgh, who repeatedly suggested their desire to retire from the Commission, wanted first to see this hearing held. They were convinced it was vitally important in itself, but no doubt were also influenced by a natural reaction to the opposition of the Department of Justice. The troubles of 1963 only increased the determination of all the Commissioners to assert their independence and carry through this piece of unfinished business. A Mississippi hearing had the primary place on the Commission's agenda.

XIV. END OF THE
BEGINNING

The Civil Rights Commission finally succeeded in holding its hearing in Mississippi at the close of February, 1965. The timing proved to be very propitious. The move in favor of a new voting rights bill was gaining headway (President Johnson would submit his proposals to Congress on March 17), and the hearing's startling revelations of the denial of Negro rights in this southern state gave fresh ammunition to the advocates of the projected bill. The Commission indeed hurried its Report and recommendations in the hope of building up still further support. Whatever impact the hearing may have had was then dramatically heightened (somewhat comparable to the course of events in 1963) by a crisis in Selma, Alabama, which led to forceful police suppression of Negro demonstrations and then a Federally protected march to Montgomery on March 21–25. With President Johnson declaring that "the tide of change is running with the American Negro," the whole civil rights movement came to a new peak in this troubled Spring of 1965.

Never reconciled to Attorney General Kennedy's veto of its plans in 1963, the Commission had continued field investigations in Mississippi and clung stubbornly to the need for an open hearing which would spread on the public record the injuries suffered by the state's Negroes. The plans were gone over again and again. The Commission was determined that this time there should be no slipup. After setting a prospective date for early 1965, it decided the hearing would center on conditions in five counties in Mississippi and cover denials of the right to register, the intimidation of potential voters, and the more general problem of law enforcement.[1]

These plans met with the apparent approval of the Department of Justice, now headed by Katzenbach, and Assistant Attorney General Burke Marshall attended the Commission's October meeting. He accepted its decision to hold the hearing, stated that the timing was satisfactory, and expressed the view that the hearing might do some good. In contrast with the prevailing attitude in 1963, he agreed to make the files of the department available (with due regard to "the sensitivity" of the FBI), and said he was personally ready to testify on the dangers of vigilante activity in suppressing civil rights and threatening civil rights workers.[2]

The staff submitted a final program for the hearing in January. It experienced great difficulty in gathering the necessary evidence; in lining up prospective witnesses, especially among the moderate elements within the state; and in assuring protection against possible reprisals for those Negroes who might testify against state officials. The members of the Commission were anxious that the hearing should be so conducted as to disclose not only what might be wrong in Mississippi but also bring out such progress as might have been made in furthering civil rights. As on other occasions in the past, they were fearful that the staff might summon too many witnesses to point up the civil rights case and that the hearing would consequently appear prejudiced. The Commission wanted to hear

1. Minutes of 59th Commission meeting, Oct. 1, 1964.
2. *Ibid.*

both sides and as Griswold especially emphasized, to be in a position to make an affirmative and constructive report.

After considerable discussion and an agreement to curtail somewhat the planned testimony, the Commission unanimously approved the overall program and set definite dates for both an executive session, to hear witnesses whose testimony might defame or degrade, and for a public session. Chairman Hannah then announced that the hearing would formally begin on February 10 and every effort would be made "to obtain a balanced picture of the status of civil rights in Mississippi."[3]

Just at this point, however, the old conflict with the Department of Justice flared up again. In spite of everything Marshall had said, Attorney General Katzenbach asked for the hearing's postponement quite as peremptorily as had Attorney General Kennedy two years earlier. The Department of Justice was involved in the proceedings against the Mississippians who were under indictment for the murder of the three civil rights workers killed the previous summer, and Katzenbach insisted that the intervention of the Civil Rights Commission in Mississippi's affairs at this juncture might prejudice prosecution of the case against the accused slayers. In these circumstances, he said, a civil rights hearing in Mississippi was impossible and he would take full responsibility for its postponement.[4]

At his own request the Attorney General appeared personally at the Commission's next meeting on January 28 to plead his case. He maintained that whether the hearing was held before or at the time of the possible murder trial, it would be "equally bad." At a tense session, during which the coals of earlier disputes were raked over somewhat acrimoniously, the Commission members stubbornly resisted the Attorney General's arguments. Hannah expressed deep concern over any further postponement. Father Hesburgh said that the Department of Justice's fears of the Commission hampering its own work had not been justified on other occasions. Griswold emphasized his conviction that the proposed hearing was more important than the trial. As a spokesman for

3. Minutes of 62nd Commission meeting, Jan. 7, 1965; news release, Jan. 7, 1965.
4. The indictment was in fact dismissed by the Federal District Judge on Feb. 25, 1965, *New York Times,* Feb. 26, 1965.

the South, Patterson stated his agreement with these views, adding that he hoped the hearing would be helpful in making known such progress as Mississippi might have achieved.

After Katzenbach left the meeting the Commissioners continued the discussion and some concern was expressed over future relations with the Department of Justice should they refuse to heed the Attorney General's advice. However, both Acting Director Rogerson and General Counsel Taylor (the latter's promotion was still in the offing) agreed that cooperation had never been really satisfactory and quoted Katzenbach as having once said the Commission should be abolished. They expressed their firm conviction that there was no alternative to risking the Department's displeasure and going ahead. The Commission then unanimously decided to hold the hearing.[5]

After the preliminary executive session at which a number of persons appeared for private testimony, the public hearing opened in Jackson on February 16 and during the next five days the Commission heard some thirty subpoenaed witnesses, including Negro protestants and state officials. The atmosphere was quite different from that which prevailed at the original voting hearings in Alabama and Louisiana. Governor Johnson, who had already urged the Mississippi officials summoned to the hearing to answer all questions and "tell the true story," made a surprise visit on the first day. While the state's Attorney General, Joseph Patterson, did not attend personally, he offered his assistance to the Commission's field agents. Mayor Thompson of Jackson made an opening statement extending "to you people one of the most cordial welcomes you have ever had anywhere." He could not be more anxious, he said, than "to give you the facts as they really exist."[6]

The Governor, described by the press as being in an "amiable mood," was unexpectedly conciliatory. He said that while most Mississippians did not like the civil rights law, any resistance to its provisions would be confined to accepted legal processes. Mississippi would continue, in his words, "to be the most law-abiding state in the nation." He expressed his confidence that the Commission would be "a real fact-finding committee" and that its report would

5. Minutes of 63rd Commission meeting, Jan. 28, 1965.
6. *Hearings Before the Commission on Civil Rights,* Vol. 1, *Voting, Jackson, Mississippi, Feb. 16–20, 1965,* Washington, 1965, 9.

bear out his own statements on Mississippi's commitment to law and order. There had been mistakes; there was now a new outlook.

"What we need from our fellow Americans," Johnson said, "is good will, encouragement, understanding, and assistance. Having accepted the will of the Nation's majority, Mississippi now asks those who have criticized our former position and actions to get off our back and to get on our side."[7]

The Commission members welcomed this new cooperative spirit as a happy augury for the future; later Negro witnesses were somewhat more skeptical. Among them were Charles Evers, the brother of the murdered civil rights leader Medgar Evers, and Aaron E. Henry, another leading NAACP official. Their testimony largely dealt with the voting registration campaign they had launched and the reprisals to which hopeful Negro voters were subjected—threats, the burning or bombing of homes and churches, beatings, and shootings. They submitted a list of fifty-five such incidents, stressed the complete failure of the 1964 Civil Rights Act to remedy things in any way, and cited the need for protection against violence and intimidation if the Negroes of Mississippi were ever to gain the right to vote.

They were singularly unimpressed by Governor Johnson's new conciliatory attitude. Mississippi was "now in a show case," and whatever his real feelings, the Governor could hardly have said anything else. "I am not at all convinced," Henry declared in a statement with which Evers promptly expressed his full agreement, "that this great change of heart he is now expressing is a genuine change. You wait until the Commission goes back to Washington."[8]

Referring again to the Governor's position somewhat later, Evers said the test of his sincerity was his attitude on voting registration. Until Johnson publicly declared that "every person in this state has a right to register and vote," Evers commented, "then, until then, the thing that he says falls on deaf ears." Henry fully agreed and gave still greater emphasis to the importance of the voting issue. "Give us a Federal registrar bill in 1965," he said, "and the Civil Rights Commission won't have to worry about Mississippi no more. We can handle it ourselves, then."[9]

7. *Ibid.*, 5–8.
8. *Ibid.*, 153ff., 160.
9. *Ibid.*, 175. Evers cited Jefferson County as one in which no Negroes at all

Evers' testimony was perhaps the most important at the hearing as he went on to develop the thesis that all that the Negroes in Mississippi wanted were their constitutional rights, and that they had no idea of changing white supremacy into black supremacy. He stated emphatically that "we aren't going to settle for anything less than equal opportunity," but he was equally forthright in declaring that there should be no racial conflict. "It is a matter of Negroes and whites together," Evers said at one point. "They must work together and live together, and no one is superior."[10]

The testimony of most of the other Negro witnesses described the obstructions, comparable to those in Alabama and Louisiana, that local registrars placed in the way of non-white voting applicants. The Commissioners heard a familiar story of delays, prejudiced administration of literacy tests, and discriminatory rejection of the Negro applicants' interpretation of constitutional clauses. At one point Commissioner Griswold asked a local registrar about his own understanding of a special clause in the Mississippi constitution. On the latter's refusal to answer, the following exchange took place:

COMMISSIONER GRISWOLD: *You decline to interpret Sec. 182?*
MR. HOOD: *On pressure being put on me before a committee like this.*
COMMISSIONER GRISWOLD: *On the ground it may incriminate you?*
MR. HOOD: *That's right.*[11]

In addition to the literacy tests, another discriminatory device employed by local officials was not to collect from Negroes, and in some instances outrightly refuse to accept the poll tax which Mississippi had enforced as a prerequisite for voting ever since 1890. When Mrs. Freeman asked one witness about the collection of this tax, he answered:

---

were registered. A year later, according to an article in the *Reporter*, their registration rocketed to 3,500, outnumbering that of whites. "Charles Evers, it is generally agreed in Fayette," this article stated, "has absolute control of the Negro vote in Jefferson County and is now in a position to secure every elective office in the county for the men of his choice." Henry Hurt, "Boycott and Ballot," *Reporter*, Aug. 11, 1966.

10. *Hearings*, 162–63, 169.
11. *Ibid.*, 78.

Well, they will ask every white person that comes in there, and every Negro they won't say a word. I was in there paying my taxes in February, and every white person come in there, white women especially, they asked about paying the tax. When I paid my tax, they handed me just my tax receipt and didn't ask for a poll tax.[12]

The result, of course, was that when such a Negro tried to vote, he was disqualified.

The Negro witnesses told many moving stories of their fruitless attempts to register. Mrs. Unita Zelma Blackwell, a housewife from Issaquena County with an eighth grade education, was one applicant who felt herself threatened for even trying to register and knew well she would always be rejected. "And you just get to the place and you know it's going to happen," she testified, "but you've just got to stand up and got to do something."[13]

Another witness, Clarence Hall, Jr., a farmer and war veteran, vividly described his concern over trying to register and his efforts to persuade other Negroes to do so:

And I tell them, without they go down there and vote, they cannot be represented. . . .
And I told them the Government will not call us monkeys, coon, and things. When the man who's running for office holler the loudest word 'nigger,' he won't get elected if we can vote like every other citizen.[14]

A second war veteran, with two battle stars, was from Tallahatchie County where eighty-seven percent of the eligible white voters were registered and only .26 percent of the eligible Negroes. He testified on the difference between the way he was treated in the Army and the discrimination to which he was subjected in Mississippi:

I had freedom to speak so long as I was in the Army. But, after I got out and got back here, my freedom run out. I didn't have freedom to speak any more after I got discharged.[15]

Even more than in Alabama or Louisiana, those Negroes who tried to register in Mississippi were subject to threats and reprisals.

12. *Ibid.*, 100.
13. *Ibid.*, 32.
14. *Ibid.*, 35.
15. *Ibid.*, 134.

Several told of how when they went to the courthouse, cars or pick-up trucks with armed white men circled the adjacent streets. One witness described how these men shouted, "You niggers get away from the courthouse. You don't have any business here." Another, a woman, told of how on returning home after trying to register, five white men drove up to her house in a car and left a placarded notice:

> *Thousands of Klansmen*
> Watching . . . . Waiting!
> KU KLUX KLAN
> *Don't be Misled?*
> *Let Your Conscience Guide You?*[16]

The situation was briefly summed up in this pointed exchange between the Staff Director and a witness who succeeded in registering but had not actually voted:

Why haven't you tried to vote?
Fear.[17]

As the hearing moved on to consider general law enforcement, other reports were given of Negroes being brutally mistreated by whites, sometimes by the police themselves. A number of witnesses —all of them under oath—told of being stripped and beaten, given castor oil, sometimes shot at. Rarely were the victims of such attacks able to obtain any redress: there were no arrests even when their white assailants could be identified.

One story with unusual undertones was that of Professor Mirza Hamid Kizilbash, a Pakistani teacher at Tougaloo College. He was with a group of Negroes driving to a civil rights meeting, when a car filled with white men forced the Negroes off the road and began beating them up. On discovering that Kizilbash was not an American citizen they left him alone. In his testimony before the Commission, the Pakistani stated that his being saved from possible murder because he was a foreigner rather than an American Negro was "the greatest irony of my existence here."[18]

16. *Ibid.,* 132, 150.
17. *Ibid.,* 141.
18. *Ibid., Vol. II, Law Enforcement,* 222–31.

A great deal of testimony was presented relating to bombings and assaults which in 1964 had led to a virtual reign of terror in McComb, Pike County. At one time ten white men, arrested following discovery of a cache of arms, acknowledged they were members of an organization called South Pike's Riflemen's Association, an undercover klavern of the Ku Klux Klan. Even though they admitted they met weekly to carry out bombing raids and were indicted for conspiracy in the unlawful use of explosives, they were never brought to trial.[19]

The hearing drew to a close with a number of panel discussions among attorneys, businessmen, and clergymen. They let in a little light on what was otherwise such a somber and depressing picture of intimidation and violence. The discussants agreed that at least some signs of a changing attitude were evident in Mississippi and that in scattered instances the authorities arrested and prosecuted whites accused of attacking Negroes. One report from Greenville in Washington County ("a breath of fresh air," Hannah commented) indicated considerable progress in allaying racial unrest in that area. Other testimony suggested that an increasing number of whites were sincerely anxious to see Mississippi "in the main stream of American life and not in backwater."[20] But while such persons recognized the need to establish communications between the white power structure and the Negro community, they faced a dilemma which was aptly characterized in the earlier testimony of Charles Evers. "These white people who want to speak out," he said, "have no umbrella of support under which to stand."[21]

The most promising development, suggesting that with time such an umbrella might become available, was evidence from various sources that the business community was beginning to feel that existing conditions had to be remedied because of their very adverse effect on Mississippi's economy. Racial tensions as exacerbated by Negro demonstrations and white counterattacks, was, in easily understood terms, bad for business. The Civil Rights Commission found some hope ("encouraging signs of change," as Chairman Hannah phrased it) in this testimony. Nevertheless, the immediate and vital problem still remained of persistent and unrelenting opposition, especially in rural Mississippi and those

19. *Ibid., Vol. II,* 30, 54.
20. *Ibid., Vol. II,* 3–4.
21. *Hearings, Vol. I,* 166.

counties where whites were in a minority, to the Negroes' exercise of their fundamental right to register and vote.[22]

The Mississippi hearing had wide coverage in the nation's newspapers; it generally evoked favorable editorial comment on its thoroughness and objectivity. William Taylor, now Staff Director-designate, reported a better press than for any previous hearing. Among other significant comments, Vice-President Humphrey congratulated Hannah on what he termed the hearing's "success." The Commission decided to submit as soon as possible a full report, with specific recommendations.[23]

After the customary staff work, suggestions and revisions, and a final discussion, the Commission unanimously approved such a Report and it was published on May 18 under the title "Voting in Mississippi."[24] It outlined the state's voting background, discussed the literacy tests and the impact of poll taxes, related the consequences of white intimidation and reprisals directed against those Negroes who tried to register, and described current campaigns, both public and private, to increase registration. In summary, it declared that ever since 1875 Negroes had been systematically excluded from the polls by legislative enactment, fraud, and violence. As a consequence, Mississippi enjoyed the worst voting record of any state in the South—no more than seven percent of its Negroes of voting age were actually registered.

In going further into the existing situation as so vividly brought out in the Jackson hearing, the Report strongly emphasized the virtually insuperable obstacles the Department of Justice faced in trying to enforce the voting provisions of existing civil rights legislation. "The history of this litigation," it said in reference to one case Justice carried to the courts, "reveals that the failure of the District Court Judge to rule upon Government applications, the need for repeated appeals, and the recalcitrance of the registrars have frustrated effective relief." No real improvement resulted from the new voting guarantees of the Civil Rights Act of 1964.

To remedy this state of affairs, the Commission wholeheartedly

22. Haynes Johnson, "Money and Mississippi," the *Progressive*, May, 1965.
23. Minutes of 65th Commission meeting, March 18, 1965; Vice-President Humphrey to John A. Hannah, Feb. 26, 1965, in Hannah files.
24. *Voting in Mississippi, A Report of the United States Commission on Civil Rights, 1965*. Washington, 1965.

and unanimously endorsed the voting rights bill currently being debated in Congress with its provision for the appointment of Federal registrars in any area where there was a pattern of discrimination. The Commissioners believed, however, that the bill should be still further strengthened. They recommended the complete elimination of all literacy tests, whether written or oral, on the ground that there was no possible way to be assured they would be fairly administered. They further proposed that in areas where Federal registrars were appointed, all prospective voters should be free to seek registration with them without prior recourse to the state registration process; urged the abolition of all poll taxes; and called for the appointment of Federal poll watchers to supervise elections. The Commission also suggested the exploration of means whereby an affirmative Federal program might be developed to encourage all eligible persons to register and vote in all elections.[25]

Before the submission of this Report but a month after the hearing at Jackson, a mounting crisis in Selma, Alabama, came to a head and dramatized even more than the hearing, or anything else the Civil Rights Commission could possibly do, the obstacles southern Negroes faced in seeking to win acceptance of their rights. Martin Luther King, Jr. had chosen this city as the focal point for a voting registration drive by his Southern Christian Leadership Conference, and on March 7, 1965, he initiated a march to Montgomery to arouse the conscience of the state—and the nation—over the continued denial of the Negroes' right to vote. On the orders of Governor Wallace, state troopers using tear gas, night sticks, and whips forcibly broke up this non-violent demonstration.

President Johnson promptly deplored the brutality of the police, which led to serious injuries to forty persons; and after complicated legal maneuvers, Federal District Judge Johnson issued an injunction against further interference with the proposed trek to Montgomery. Hundreds of Negroes and white sympathizers in the meantime gathered in Selma, including such prominent figures as Ralph Bunche and the veteran labor leader, A. Philip Randolph, and on March 21, Dr. King started a new "freedom march" on the Alabama capitol.

The demonstrators were now protected by some three thousand

25. *Ibid.*, 59–63.

Federalized National Guardsmen and regular troops. With their number varying day by day from several hundred to a thousand or more, they trudged the fifty miles to Montgomery, at night pitching their tents or sleeping on the open ground, sometimes in the pouring rain. All the world watched their progress over television or read of it in the newspapers. No further violence occurred. After five days Dr. King led an estimated crowd of thirty thousand to the steps of the capitol in Montgomery.

"We are not about to turn around," Dr. King told his immense audience. "We are on the move now. Yes, we are on the move, and no wave of racism can stop us."

Perhaps no other demonstration aroused the country as did the Selma march. It was in support of an unquestioned constitutional right—the right to vote. It was orderly and peaceful. A number of southern newspapers, as well as those throughout the North, recognized its importance. The Atlanta *Constitution* described it as "a great catalyst. . . . We can be thankful for the great outpouring at Selma."[26]

It was on March 15, as the Negro leaders were making ready to resume their march on Montgomery, that in a televised address before a joint session of Congress, President Johnson first called for the new voting legislation embodying the recommendations of the Civil Rights Commission and the current demands of Negroes in both Mississippi and Alabama. He recognized the inability of existing laws to protect voting rights; he accepted the need for prompt action to make good constitutional guarantees that were not being enforced. "The time for waiting," the President declared, "is gone. . . . For outside this chamber is the outraged conscience of a nation—the grave concern of many nations—and the harsh judgment of history on our acts." Two days later he submitted the text of his proposed bill. Its purpose, he said, was to "strike down restrictions to voting in all elections—Federal, state and local—which have been used to deny Negroes the right to vote."[27]

The heart of what was to become the Voting Rights Act of 1965 was the appointment of Federal registrars—or what were

26. *Revolution in Civil Rights,* 84; *New York Times,* March 14, 21, 28, 1965.
27. *New York Times,* March 16, 18, 1965.

now called Federal examiners—to combat discrimination in the registration of southern Negroes. Wherever the Attorney General found that literacy tests were in effect and that less than fifty percent of the population of voting age were registered or had voted in the 1964 election, and so certified to the Civil Service Commission, the latter agency would appoint Federal examiners to handle all voting registration. On the basis of existing statistics, this provision of the bill would apply to six southern states: Mississippi, South Carolina, Alabama, Georgia, Louisiana, and Virginia; to Alaska, which represented a very special case; to thirty-four counties in North Carolina; and to a few scattered districts in some other states. This was a tough and realistic bill. Its purpose was to circumvent the laborious processes of litigation by authorizing direct executive action in securing the right to vote. In the words of one commentator, it was "an end run around the judicial process."[28]

The law was in the making more than five months. However, the final result of the seemingly interminable hearings, political maneuvering, and congressional debate, following the pattern of all civil rights legislation, was to strengthen rather than weaken the Administration's original draft. At one point Representative Lindsay of New York (the future Mayor) proposed making the Civil Rights Commission, whose life he would have extended for ten years, the agency to certify the patterns of discrimination which would lead to the appointment of the Federal examiners. This move was defeated. Congress did, however, accept the Commission's recommendations in respect to sanctions against anyone interfering with persons seeking to vote, the appointment of Federal poll watchers, and, on the poll tax issue, declared that since such taxes were used to abridge the right to vote, the Attorney General should initiate immediate suits to determine their constitutionality. Congress also added a provision, affecting particularly Puerto Ricans in New York, making a sixth grade education in a foreign language, not only in English as stipulated in the 1964 Civil Rights Act, substantive proof of literacy.[29]

The Senate started formal debate on April 13 and passed its bill six weeks later; the House acted favorably on a somewhat different measure on July 9. After the necessary Senate-House conference, both branches of Congress approved a final version of the bill early

28. *Revolution in Civil Rights*, 84–87; *New Republic*, April 3, 1965.
29. *Public Law, 85–315.*

in August. The vote in the Senate was 79 to 18 and that in the House 328 to 74—once again approximately the same divisions as in every previous civil rights law. President Johnson signed the bill on August 6.[30]

While the Civil Rights Commission did not directly participate in drawing up the Voting Rights Act of 1965, Father Hesburgh testified extensively in its support before a subcommittee of the House Judiciary Committee. He stressed in his testimony the lack of any real progress in guaranteeing the right to vote through previous legislation. Declaring that on no other issue had there been such complete agreement within the Civil Rights Commission, he expressed its members' strong conviction that action could no longer be delayed. "For the past six years," he told the House committee, "we have recommended such legislation. We have done so in the belief that nothing less will suffice to root out the evil of discrimination in voting."[31]

Direct evidence of the Commission's influence in the course of the congressional debates is found in a statement by Senator Edward Kennedy. "You may be assured," he wrote Hannah, "that your assistance in this matter was of real significance in our attempts to strengthen the bill."[32]

Some three months after passage of the Voting Rights Act, the Commission drew up a report seeking to analyze the immediate effects. It found that in many areas of the South the new law was meeting with full compliance, and that its administration by the Civil Service Commission was "imaginatively planned, vigorously executed, and closely supervised." However, the Commission reported that in the opinion of staff investigators, the Attorney General was moving very slowly in assigning Federal examiners. The Department of Justice was gradually broadening its policy, but it had at first designated for Federal intervention only such counties where there had been flagrant violations of the right to vote and ignored those where discrimination was less overt but nonetheless real.[33]

Attorney General Katzenbach promptly answered what the

---

30. *The Voting Rights Act . . . the first months,* United States Commission on Civil Rights, 1965, Washington, 1965.
31. Files of Civil Rights Commission.
32. Senator Edward Kennedy to Hannah, May 15, 1965, in Hannah files.
33. *The Voting Rights Act . . . the first months,* 3, 40, 44–46.

New York Times described as this "biting criticism" in a strong statement defending the policies of his Department and denying the validity of the report's charges that it had been moving too slowly. All of the old antagonisms between the Commission and Justice were revived. When Staff Director Taylor tried to reassure Katzenbach that the Commission had no intention of attacking his department, the Attorney General was not appeased. An always touchy problem was not resolved but only pushed into the background when on December 20 Katzenbach wrote Taylor that he felt it would not serve "any constructive purpose to pursue these matters."[34]

Apart from such immediate and controversial questions, the Report pointed out that what was presently being done constituted only the first steps in a long continuing process and that the real test of the new law lay in the future. To assure full success, the Commission recommended the appointment of Federal examiners in all political subdivisions covered by the law, rather than just those practicing demonstrable discrimination; once again urged an information program to acquaint Negroes with their rights and to encourage them to register; and called for adequate preparations to assure the law's strict enforcement during the elections of 1966.[35]

The next year demonstrated the value of the Voting Rights Act far beyond immediate results in the first few months after passage. The growth in Negro registration throughout the South, the role of these new voters in both the primaries and the elections, and the consequent changes in the attitudes of white politicians all presaged a revolution, albeit a gradual one, in southern politics.

The Mississippi hearing, with its close relationship to passage of the Voting Rights Act, was the most conspicuous activity of the Civil Rights Commission during 1965. It was engaged on other fronts as well. The staff, as well as the State Advisory Committees, continued investigations and surveys along the general lines mapped out when the Commission was initially set up in 1958. New studies ranged from an examination of segregation in northern urban areas, involving a public hearing the next year in Cleve-

34. *New York Times*, Dec. 5, 1965; Katzenbach to Taylor, Dec. 20, 1965, in Hannah files; Minutes of 72nd Commission meeting, Jan. 6, 1966.
35. *The Voting Rights Act ... the first months*, 4.

land, to an inconclusive investigation of civil rights among Spanish-speaking people of the Southwest. With the expansion of the clearing-house functions assigned the Commission in the Civil Rights Act of 1964, the staff closely cooperated with some twenty-five Federal agencies and helped them to establish non-discriminatory guide lines. It also disseminated information to any number of state agencies and private groups engaged in civil rights activities.[36]

The most important report of the year, other than that on Mississippi voting, grew out of the hearing at Jackson as supplemented by staff investigations in Alabama, Georgia and Florida.[37] Titled "Law Enforcement—A Report on Equal Protection in the South," it brought together a great mass of material on the failure of both Federal and state authorities to solve incidents of racial violence and effectively to prosecute whites charged with crimes against Negroes. The Report examined state and local law enforcement, the availability of Federal remedies when local action was ineffective, and the general policies of the Department of Justice.

The Commission's findings, as published on November 4, 1965, were highly critical of state authorities, whose attitude appeared to be based on a continuing hostility to the Negroes' attempted assertion of their rights, and also of Federal law officers. While recognizing the inadequacies of existing legislation, which seriously hampered prosecutions by the Department of Justice, the Commission maintained that the sources of presidential power were broad enough to provide more Federal protection against violence than was currently being given. By limiting the use of force to cases covered by a Federal court order, the possibilities of forestalling racial violence remained very limited.

To meet this need, the Commission recommended not only stronger criminal and civil remedies but more forthright executive action in providing equal protection of the laws. It asked for legislation making any interference with the activities of persons engaged in safeguarding their civil rights a Federal crime and for prosecution in cases of racial violence whenever local officials failed to act. It called for increasing the authority of the Attorney Gen-

36. Minutes of Commission meetings; Staff Activities Reports.
37. *Law Enforcement—A Report on Equal Protection in the South, United States Commission on Civil Rights, 1965,* Washington, 1965.

eral to intervene in other cases and to protect persons subject to state prosecutions for exercising their First Amendment rights of free speech and free assembly. Finally, the Commission recommended that the President direct the Attorney General to station Federal law enforcement officers at places of likely racial violence and authorize them to make on-the-scene arrests for any violation of Federal law.[38]

Congressional and newspaper reactions to this Report were generally approving. However, its scarcely veiled criticism of the failure of the Department of Justice to act more vigorously—as in the voting report—inevitably aroused the ire of the Attorney General. Even though the Commission members "muted" the treatment of this issue as included in a first draft of the Report, Katzenbach was unhappy.[39]

Two further reports prepared in 1965 and submitted to the President and Congress in the following February may be noted. With special reference to possible sanctions under Title VI of the Civil Rights Act of 1964, the first was a survey of desegregation in health and welfare services in the South, and the second still another study of school desegregation in southern and border states.[40]

The findings in the health and welfare report indicated that while agreements to do away with discrimination were supposedly operative in most Federally assisted programs, widespread segregation still existed in practice. The Department of Health, Education and Welfare had issued the appropriate regulations, but not taken the necessary steps for their enforcement. Negroes were still assigned to separate rooms or wards in southern hospitals, discrimination continued in many local health programs, and a majority of the children in Operation Head Start were enrolled in segregated schools.

The Commission recommended as a result of these findings

38. *Ibid.*, 177–81.
39. Minutes of 69th Commission meeting, Oct. 7, 1965; 70th Commission meeting, Nov. 4, 1965.
40. *Title VI . . . one year after: a survey of desegregation of health and welfare services in the South,* United States Commission on Civil Rights, 1966, Washington, 1966; *Survey of School Desegregation in the Southern and Border States, 1965–66,* A Report of the United States Commission on Civil Rights, February 1966, Washington, 1966.

the immediate application of sanctions under Title VI wherever negotiations failed to correct violations of the law, and further studies to determine the extent to which discrimination still existed.[41]

The educational survey showed that some progress was being made in school desegregation, but the most reliable estimates still indicated that only one Negro child out of every thirteen in the southern and border states was as yet attending school with white children. The tortoise-like pace of integration was primarily attributed to the operation of freedom of choice plans. White students rarely elected to attend Negro schools, and Negro students remained almost equally reluctant to transfer to white schools. The Report revealed that in some areas where Negro students elected to transfer, they and their parents were still subjected to retaliatory threats, intimidation, and violence.

The Commission made a long series of rather inclusive recommendations to speed up the processes of school integration. It called upon the Office of Education to reevaluate its policies, make clear that other ways of encouraging integration than freedom of choice were available, and require school districts desegregating under court order not only to file acceptable plans but also publicize them. On a more specific issue, it asked for new legislation authorizing the Attorney General to enjoin private persons from harassing or intimidating Negro parents or children seeking to exercise their rights under approved desegregation plans.[42]

The Commission members were not very happy over this Report as originally drawn up by the staff. They considered it vague and inconclusive, not wholly fair to the South, and too limited to be of great significance. They finally accepted it, but in critical accompanying statements Hesburgh and Patterson made their doubts very explicit. Both men agreed that shifting students about from one school to another could not really solve the long-term problem, and emphasized the need for improvement in all schools, together with the upgrading of teachers regardless of race. Father Hesburgh stressed the importance, within a context of equal opportunity, of "better teachers, better facilities, better educational

41. *Title VI* . . . 45–47.
42. *Survey of School Desegregation,* 53–61.

programs, for all Americans, North and South, white and Negro."
In the same vein, Patterson said he did not think "social tensions
will be relieved until we improve the bad schools, not simply regulate them." He concluded that the Commission survey merely
touched on the "legal periphery of a vast substantive field."[43]

With its activities, especially the clearing-house functions,
greatly expanded, the Commission was once again hard put in persuading Congress to grant the necessary funds. Its traditional foe,
Senator McClellan, questioned the value of the new operations,
brought up the Commission's strained relations with the Department of Justice, and as he had so often in the past, concluded that
there was no need for the Commission at all. Nevertheless, additional funds were eventually obtained. Early in 1966 the Commission received a budget allowance for the next fiscal year of
$2,703,000, with 156 staff positions.[44]

No changes occurred in the Commission membership or in its
major staff personnel during 1965. In spite of repeated suggestions
that they were about to resign, both Chairman Hannah and Father
Hesburgh continued in office—the only survivors of the group
originally appointed by President Eisenhower. The remaining four
members—Griswold, Rankin, Mrs. Freeman and Patterson—gave
no indication of giving up their posts. Sometimes compelled to
resort to telephone "conference calls" to supplement the monthly
meetings, all six were always ready to give a high priority to Commission affairs in spite of their many other responsibilities.

The real burden of conducting general operations still lay on
the shoulders of the Staff Director. Whatever the Commission
might do, Griswold wrote Taylor in late August, 1965, as the Senate finally got around to confirming the appointment President
Johnson had made on February 26, "most of the ideas, and most
of the motive power are going to have to come from or through the
Staff Director."[45] Taylor remained responsible not only for handling current business, but for developing new programs.

The usual question arose as the summer drew to an end as to

43. *Ibid.*, 63–65. See also minutes of 72nd Commission meeting, Jan. 6, 1966.
44. *Departments of State, Justice, and Commerce, the Judiciary and Related Agencies Appropriations, 1966*, 721–45; minutes of 70th Commission meeting, Nov. 4, 1965; and 72nd Commission meeting, Jan. 6, 1966.
45. Erwin N. Griswold to William L. Taylor, Aug. 25, 1965, in Hannah files.

what such future programs might be over and beyond those on which the staff was already engaged. The Commissioners asked at their September meeting whether the results of current activities were wholly commensurate with an expanding budget.[46] Even as such doubts and misgivings were being expressed, however, a reorganization of the whole civil rights program of the Federal Government helped to mark out the path the Commission might be expected to follow.

In a report to President Johnson in late September, Vice-President Humphrey stated that compliance with the terms of the Civil Rights Act of 1964 "exceeded all expectations," and that implementation of the Voting Rights Act held out every promise of providing the Negro in southern states the opportunity to register and vote. In these circumstances he suggested that the continuing problem for the Federal Government was in the field of more effective enforcement of existing legislation rather than new laws (except possibly in the administration of justice), and that this seemed to call for a new centralization of authority over civil rights matters in the Department of Justice.

The President thereupon abolished by executive order the President's Council on Equal Economic Opportunity, transferring its responsibilities to the Attorney General, and also removed the Community Relations Service from the Commerce Department to the Department of Justice. He supplemented these moves by instructions calling for mutual assistance and cooperation on the part of all other Government departments or agencies in combating any laxity in upholding the compliance provisions of Title VI under the 1964 Act.[47]

The Commission on Civil Rights retained its special and distinct status as a wholly independent agency in this reorganization. Its functions were somewhat enlarged by the transfer from the Community Relations Service of such clearing-house or data collecting activities as the latter agency had undertaken, but no significant change was made in its overall responsibilities. Some two months later, however, the President assigned it a new task. He asked the Commission to make a new intensive survey of "the prob-

46. Minutes of 68th Commission meeting, Sept. 8, 1965.
47. *Weekly Compilation of Presidential Documents,* Sept. 27, 1965, 305–10.

lem of race and education" throughout the entire country. It was to carry this out as rapidly as possible with the underlying purpose, as phrased by the President, of developing "a firm foundation on which local and state governments can build a school system that is color blind."[48]

In some ways this new task no more than supplemented work on which the Commission had been engaged ever since it was first established. It was another investigation. The proposed survey's scope, however, was broader than anything yet undertaken. It held out the possibility of delving much deeper into the whole educational problem than the limited study of desegregation in the South on which the Commission was about to report. Going far beyond the usual appraisal of Federal policies, what was now called for was a really comprehensive study of racial isolation in the nation's schools —North and South—as it might affect the whole broad field of public education.

The Commission accepted this new assignment. Terming it "a great challenge," Staff Director Taylor promptly began to make the necessary plans. Chairman Hannah declared that it was "perhaps the most important assignment this Commission has ever undertaken."[49]

Wholly apart from Commission affairs, something further was happening to the Negro Revolution and the civil rights movement in the late summer of 1965. The demonstrations of southern Negroes, where disorder resulted from white attacks upon such nonviolent protests as sit-ins, freedom rides, and peaceful marches, were more and more giving way to the riots in northern cities in which frustrated Negroes assailed the police, broke into stores, burned and looted with unrestrained violence. But while there was a sharp contrast in this shift of protest from the South to the North, the basic causes underlying the non-violent demonstrations and the unrestrained rioting were very much the same. Negroes long denied equality were in both cases demanding respect for their rights. Those in the South were most concerned with voting, segregated schools, and discrimination in public accommodations; those in

48. *New York Times,* Nov. 17, 18, 1965.
49. Minutes of 71st Commission meeting, Dec. 2, 1965; Hannah to President Johnson, Dec. 9, 1965, in Hannah files.

the North were rebelling against slum conditions, poor schools, and lack of economic opportunity in the black ghettos.

The forewarnings of trouble in the North had long been apparent. Even though its mandate led to a considerable concentration of its energies in investigating the denial of equal protection of the laws in the South, the Civil Rights Commission, as has been shown, had since 1958 been calling for concrete action to meet the problems of the northern cities. It held its housing hearings in New York, Chicago, and Washington; conducted general civil rights hearings in Los Angeles, San Francisco, Detroit, and other northern and western cities. It repeatedly emphasized in its reports the inherent danger of violence in the overcrowded, unsanitary, crime-breeding slums where so many Negroes found themselves helpless and hopeless in trying to better their conditions. It early declared that segregated housing in the North, with its concomitants of segregated education and segregated social life, were at the very frontier of the struggle for equality. Except, however, for President Kennedy's rather belated Executive Order seeking to eliminate discrimination in Federally assisted housing, virtually nothing had been done. The plight of northern Negroes remained unrelieved by the civil rights legislation from 1957 through 1965.

What most dramatically brought this home to a still apathetic nation, in spite of the earlier outbreaks in northern cities, was the devastating riot in the Watts section of Los Angeles during mid-August, 1965. Serious portents of possible violence in Los Angeles were on record. The testimony of witnesses at the hearing of the Commission five years earlier told of the breakdown in communications between a restive Negro community and the Los Angeles officials. The State Advisory Committee in California subsequently reported that racial tensions were dangerously increasing. However, both Mayor Yorty and Police Chief Parker discounted such warnings; they agreed that there was no real problem.

The Watts riot grew out of the arrest of a Negro charged with drunken driving. A crowd promptly gathered and began to throw rocks at the police. It quickly grew until a mob of several thousand was on the rampage, stoning and overturning cars and buses, smashing windows, breaking into stores, starting fires, and indiscriminately looting. With the outnumbered police unable to maintain order, the rioting Negroes took control of a 150-block area, shouting "Burn, Baby, Burn" and greeting the appearance of any white man with cries of "Here comes Whitey! Get him!" Mayor Yorty called for state aid and only after a force of twelve thousand guardsmen was assembled, together with some twenty-five hundred city police, highway patrolmen, and sheriff deputies, was anything like order restored. During five days of insensate rioting—August 11–16—thirty-four persons were killed, one thousand injured, and nearly four thousand arrested. With whole city blocks burned out, the total damage was estimated at forty million dollars. Watts was the worst racial outbreak the country had as yet ever known.[50]

Whatever the catalytic incident or the role played by irresponsible teen-agers and hoodlums in the looting and destruction of property, the basic cause for the outbreak in Watts, as in the case of earlier and subsequent rioting in northern cities, was the sense of frustration among Negroes in the urban ghettos. Watts stood as a symbol of a new phase of the Negro Revolution. It was marked by a militancy which soon eclipsed the non-violence that had heretofore characterized Negro protest and kept the civil rights movement within peaceful bounds. With the leaders of the more assertive Negro organizations raising the emotion-packed cry of Black Power, justified as it might be as an expression of self-respect and independence, racial conflict was greatly intensified.

The answer, if there were an answer, lay far beyond civil rights legislation going no further than to provide legal safeguards for equal protection of the laws. President Johnson realized this. In a notable speech at Howard University on June 4, 1965, he declared that the nation had reached only "the end of the beginning." He insisted upon additional efforts to meet the needs of the great majority of Negro Americans—"the poor, the unemployed, the uprooted and the dispossessed." With the walls rising and the gulf widening between this "other nation" and the rest of American society, the President called for a more far-reaching approach to the "seamless web" of problems that the country faced in seeking to overcome inequality in American life. "We seek not just freedom," he said, "but opportunity."[51]

50. *New York Times,* Aug. 12–17, 1965.
51. *Ibid.,* June 5, 1965.

This surely involved a vast program promoting urban renewal and creating new jobs—the expenditure of billions of dollars—as the only way to combat what was the crisis of the cities rather than simply an issue of civil rights. Nothing less could assure those presently condemned to live in the black ghettos the equality in housing, in education, and in economic opportunity which alone could assuage their frustrations, their discontent, and their spirit of rebellion.

The development of such a program did not fall within the province or the responsibilities of the Civil Rights Commission. It still had its prescribed duties and the new tasks assigned it either by Congress or by the President. The enlarged clearing-house functions, further investigations, the new educational survey, the informational program, and its traditional role in seeking to assure full compliance with existing legislation, were a promise of the Commission's continuing usefulness. Changing conditions, however, had seemingly transformed the original drive for civil rights as equality under the law into a movement involving even deeper problems affecting the basic structure of American society.

XV. THE COMMISSION'S ROLE

Subsequent events have tended to overshadow the importance of the progress made during the 1950's and early 1960's toward assuring the Negroes equal rights. The rioting and violence in the North, so dramatically underscoring the crisis of the cities and the paramount need for action on a massive scale in urban renewal, obscure the advances made in securing Negro voting rights and eliminating segregation in so many aspects of American life. Granted that what had taken place by the close of 1965 was only the end of the beginning, these earlier developments greatly changed the basis of racial relations within the United States, made the Negro Revolution one of constantly rising expectations, and laid the foundation for the further progress that was so vital in realizing the democratic dream of equality. The role of the Civil Rights Commission must be judged in the circumstances of the time—its congressional mandate, the climate of opinion when it was originally created, and its practical achievements during this period when the civil rights movement as a whole was first getting under way.

The Commission's responsibilities, as outlined by Congress, were to investigate complaints of citizens deprived of their right to vote by reason of race, color, religion, or national origin; to collect information on legal developments constituting a denial of equal protection of the laws; and to appraise Federal policies in the general area of the legal enforcement of the provisions of the Fourteenth Amendment. For some eight years it had conducted far-flung investigations into every phase of legal discrimination and issued a series of reports with specific recommendations for both congressional and executive action to remedy the infringements of equal rights so carefully documented by the staff's findings. In very considerable part as a result of these findings and recommendations, Congress passed the Civil Rights Acts of 1960 and 1964, and the Voting Rights Act of 1965, while the Executive Branch initiated a broad program to eliminate discrimination in governmental agencies and Federally controlled programs of aid and assistance to the states. These measures did not go far enough to meet the underlying problems of still continuing segregation, especially in education and housing, or those involving the lack of equal employment opportunity. The Commission itself repeatedly and forcefully emphasized the compelling need for broader and more imaginative approaches to inequality than anything Congress had yet done. Against a background of close upon a century of apathy and indifference, however, the actual progress made by 1965 in elevating the status of the Negro in American society was of utmost importance and revolutionary in its consequences.

The tributes of presidents, congressmen, and civil rights leaders all attest to the significant contribution the Civil Rights Commission made in bringing about the new legislation and stiffening the resolve of Federal administrators to enforce the law effectively. As the *New York Times* stated on one occasion, the Commission had through its careful fact-finding played a primary role in seeking to discover answers for what was wrong and thereby shifting the emphasis in the civil rights movement to how the problem of inequality could really be solved.[1]

1. *New York Times,* Feb. 21, 1965.

Berl Bernhard, the Commission's one-time Staff Director, was not of course an impartial witness. But in a commencement address at Central State College, Wilberforce, Ohio, in 1963, he eloquently expressed what the Commission felt about its role. He said:

> *Though the Commission is a fact-finding agency alone and has no powers of enforcement, it will, I believe, be seen by history as a major and dynamic force for the realization of civil rights in America. It has done things that no group or other agency could do. It established national goals, conceived legislation, criticized inaction, uncovered and exposed denials of equality in many fields and places, prodded the Congress, nagged the Executive, and aided the Courts. Above all, it has lacerated, sensitized, and perhaps even recreated the national conscience.*[2]

Once again it may be noted that the tide of Negro protest, first swelling to a crescendo in the non-violent demonstrations in the South and then reaching a new climax with the rioting in the ghettos of northern cities, was more effective in arousing the country than anything else. Or perhaps of even greater impact in the initial stage of the civil rights movement was the shocking spectacle of attempted suppression of such protests in the South by police brutality—the cattle prods, the whips, the police dogs. There was President Kennedy's statement that "Bull" Connor had done more for civil rights than anybody else. It was nevertheless the Commission which kept up the steady, insistent pressure, with its facts laid on the line, which gave a substantive basis for transforming the emotional reaction to the demonstrations and protests into remedial measures.

The role the Commission played was hardly that envisaged when it was first created. President Eisenhower and the Commission members themselves originally thought in terms of a contribution to the civil rights movement which would help to keep things under control through recommendations taking into consideration both northern and southern views. Chairman Hannah accepted this approach when he spoke of the difficulty in following a moderate course between the conflicting pressures of the two sides. But the Commission progressively became a more outspoken champion of civil rights and this early concept of its role gave way

2. Berl Bernhard, "Equality and 1964," *Vital Speeches,* July 15, 1963.

to a far more positive, affirmative one. Its southern critics were entirely right that in its wholehearted support for equality, it soon
abandoned any pretense of seeking to safeguard the southern way
of life and fully accepted the prevailing philosophy of the North.

This shift of viewpoint during a checkered career which three
times found the Commission so narrowly escaping extinction, was
due to several factors. The staff, wholly committed from the very
first to civil rights, exerted a constant pressure in favor of what
sometimes proved to be a more uncompromising position than some
of the Commissioners themselves felt to be advisable. The replace-
ments made in the Commission after 1959 marked a steady pro-
gression toward a membership increasingly sympathetic to the
justice of the Negroes' demands. Finally, and most important, was
the growing realization of the Commission as a whole that the challenge to democracy in the indisputable gap between promise and
performance in upholding the principle of equality had somehow
to be bridged. Nothing was deemed more important on the American scene, both in its domestic and international implications.

The self-education of the Commission, as its members reviewed the harsh and incontrovertible facts disclosed by staff investigation and surveys, accounted for the increasingly forthright
nature of the recommendations in the periodic Reports. And this
in turn helped to convince Presidents Kennedy and Johnson, the
Congress, and a growing majority of the American people that the
time for temporizing, compromise and accommodation had passed.
The issues raised by the denial of equal rights had to be met realistically not only because it had become politically advisable or
expedient to do so, but because it was morally imperative. The
Commission's fact-finding and recommendations were an essential
part of this whole process which in the 1960's led to a national
awakening to the vital importance of this fundamental domestic
problem.

The members of the Commission not only realized that the
legislation they encouraged hardly touched upon the economic
problems of discrimination, so clearly indicated by a continuing
rate of unemployment twice as high among Negroes as among
whites, and that the new laws did very little if anything to combat
de facto segregation in the black ghettos of the North. They also
well understood that in seeking to meet the general issue of dis-

crimination, other approaches than Federal laws and Federal subsidies were necessary, however important they might be. If it were essential that Washington take the initiative, its lead had to be followed by other governmental units and private agencies.

"If my years of experience have taught me one thing," Chairman Hannah stated in an address in November, 1965, "it is that problems of civil rights will be solved, not by national programs, but by local programs; not by Federal action, but by community action."[3]

Father Hesburgh repeatedly emphasized at the Commission hearings and in his public statements a further consideration. The ultimate answer to what was basically a moral problem lay in the minds and hearts of men of goodwill rather than in laws or in executive orders. But together with his colleagues he believed that the law, to whose enforcement the Commission was above all committed, was finally pointing the way. Legislation was providing that umbrella under which men of goodwill could more effectively act upon the courage of their convictions.

The movement to ensure equality in American life had indeed only begun as 1965 drew to an end. The issues over the near horizon were even more pressing and more urgent than those with which the legislation of the previous decade sought to deal. If a legal foundation for upholding the equal protection of the laws guaranteed by the Fourteenth Amendment was finally secure after a century of indifference, the economic and social challenge which the Negroes were raising with their militant demands and the divisive, provocative slogan of Black Power still remained.

This is not the place to discuss this new phase of the Negro Revolution born of the riots in northern cities and the consequent weakening of the civil rights movement as a cooperative, non-violent venture of moderate Negroes and liberal whites. The question is rather how effectively the Civil Rights Commission operated during its first eight years before the national scene was transformed by events so threatening to the nation's domestic stability. Viewed with any sense of historical perspective, against the background of the long past, its activities stand out conspicuously. The Civil

3. John A. Hannah, "Civil Rights and the Public Universities," Talk before National Association of State Universities and Land Grant Colleges, Minneapolis, Nov. 16, 1965, in Hannah files.

Rights Commission faced squarely and honestly the issues with which it dealt, opened its hearings to testimony from every quarter, stood up against criticism from its friends and virulent attacks by its foes, carefully and conscientiously reviewed the findings of its staff on every aspect of discrimination, and made to Congress and the President those constructive recommendations which in so many instances were written into law or enforced by executive orders. It ploughed new ground in opening up fresh vistas for effective action. Although the steps which it so significantly influenced during these years sometimes appear in retrospect as tentative and halting, they were gigantic strides in any comparison with the past. And they were indubitably in the right direction—along the road to the ultimate achievement of equality in American society.

BIBLIOGRAPHICAL
NOTES

A first source for a history of the United States Commission on Civil Rights is its own Reports. Three biennial statutory Reports—1959, 1961, and 1963—have been published, summarizing in each case the investigations, surveys, and hearings of the previous two years and making specific recommendations to the President and Congress. That for 1959 has an abridgement—*With Liberty and Justice for All;* the 1961 Report was published in five volumes—*Voting, Education, Employment, Housing,* and *Justice,* with an additional volume of excerpts, and the 1963 Report was published in one briefer volume.

There were also in the period 1958–1965 a number of interim reports or special publications. Among the most notable are those dealing with equal protection of the laws in higher education (1960), housing in Washington (1962), conditions in Mississippi (mimeographed, 1963), a history of civil rights —*Freedom to the Free* (1963), law enforcement in the South (1965), Equal Opportunity in Farm Programs (1965), Voting in Mississippi (1965), and Civil Rights under Federal Programs (1965).

The Commission has also published the transcripts of its hearings and conferences—on voting in Alabama (1959), Louisiana (1961), and Mississippi

(1965); on housing in New York, Atlanta, and Chicago (1959), and in Washington (1962); on civil rights in general in Los Angeles and San Francisco (1960), Detroit (1960), Phoenix, Arizona (1962), Memphis, Tennessee (1962), Newark, New Jersey (1962), and Mississippi (1965). There are also transcripts of four annual conferences on education dealing primarily with the problems of schools in transition, and a number of staff reports have been printed which deal with problems of desegregation in schools throughout the country.

Another category of publications are those of the State Advisory Committees. They include a summary of individual state reports, with various documents, published in 1959, and a special volume entitled *The 50 States Report*, which appeared in 1961. Other printed documents from State Advisory Committees range over the entire field of civil rights in their particular communities—education, employment, housing, the administration of justice, and other related topics. Among such reports, for example, are studies related to Rapid City, South Dakota; urban renewal in Connecticut; housing in Boston; health facilities in New York City; urban renewal in Iowa cities; civil rights in Buffalo; imbalance in Boston public schools; equal opportunity in Maine. . . .

Since its assumption of new responsibilities as a national clearing house on civil rights information, the Commission has issued periodically pamphlets and booklets in two series of special publications and bulletins dealing with new legislation, the enforcement of the laws, statistical data on civil rights, and other material for general distribution.

A complete catalog of all publications to date was issued in 1964, and supplementary addenda are available for later years.

Further information for this study has been drawn from unpublished material at the headquarters of the Civil Rights Commission and from the files of its chairman, John A. Hannah, at Michigan State University. This has included the minutes of the Commission's monthly meetings, reports and memoranda from the Staff Director, an intraoffice *Newsletter*, Staff Activities Reports, early drafts of the biennial reports, special office documents, the correspondence of Chairman Hannah, and other miscellaneous and uncataloged data.

Government publications helpfully supplement the official Reports and other publications of the Commission. They include most significantly the hearings before both Senate and House committees on proposed civil rights legislation; the debates over such legislation as found in the *Congressional Record;* and the official texts of the civil rights laws as they were ultimately passed. With special reference to the Civil Rights Commission, such material also embraced the committee hearings dealing with the Senate confirmation of the Commission's members and Staff Directors, and those concerned with the annual appropriations. There was also in 1961 a special investigative report on the Commission—Senate Report 438, 87th Congress, 1st Session. On other occasions, when Congress was considering the extension of the Commission's life, considerable information became a part of the public record through additional special hearings or congressional debate.

The *Public Papers of the Presidents* have been consulted for statements in regard to both civil rights in general and on the Commission itself.

The files of the Commission have extensive newspaper and magazine clippings providing the source for many of the quotations in this study. In addition, the *New York Times* has been followed with special care both for news articles and editorials; and also the Washington *Post, Time, Newsweek, U.S. News and World Report,* and the *New Republic.* A few articles dealing specifically with the Civil Rights Commission have appeared. Two of the best are Berl I. Bernhard (for a time Staff Director), "Role of the United States Commission on Civil Rights," *Law in Transition,* 23, Summer 1963, and Barbara Carter, "The Role of the Civil Rights Commission," *Reporter,* 29, July 4, 1963.

A very valuable publication has been *Revolution in Civil Rights,* published from its digests by the Congressional Quarterly Service, Washington, 1965.

Among books with historical source material bearing on the Civil Rights Commission are most importantly Dwight D. Eisenhower, *Waging Peace,* New York, 1965; Sherman Adams, *First-Hand Report,* New York, 1961; Emmet John Hughes, *The Ordeal of Power,* New York, 1963; Arthur M. Schlesinger, Jr., *A Thousand Days,* Boston, 1965; and Theodore M. Sorenson, *Kennedy,* New York, 1965.

The number of volumes dealing with the position of the Negro in American society, the civil rights movement, and the Negro revolution is rapidly mounting every year, and no attempt will be made here to list them. However, among those found helpful for background material in writing this account of the Commission were Gunnar Myrdal's classic *An American Dilemma,* 2 vols., rev. ed., New York, 1954; C. Vann Woodward's highly provocative and valuable *The Strange Career of Jim Crow,* rev. ed., New York, 1965; E. Franklin Frazier, *The Negro in the United States,* rev. ed., New York, 1957; Rayford W. Logan, *The Negro in American Life and Thought, The Nadir, 1877–1901,* New York, 1954; Alan P. Grimes, *Equality in America,* New York, 1964; William Gillette, *The Right to Vote,* Baltimore, 1965; Albert B. Blaustein and Clarence Clyde Ferguson, Jr., *Desegregation and the Law,* New Brunswick, 1957; John Hope Franklin, *From Slavery to Freedom: A History of American Negroes,* New York, 1956; Louis E. Lomax, *The Negro Revolt,* New York, 1963; Robert Penn Warren, *Who Speaks for the Negro?,* New York, 1965; and Talcott Parsons and Kenneth B. Clark, eds., *The Negro American,* Boston, 1966.

In a somewhat different category there may be noted among many others dealing with the status of the Negro in America: Martin Luther King, Jr., *Why We Can't Wait,* New York, 1964, and *Where Do We Go From Here,* New York, 1967; James Baldwin, *The Fire Next Time,* New York, 1964; Carl T. Rowan, *Go South to Sorrow,* New York, 1957; Langston Hughes, *Fight for Freedom,* New York, 1962; J. Saunders Redding, *The Lonesome Road: The Story of the Negro's Part in America,* New York, 1958; Walter F. White, *How Far the Promised Land?,* New York, 1955.

INDEX

Acheson, Dean: on the 1957 Civil Rights Act, 2

ACLU. *See* American Civil Liberties Union

Adams, Amelia JoAnne: testimony before Commission voting hearings, 35

Adams, Charles Francis: on the Negro, 6

Adams, Sherman: Eisenhower's request for commission on civil rights, 11; and Federal intervention in Little Rock, 17

Africa: rise of nationalism and the American Negro, 8

Alabama: hearings on voter registration, 32–33; testimony in, 33–37, 39; impasse reached, 37–38; defiance of registration officials, 38–39; Hannah requests Federal action, 39–40; orders to destroy rejected registrations, 40–41; renewed demonstrations in Birmingham, 187–188; University of, de-

segregated, 189; march on Montgomery, 242–243

Alinsky, Saul D.: suggestion for handling urban segregation, 60–61

American Civil Liberties Union: pressure to pass civil rights bill (1957), 13; statement on police brutality, 120–121

Area Redevelopment Act, 200

Arizona: Commission's general hearing in, 162–164

Armed services: course of integration in, 206–207

Arth, Carol: loaned to Commission, 27; remains with Commission, 28

Atlanta: housing facilities in, 51; hearing on fair housing, 56–58

Barnett, Ross: tries to block Meredith, 172–173

Battle, John S.: designated Commission member, 18; qualifications of, 21;

controversy with Wilkins, 28; in Chicago hearing, 60; dissent on tenor of Report, 64–65, 66; resignation, 85; support of Bernhard, 102

Bergmann, Harry P.: testimony in Washington housing hearing, 159–160

Bernhard, Berl I.: appointed Staff Director, 101; Senate confirmation, 101–103; on character of Commission, 154; on Federal-aid projects in Mississippi, 186; resignation, 213; on Commission's role, 258

Birmingham: renewed demonstrations in, 187–188

Black Belt survey, 91

Black Power, xi

Blackwell, Unita Zelma: testimony in Mississippi hearing, 238

Block-busting, practice of, 55

Brown, Claude, 52

Brown v. Board of Education, 9

Brownell, Herbert: draft on Civil Rights Commission, 11–12

Bunche, Ralph: in Selma, 242

Bus terminals: order desegregating, 95

Cahill, Thomas J.: testimony at San Francisco, 123

California: general hearing in Los Angeles, 119–122; state laws supporting civil rights, 122; hearing in San Francisco, 122–125

Campaign, presidential: and issue of civil rights (1960), 98–99; (1964), 224

Canham, Edwin D., 29

Canino, Pedro: description of East Harlem, 54

Carleton, Doyle E.: designated Commission member, 18; qualifications of, 22; at Atlanta hearing, 56; in support of Commission, 83; resignation, 99; support of Bernhard, 102; against withholding Federal funds, 112

Carter, Barbara: article on Mississippi Report, 186–187

Charlottesville (Va.): progress of school integration, 115–116

Chicago: housing facilities in, 51; fair-housing hearing, 58–61

Civil rights: beginning of movement, x; and the Commission on, x; mounting aggressiveness, xi; World War II and its aftermath, 8; constitutional background of, 67–69; 1960 campaign issue, 98–99; omnibus bill

on, 189–191; relationship of Commission to progress of, 210–211; in 1964 campaign, 224

Civil Rights Act of 1875, 4

Civil Rights Act of 1957: signed, 1; provisions of, 2–3; struggle for passage, 12–15

Civil Rights Act of 1960, 96–98

Civil Rights Act of 1964: mentioned, xi, 136; passage of, 218–220; the Commission and, 220–222

Civil Rights Commission: initial phase, ix; role of, x–xi; purpose of this study, xi–xii; creation of, 2, 3, 12–15; responsibilities and powers, 15; appointment of members, 16–19; qualifications of members, 19–22; confirmation of members, 22–23; delay over confirmation of Staff Director, 23–25, 27, 29–30; delay in providing funds, 25–26; getting under way, 27–28; setting up State Advisory Committees, 28–29; areas of concentration, 30–31

Hearings on voter registration, 32–42, 127–131, 235–241; conference on progress of school integration, 44–50, 110–113, 113–119, 170–171; hearings on housing (1959), 50–61; other activities during 1959, 61–62; first Report completed, 62 (*See also* Reports of the United States Commission on Civil Rights)

Struggle for extension, 81–85; Battle resigns, Rankin succeeds, 85–86; McClellan's investigation of staff and management, 86–88; friction with the Department of Justice, 89, 179–181, 186, 187, 234; and Supreme Court decision, 89–91; expanded program, 91–92; recommendations of, and 1960 Civil Rights Act, 96–97; recommendations to President, 99; new appointments, 100–103; second extension, 103–108; closer Executive cooperation, 110

General hearing in Los Angeles, 119–122; in San Francisco, 122–125; Detroit conference, 125–127; further reorganization of administrative set-up, 154; zeal of staff members, 155; steady flow of complaints, 156; survey of housing in Washington, D.C., 157–162; general hearing in Phoenix, 162–164; hearing in Memphis, 164–168; hearing in Newark, 168–169;

tioned, 117; purpose of organization, 118

Henry, Aaron E.: on apparent cooperation of Governor Johnson, 236

Hesburgh, Father Theodore M.: designated Commission member, 18; qualifications of, 21; presides over New York hearing, 52–56; in Chicago hearings, 58–59, 61; letter to Wofford, 104; on contradictory statements in Detroit hearing, 126; note in Vol. V, second Report, 151; on Justice Department and Mississippi hearing, 234; testifies in support of Voting Rights Act, 245; on improving the schools, 249–250

Higher education. *See* Education, higher

Higher Horizons Program, 114

Hill-Burton Act: study of, in Commission's third Report, 203–204

Hirsch, Rabbi Richard G.: on fair housing, 60

Hoover, J. Edgar: anger over Commission's second Report, 149–150

HOPE. *See* Help Our Public Education

Horne, Frank S.: quoted, 56

Hospital services: discrimination in, in Memphis, 164–165; racial discrimination in, 204; report on progress of desegregation in, 248

Housing: issue of segregation in, 31; 1959 hearings on, 50–61; Commission's recommendations, 74–78; segregation in, and schools, 114–115; root of civil rights problem, 120; situation in San Francisco, 123–124; findings and recommendations in second Report, 144–146; survey of, in Washington, D.C., 157–162; segregationist pattern in Memphis, 167; contradictions in Newark, 169; Executive Order on non-discriminatory housing, 174; discussion of Executive Order on, 201–202

Humphrey, Hubert: support of Civil Rights Commission, 13; praises the Commission, 64; named coordinator of civil rights agencies, 224; on Mississippi hearing, 241; on compliance with 1964 Civil Rights Act, 251

Indians: discrimination against, 124; status of, 150–151; problems of, in Phoenix, 164

Integration, school: conference on progress of, 44–50; Commission's findings and recommendations, 72–74; provisions for, in 1960 Civil Rights Act, 96; second and third conferences on Problems of Schools in Transition, 113–119; resistance to, in Virginia, 115–116; programs of, discussed in second Report, 137–138; recommendations of Commission, 139–140; lack of progress in Memphis, 166; support of, in omnibus bill, 190, 191; Commission's recommendations in third Report, 198–200; report on progress of, 249–250

International consequences of housing discrimination, 160

Ishimaru, Haruo: on discrimination in housing, 124

Japanese Americans: and housing discrimination, 124

Javits, Jacob: support of Commission, 13; on discriminatory policies, 54; on Mississippi Report, 183–184

Jim Crow laws: proliferation of, 5

Johnson, Frank M.: orders Alabama registration records open, 40

Johnson, George M.: succeeds Wilkins, 22; mentioned, 28; at Atlanta housing hearing, 56; in Chicago hearing, 59; resigns from Commission, 99

Johnson, Lyndon B.: role in passage of 1957 Civil Rights Act, 12; on support of Commission, 13–14; on discrimination in housing, 50–51; for renewing Commission, 82; mentioned, 84; presses passage of civil rights legislation, 214; on passage of 1964 Civil Rights Act, 219; civil rights stand in 1964 campaign, 224; "the tide of change . . . ," 232–233; calls for new legislation on voting, 243; "end of the beginning" of search for equality, 254

Jones, Howard Mumford: quoted, 139

Justice: minority groups and (Vol. V, second Report), 146–151

Justice, administration of: lack of equity in (third Report), 202–203

Justice, Department of: Civil Rights Division established, 2; friction with Commission, 89; deepening feud with Commission, 179–181, 186, 187, 234; increased Negro employment in, 203

as described in first Report, 75–77; the Commission's recommendations, 77–78; effect of sit-ins and related movements, 93–94; and freedom rides, 94–96; tenacity of, in southern schools, 198–199; extent of, in urban areas, 205

Selma: mentioned, *ix;* crisis in, 242–243

Senate: debates over new appointments, 101–103. *See also* Civil Rights Act(s); Voting Rights Act

Senate Judiciary Committee: hearings on members of Commission, 22–23; delay over confirmation of Staff Director, 23–25

"Separate but equal" status, 5

Services, armed: course of integration in (third Report), 206–207

Shine, Henry M., Jr.: and development of State Advisory Committees, 29

Siegfried, André: on the Negro problem, 7

Simmons, Samuel J., 226

Sit-ins, 93–94

Slavery: doctrine of equality and, 3–4

Slums: fostering delinquency and crime, 54

Smith, Ben L.: testimony on progress of school integration, 48

Smith, Howard K.: opposition to 1964 Civil Rights Act, 219

Smith, W. Edward: testimony before third educational conference, 117

SNCC. *See* Student Nonviolent Coordinating Committee

Sorensen, Theodore: on Kennedy and civil rights, 105, 153, 176

SOS. *See* Save Our Schools

South Pike's Riflemen's Association, 240

Southern Christian Leadership Conference, 10

Spanish surname, people of. *See* Mexican Americans

Spellman, Francis Cardinal, 54

Sproul, Robert G., 29

Stallings, Frank H.: on integration and increased motivation, 116

State Advisory Committees: establishment of, 28–29; conference of, 83; *The 50 States Report,* 110; activities of, outlined in third Report, 207–208; some 1964 activities, 226–227

Stevenson, Adlai: mentioned as possible appointee, 18

Storey, Robert G.: appointed to Commission, 18; qualifications of, 20; on State Advisory Committees, 28; at Montgomery hearings, 33–40 *passim;* in Atlanta hearing, 56, 57–58; testimony before Senate Judiciary Subcommittee, 83; on Commission's fact-finding, 208; resignation, 212–213

Student Nonviolent Coordinating Committee, 9

Supreme Court: decision of 1954, *x;* effect of 3; declares Civil Rights Act constitutional, 89–91

Sussmann, Peter M., 214, 226

Taylor, William L.: appointed General Counsel to Commission, 213; appointed Staff Director, 230; on press coverage of Mississippi hearing, 241

Tennessee: general hearing in, 164–168

Thurmond, Strom: against establishment of a civil rights commission, 14–15; attacks Commission's Report, 64

Tiffany, Gordon M.: hearings on appointment as Staff Director, 23–25; during production of first Report, 66; resigns from Commission staff, 87–88

Truman, Harry S.: report of his committee on Civil Rights, 8–9

Tuition grants: for white children, 116, 117

Unemployment: issue of, at Los Angeles conference, 120; as discussed in Commission's second Report, 141–143; Commission's proposals, 143–144

United States Commission on Civil Rights. *See* Civil Rights Commission; Reports of the United States Commission on Civil Rights

United States v. Raines, 90

University education. *See* Education, higher

Urban areas: treated in Commission's third Report, 205

Urban League: formation of, mentioned, 7

Urban Renewal Administration, 145

Vardaman, James: doctrine of white supremacy, 6

Varner, Probate Judge: testimony in registration hearings, 36